ACHILLES

Son of Peleus, Scourge of Troy

To Fred —
I hope you
enjoy this
trip back in time!
Mike Chignon

Also by Mike Chapman

Two Guys Named Dan
Kings of the Mat
Toughest Men in Sports
Evy and the Hawks: The Glory Years \(co-author)
Gotch to Gable: A History of Iowa Wrestling
Iowans of Impact
Nick and the Cyclones
Gotch: World's Greatest Wrestler
Encyclopedia of American Wrestling
Fighting Back
Gotch: An American Hero
Please Don't Call Me Tarzan
The Gold and The Glory
The Sport of Lincoln
Lowell Park

ACHILLES

Son of Peleus, Scourge of Troy

By
Mike Chapman

CULTURE HOUSE BOOKS

ACHILLES: Son of Peleus, Scourge of Troy

A Culture House Book / April 2004

For information address: Culture House Books
                             P O Box 293
                             Newton, IA 50208

Library of Congress Cataloging-in-Publication Data
Chapman, Mike, 1943 -
    ACHILLES: Son of Peleus, Scourge of Troy / Mike Chapman
1. Achilles. 2. Trojan War. 3. The Iliad. 4. The Odyssey.
5. Greek Mythology.

ISBN   0-9676080-5-8

PRINTED IN THE UNITED STATES OF AMERICA

First edition

Cover artwork by Carole Bender

"For who can match Achilles?
He who can must be more than hero,
more than man."
— *Homer*

Prologue
(1186 B.C.)

The beautiful woman and the old man walked briskly along the top of the high and massive wall that overlooked the war-torn plain below. His best years were now far past and he was in the twilight of his life. His face, much of it covered by a thin, white beard, was gaunt and wrinkled; yet, there was evidence in his manner and in his bearing that he was once an imposing figure. Royal blood flowed in his veins and it was clear at a glance to all that saw him, up close or at a distance, that he was still a king.

She, on the other hand, was well into her prime years. Of medium height, she had become perhaps a bit soft with the passage of time, but her beauty was dazzling and captivating. Many seeing her for the first time could not look away; some even gasped as she moved past and followed her for a few steps, just for the pleasure of having their eyes rest on her.

While her body had many contours, it was her face that set her apart from all others. It was exquisite…beautiful beyond words, perfectly formed in every way. Her dark blue eyes sparkled, and her lips were full and sensuous and smiled easily. Her hair was light brown with a hint of red, and swirled around her head in a fashion that was created by her and reserved for her alone. She walked with a style and grace that told everyone that she was unlike any other woman. There was an air about her that made men weak and women envious. It was rumored that she was the daughter of Aphrodite, goddess of love. It was also rumored that she knew all of Aphrodite's secrets, and knew them well.

On this day, he wore a purple robe which hung to his ankles, held about his waist by a leather belt trimmed in gold, secured by an enormous silver buckle. A thin white chiton, trimmed with green lace, covered her body and little bells hanging from her ears jingled lightly. As they walked together along the high wall, her hand resting on his arm, they gazed out over the terrain below. For ten long years, the plain had been battered and bruised by thousands of warriors fighting furiously. It had endured battles almost beyond belief in their brutality. Chariots racing madly in every direction, horses pounding in a frenzy, and thousands of men screaming in pain and in the death rattle were all common sights on this plain.

Their attendants and servants, six for him and two for her, followed close behind them as they walked. They kept a respectful distance, but watched every move of the two in front of them, anxious to serve immediately if needed. The others who had come to the wall to observe the spectacle below nodded in deep respect as the pair passed, aware that only the gods on Mount Olympus outranked them when it came to their station in life.

For he was Priam, long-time ruler of Troy, and she was Helen, the daughter in law that came to him from the mainland across the sea, stolen from her husband by the audacious Alexandros. At first, Priam was furious that his rebel son had dared to kidnap the wife of such a powerful king as Menelaus of Sparta. But eventually Priam, too, had fallen under the spell of Helen. Now he loved her dearly and, it was said, would send thousands of his warriors to death in order to protect her. Of course, the truth of the matter was far more complex, as it always is when men go to war.

They finally halted, resting their hands on the thick wall before them, and peered out over the land that lay before the great walls of Troy. It was a huge, grassy expanse where, in happier times, Trojan families had dallied in the bright light of day, racing horses and playing leisurely games. For generations, Trojans had strolled across the plain to the seashore, frolicking in the ocean and spearing fish for supper. And they had watched the great ships sail past, on their way up the Hellespont, to the fabled Back Sea and beyond.

Those glorious days were now long gone. They ended when Alexandros and Helen rode in his chariot through the Scaean Gates below, bringing in their wake one thousand ships filled with the finest warriors from the land of the Achaeans. Day after day, for nearly ten long years, the Invaders fought with the Trojans and their allies. During those years, the windy Troad had ceased to be the secure homeland of the citizens of the fabled city and had become instead the killing fields of the Achaeans.

On numerous occasions such as this, Priam and his favorite daughter in law, out of the fifty wives his sons had selected, walked between the watch towers, on the walls. He enjoyed being in her company and drinking in her beauty; and she enjoyed the majesty of his presence. He was, after all, the most famous and powerful ruler in the entire world.

Now he turned his gaze once again upon the plain, where thousands of his men had died or had been sorely wounded. Then his eyes moved to the long, wooden wall that sprawled along the seashore. Behind it, he saw the masts of the ships.....like giant fingers pointing to the heavens. They went on and on and on, for what seemed like forever. He turned his head to the right, and saw ships, then turned to the left, and saw more ships. A thousand in all, he had been told.

Suddenly weary, he glanced at Helen.

"Will it ever end, this terrible war?" she said softly, leaning closer to him, hugging his arm. He looked into the cool blue eyes that had seduced so many others and smiled, patting her hand with his gnarled fingers.

"There will be an end to it, when the gods have grown weary of the game," he said, his voice low. "They use us like children play with their toy sticks....and maneuver us as suits their pleasure. When they have played with us long enough and they become bored, then the war will end."

She sighed, and looked out over the plain. She gasped. Her eyes narrowed and her fingers tightened on his arms. He turned away from her to follow her stare and he tensed.

"He comes," she said stiffly.

The old king saw and nodded.

"Deathdealer," she murmured. "He comes again, and there is no stopping him. He is like the wind that cannot be contained. He has become Ares, god of war, and his hunger knows no limits."

Priam squinted into the sun, and lifted a trembling hand to shade his eyes. He nodded again, his mind reeling with memories that sent a searing pain through him. His dry lips quivered and he swallowed heavily.

"Achilles," he murmured. "How the gods favor you, against us. Zeus surely must love you, to have blessed you with such formidable skills of war and with such an all-consuming anger."

The old king watched with growing trepidation as the gleaming chariot raced across the land, passing the river that cut the plain in half. Behind it came dozens of other chariots, and a mass of warriors running, all dressed in black armor, a cloud of dust rising behind them. And then those on the wall heard the war cry, faint at first, and then growing like thunder from Olympus.

"The Myrmidons," said Helen, shaking. "Let us go, dear father in law. I cannot bear to see what this day will bring."

They moved quickly back over the wooden timbers they had just traversed. Before taking to the stairs that would lead them down to the dirt-packed streets and then back to the security of the proud citadel on the hill, Priam turned for one last look. The war chariot was nearing the walls of Troy, and Priam could see the golden armor of Achilles shining in the sunlight.

"All men must die," he said softly, to himself. "Even Deathdealer will some day die."

And then Priam was gone, not daring to dream that today was that day of days....

The sea nymph

The light mist of night lay softly on the dark and gently sloping hills. Overhead, Diana the moon goddess, weary after hours of forcing her silver chariot in and out behind the scudding clouds, was still casting a dim light over the earthly landscape far below. Soon, she would be fast asleep in her abode beneath the deep waters of Ocean, while her brother, Helios, drew the first light of the sun across the day sky in his chariot of fire.

As the moon rode high over Phthia, in the hills of southern Thessaly, a lithe figure moved quickly through a dense forest. The figure cast nervous glances over her shoulder as she ran, clutching a tiny bundle to her bosom. She stopped several times to catch her breath and to listen for any sounds of pursuit. Once, she felt she heard the crunching of a horse's hooves on the thick forest carpet behind her and she leaped behind a large, gnarled tree, fighting for her breath, breasts heaving, waiting. When she felt assured she was alone, she ventured back onto her dark path.

The moon offered an ominous presence, and twice she paused to look up at the silver chariot. The moon goddess appeared to be observing her flight with an unemotional detachment.

"Diana, protect me," she whispered softly, "and I will honor you unceasingly, forever." She continued her journey. She moved quickly, her strong, young thighs steady and forceful. She felt strangely empowered, as though she could run all night without stopping, if need be. She glanced down at the bundle she held tightly and was relieved to know the baby still slept. The drugs worked well, she thought.

Finally, she saw the large clearing and stopped abruptly. This was the area she feared most. She had felt reasonably secure among the trees of the forest, but here there was no place to hide. If anyone was following, or if anyone had learned of her plans, this would be where they would be waiting. She slid behind a tree, listening intently for any signs that would suggest danger.

For nearly ten minutes she stood, marshalling her forces for the burst across the open land. There was an eerieness to the clearing she had never known before; but then again, she had never been on such a perilous mission. Never in her twenty years of life had she faced a journey of such overwhelming danger. She checked the baby again; it was starting to stir, but it was still under the power of the drug.

She sighed and gathered herself for the flight ahead that would determine her future, and the destiny of her baby. She looked up at the moon again; the chariot was starting to slip behind a large cloud. She smiled faintly. It was a good sign that Diana was with her, would hide her brilliant face, and would help to protect her.

The moment of truth had arrived. She stepped from behind the tree and entered the open field cautiously, glancing every which way. The gentle wind made the tree limbs sway slightly and she thought she saw movement at the left side of the field. She stopped, staring intently, then began moving slowly again, eyes leveled at the tree line. Nearly one fourth of the way across, she began to move faster. She was feeling confident. Perhaps she had indeed been successful in fooling her lord and master.

A terrifying cry cut the night air and she froze, temples pounding in fear. It was just one word, but it had been shouted with resounding fury: "Thetis!" Gasping, she twisted to the right, and saw that her worst fears were suddenly realized. The man-horse had found her!

Out of the depths of the forest came a short, four-legged creature, and on its back, bent over and clinging to its mane, sat a squat, powerful man with a long flowing mane of his own. At this distance, they gave the appearance of being just one creature – a gruesome combination of man and horse known to the hill people as centaurs. It was a sight that bred fear in the hearts of the bravest warriors…a vision from the past, from the legends of the caves. For eons, the hill people had told chilling stories of the race of man-horse that haunted the deepest forests on the highest mountain. Now, the centaur had found her and he was coming for her!

She turned and ran at an angle, trying to reach the left side of the high grass area, making the centaur race the full width of the space. She could hear the pounding hooves and the war cry of the man-horse; the sounds gave fury to her legs. She ran like a deer and reached the forest's edge far in advance of the centaur. She flew into the thick stand of trees, twisting and turning, hoping to confuse the centaur. His blocky horse could not maneuver in the woods as easily as could her lithe form, and they both knew it. She heard him curse loudly as he pulled up at the forest's edge.

She froze in her tracks, gasping and straining to hear. She could detect the horse panting and pawing the earth with its hooves, the man growling, searching for clues. She glanced through the thick branches and saw his shadowy form, stalking the edge, peering into the dark forest. She saw the powerful four legs of the horse and the bent body of the human, blending together into one terrible image. It was no wonder that those who loved tall tales would easily believe centaurs were indeed one beast, united through some unfathomable scheme of the gods.

But even if they were not one beast, the men were fierce warriors and would die for a cause they believed in. In a long distant time, the centaurs had sworn their allegiance to the kings of Phthia, and now her husband Peleus, as their king, had commanded them to find her and carry her back to his palace. This centaur was nothing if not loyal; once on a mission, not even the gods could deter him.

The man sat up tall on the back of his steed and lifted his head, nostrils flared, sniffing the night air again and again. She began inching away, backwards; the baby was stirring and she felt a jolt of terror the length of her back. She was running out of time. She backed away quickly and then the baby let out a whimper. She froze, staring through the foliage. She heard the man-horse snort; she turned and raced through the forest breathlessly. Branches struck her face; she ducked beneath some and ran full force into others. She tumbled to the ground once and sprang back to her feet, clutching the baby to her breast. It cried and she glanced down at it, tears in her eyes. Was there any hope for them, she asked herself as her legs and lungs pumped feverishly.

Suddenly, she saw the small entrance to the cave and a great wave of relief washed over her. She broke into another small clearing and raced for the cave's mouth and felt a sense of security as she disappeared into it. The cool air was wonderfully uplifting. She stumbled along the stony floor, glancing back over her shoulder. The centaur had not yet found the cave. She was safe!

She moved silently to where the torches were stashed and pulled one from the wall. She began to descend into the bowels of the cave. Though it was now pitch dark, she knew the path well. She had come here many times over the years, to sit with the other sea nymphs and to worship the great god Poseidon. This was home and she was beginning to believe that she had triumphed.

A dim light flickered ahead and she knew it was the first of the torches to light her path. She moved to it, then held her torch to it, waiting for it to spark. The warmth of the flame struck her face and she glanced down again at the baby. His eyes were open and he stared up at her, his little hands moving slightly.

"Stay still, my prince," she whispered. "We are almost home and you will soon be in the company of the gods."

She stepped quickly down the steep path, the torch lighting her way. There were long periods of darkness, broken by the flickering light of the torches hanging on the walls. She was no longer worried about pursuit. Even a centaur would think twice about entering the cave of Poseidon. The sea god was a powerful deity and was given to severe acts of revenge for those who invaded his private domain.

At last, she stood at the entrance to the great room. She heard the soothing voices of her sisters, singing softly, mingled with the gentle sounds of the flute. Her eyes devoured the familiar scene; twenty young women sat in a circle, with nothing but linen cloths over their thighs, their breasts free of any clothing. Their long hair hung straight down, uncombed and unbraided, and their bodies swayed slightly, in a trance, eyes shut. She recognized the young man playing the flute as the former sheepherder who had joined their group only recently.

In the center, next to the fire, was Nereus, the aged and wise sage she had come to adore. He was holding his arms open, hands reaching upward, offering praise to Poseidon. She felt a stirring in her heart, something akin to love. It was a feeling she had once experienced for Peleus, what now seemed like eons ago, but had long since extinguished. With a sigh, she moved toward the rough steps and floated down toward the fire. Nereus was the first to see her and a wide smile broke across his craggy face. He chanted, eyes wide, and motioned toward her. The others opened their eyes and saw her; they smiled too, without a break in their singing.

She approached the circle and held out her baby for all to see. Four of the women stood, reaching for her and the infant. They embraced her and their hands eased over his tiny feet and hands, caressing him. They murmured to him, chanting of immortality. A warm glow sparked inside her and began to blossom. Nereus stood, chanting, and walked toward her, embracing her and the baby in his thin arms. His shaggy beard smelled of smoke and his body wreaked of the drug. She breathed in heavily, eyes closed, savoring the joy of homecoming.

"It's been soooo long, Nereus," she murmured. He nodded, glancing down at the baby, who was beginning to stir again.

"You have come to make your son immortal," he croaked, eyes growing wider. She smiled down at her son and then nodded at Nereus.

"As Poseidon ordered," she said.

Nereus took the baby from her and held it aloft, above his head, eyes closing. He mumbled words that even she did not understand, undoubtedly a special message to Poseidon, known only to the high priest, she reasoned. The others gathered around, forming a tight circle. Nereus moved from the group, bent over, still holding the baby at arm's length. He moved to the fire and turned the baby toward it. Feeling the heat, the baby screamed and kicked feebly.

She gasped, but said nothing. Nereus mumbled more words, then came back and handed the baby to her.

"Give him to the Lord Styx," he said, voice cracking, eyes wide. "The fire took your other babies; we will give this one to the River....where Poseidon can protect him forever, against all harm."

She clutched the struggling baby and walked to the edge of the fast-flowing river. She had often sat by the river's edge, watching it flow past, mesmerized by its quiet murmurs and dark color. She often wondered where it came from and where it went; Nereus told them it was the River of Death and actually flowed into Hades, the land of departed souls. He told them that one night, long ago, he had awakened to see the ferry going past, full of dead souls, wailing pitifully and staring at him as they sailed toward the underworld. He confessed he wanted to follow them, but Poseidon had warned him against such folly. Even though Poseidon and Hades were brothers, the great sea god could not save mere mortals from Hades' clutches once they were in his realm. No, going into the underworld was not a wise plan, even for a priest with the powers of Nereus.

Now, she stood by the waters, clutching her baby. Nereus moved to her side, gazing rapturously into the river. He muttered many more words; finally, he turned to the young woman.

"Now....hold him securely, by the heel of one foot, and immerse him fully into the river, if you would protect him, and make him immortal," he grunted. "Now!"

She paused, gripping the baby by his right heel, and then plunged him into the dark waters, head first. She bent over, gaping as the baby's arms flailed wildly, then she jerked him out. The baby gasped, fighting for its breath. She felt a stab of remorse.

"Now! Again!" Nereus shouted.

She thrust the squirming body into the water again.

A voice rang out, loud and shrill; she gasped, twisting in terror.

"Thetis! Stop!"

A powerful figure leaped from the very place she had stood minutes before and raced into the circle of startled women. Knocking them aside he ran to the river's edge. Nereus tried to block him, but the larger man backhanded him. The priest flew sideways and then sprawled into the dirt along the river's bank, unconscious.

The man jerked the baby from the hands of the startled woman, who gaped at him through eyes grown wide.

"Haven't you killed enough of our children?" the man shouted, veins in his neck straining against the thick flesh. He wore a purple tunic, which exposed his muscular arms. He held the baby at arm's length, watching him writhe and gasp. Then he pulled the infant to his chest and turned his eyes, cold and angry, on the woman.

"You are an unfit wife and unfit mother," he spat through clenched teeth. "To think I once loved you and entrusted our sons to you."

He turned to leave and she reached for him.

"Peleus!" she gasped. "I want our son to be immortal, to never face death. To live forever as a god, with the gods."

He turned on her, hate filling his eyes.

"Evil woman," he growled. "Your love of the drug has made you weak and foolish. But you will not kill this son. He is not immortal, but he will be great. He is the son of Peleus, king of Phthia, and one day his fame will spread throughout all Hellas."

She clutched at Peleus's arms, weeping, but he jerked his arms free and she flew to the ground. She looked up, sobbing as her husband strode away. She saw him approach the small ledge from which he had sprung, and then she saw the centaur, glaring down at her.

Peleus climbed up to the ledge and held the baby for the centaur to see. Chiron nodded at Peleus. The two of them turned and disappeared into the black of the long tunnel they had all just come down.

Thetis watched them go and then collapsed, her face pressed against the soft dirt, her body wracked by sobs.

The land of the centaur

The lad walked quickly across the grassy field, strands of long, blond hair flowing gently across his handsome face. The heat of the sun caressed his nearly naked body and he gazed up at the bright orb overhead as Helios pulled the sun behind his chariot. The boy welcomed the stunning light and the heat that ran over his flesh, making him feel alive and powerful.

The gentle breeze blew almost constantly on Mount Pelion, high above the tree-dotted lowlands of Phthia. It stirred his hair again and then disappeared as quickly as it had come. He stood silent, head held high; he juggled the long shaft in his hand. It was a beautifully-crafted spear that could slice through the air, if thrown correctly. He ran his eyes over the bright point, sharpened by the hammer and the anvil of a master blacksmith to perfection. It was a gift from his father and he meant to use it as only the son of a king should.

Suddenly, he was keenly aware of the strange power that had first visited him one day over a year ago, and had never left him for long. It was as though Zeus himself, the king of all the gods, had breathed into him a form of power that only he could sense and only he possessed. At moments like this, he felt incredibly close to the Cloudgatherer

He sprang into action. He ran with ease, floating over the grassy knoll, the young muscles flowing beneath his bronzed skin. His right arm jerked backwards, his head titled upward. His hand gripped the shaft loosely and his arm muscles tensed. He was at full speed, racing like the wind; the arm flew forward, and the hand released the shaft. It arched high into the air....streaking majestically....and he sped beneath it, his eyes locked upward, marking its flight.

He flew over the knoll, right hand reaching out. The spear was descending and he was determined to catch it as it struck the ground.

Lungs bursting, legs straining mightily, he leaned forward, mouth open, gulping in great quantities of air.

The spear's point struck the ground and at the exact moment his hand closed on the shaft. He ran past the quivering spear, jerking it from the earth. He slowed, raising the spear overhead, his body gleaming with sweat, prancing in a tiny circle, his heart pounding. He came to a halt, and was, suddenly, hardly breathing; that was the gift from Zeus....the way his body was able to recover from such strenuous outbursts. His body was lean and hard and incredibly shaped. To the centaur watching from afar, he looked more like a god than any human he had ever seen.

"Well done, Peleusson," the centaur shouted. He ambled forward on his bent legs, his horse standing behind him, grazing on the thick grasses. "Well done, indeed."

Young Achilles watched his mentor approach, a great pride swelling up in his chest. Chiron was the leader of the small band of centaurs who chose to live in the rugged highlands of Phthia, well above the palace, the farms and even the scattered huts of the herdsmen. The rocky terrain made chariot travel impossible; the wooden wheels would shatter within moments of the start of any trip. These hardy men had learned ages ago to travel by horseback and had developed a relationship with the small, sturdy horses that made them seem, at times, like one beast.

The men wore their hair long and wild, in a mane, like the horses they rode. They were small in numbers but were held in awe by all who knew of them. Not only were they fierce warriors but they were considered highly intelligent, as well. It was said they often communed with the gods, high up in the terraces above the common folks; even Peleus, the great king, and his father-king before him, had turned to the centaurs for advice and counsel.

For almost as long as he could remember, Achilles had lived in the cave of Chiron, learning all he could about the ways of the forest, the hills and of the centaur. He was confident that Chiron was the wisest man in the entire world, wiser even than his own father, the king. Why else would Peleus choose to send his only son into the high reaches of the mountains to live, away from the palace he so dearly loved, if not to learn from the wisest of all men? To attract praise from Chiron was his heart's desire. Nothing could make Achilles happier than to know he had earned respect of the aged centaur, the very man who had tutored the great heroes Heracles and Theseus many years before.

"Your running....is amazing," said Chiron, shaking his head in wonderment. "I have never seen anyone with such speed." He paused, and arched a thick eyebrow. "At least, I have never seen a mortal run like that."

Achilles wiped the blade clean with a handful of long grass and glanced up at the centaur, smiling.

"Maybe I am not mortal," he said, seizing the opportunity to talk of the gods. "Perhaps my father is really a god. Even Zeus Cloudgatherer."

Chiron chuckled, laying a thick hand on the lad's shoulder.

"Yes, that must be the answer," he said. "But, let's not talk of it too loudly. Peleus may get angry and then he will never let you come back home."

Achilles felt a stab of angst when he heard his father's name. It had been over ten years since he had lived with Peleus in the small and ancient palace down in the valley. Peleus had visited him and Chiron once a year for each of the ten years, but always the visits were too brief for Achilles. He greatly admired his father and loved to sit by the fire and listen to Chiron tell stories of the great deeds of Peleus and his brother, Telamon. The story he liked the most was of their journey to the land of the Colchins, far beyond even the city of Troy. The brothers had sailed to the Black Sea with Jason and his argonauts in search of the mysterious fleece of the golden ram. The story had become legend already, throughout all the land. Achilles was proud that his father had been a part of such a grand adventure, and that he was regarded as a powerful ruler and fearless warrior.

But he also saw the gentle nature of his father, when the three of them would sit by the crackling fire in Chiron's cave, eating the meat of wild boar and partaking of the wine. Peleus and Chiron would chuckle and swagger, spinning their tales well into the night, while young Achilles sat spellbound. When he fell asleep, Achilles dreamed of wonderful adventures and great battles... where he was the central figure and always emerged victorious.

They ambled slowly over the grassy highlands, heading back to the cave, Chiron and Achilles side by side. The stocky brown horse that was Chiron's constant companion straggled along behind. Several times, Chiron turned and whistled...a low, eerie sound. The horse's ears stood at attention and it moved quickly to the man's side. Achilles knew that Chiron and his clan had a way with horses that no one else could understand. It was as though they were of one mind and that Chiron could communicate with the horses at a level no one else could ever hope to do.

Achilles often asked Chiron to teach him the secret of communicating with the horses that grazed in the thick pastures near the cave and Chiron had promised to do so. But the days were always filled with other matters. Achilles had to learn to hunt, for their meals were dependent largely upon his skills with the bow and arrow and the lance. The hills and dense forests below were filled with various game, from fox and large rabbits to deer and wild boar. There were also small bears and scrawny mountain lions, all worth eating if one was starving.

And there were plenty of berries and figs to be gathered by the women who lived in the nearby wood huts and who came late at night to share Chiron's cot, when Achilles was supposed to be sleeping. The centaurs loved to race their horses and fight, and to engage one another in long and impassioned discussions about the gods; but they also loved women. Achilles would often hear Chiron singing softly to his woman, late at night, before they both surrendered to the sweet charms of the goddess Aphrodite.

Women was a subject that Achilles had not spent much time thinking about, largely because he didn't know what to think. After considerable prodding, Chiron had finally told him about his mother. Thetis, he explained, was so beautiful that it was said even Zeus was in love with her at one time; she had been a forest nymph who eventually turned to the worship of Poseidon. She had met Peleus when they were both very young and they had quickly fallen in love. In fact, it was Chiron who had introduced them to one another. Their marriage was a tremendous event, celebrated far and wide, for Peleus was a popular ruler and Thetis was from a good family. There were even rumors that the gods and goddesses of Olympus attended, in disguises, of course.

The wedding had been held on Mount Pelion, not far from Chiron's cave where they now sat. Guests came from far and wide and it was a wonderful event that lasted seven days. But there were bitter feelings among those who were not invited and many arguments broke out between rival chieftans and tribes after Peleus and Thetis had left to consummate their vows. There had been many battles and even a few deaths. Since they were the hosts, the centaurs had been blamed, for they were a rowdy lot to begin with, who loved parties and drinking and wenching, as well as brawling.

Something strange happened to Thetis during her first pregnancy and she had turned against Peleus. She departed from the worship of Artemis, the goddess of the hunt and the forest, and embraced Poseidon. She became consumed by the thought of making her sons immortal. Determined to burn away their mortal parts, she had immersed three of them in fire in the caves of Nereus. Each died a terrible death and at last Peleus placed her under constant surveillance in the palace. Thetis rebelled and ran away several times, only to be captured by Chiron and carried back to Phthia.

Chiron told Achilles that when Thetis was carrying him inside her, she tried to hide the knowledge from Peleus, claiming that this son – and she was certain it was another son – was born of a god, and not Peleus.

She was convinced that Zeus had visited her one late night and, disguised as Peleus, had entered her.

"She is not an evil woman, just spoiled by worship of the drug and no longer a fit wife for a king," said Chiron, stripping meat from a piece of bone, eating casually while telling Achilles the story of his birth. "Peleus had instructed me to watch her every move, and she knew that was my mission. But she was clever and stole away from the palace shortly after you were born. I followed her through the forest, trying to prevent her from subjecting you to the flames. She was under the power of Nereus, a truly stupid old man who thought he was chosen by Poseidon to rule the world." Chiron paused to chuckle at the thought, then continued.

"Your father followed us....and we entered the cave of Nereus at just the right moment. Peleus could move down the slope faster than I could and he arrived just as Thetis was dipping you in the river Styx. They had given up on the fire method, apparently... and to your good fortune. Maybe the god who Thetis claims is your real father was looking out for you, Peleusson."

The centaur smiled faintly at the young boy who was hanging on every word and continued, his voice low and powerful.

"Your father leaped down into the midst of Nereus's followers, scattering them every which way, and clutched you from the river. I think to this day that your mother would have drowned you if Peleus had not intervened."

The story was over and the two sat in silence, each reflecting on the way events had transpired that day. And then Achilles asked the old man, "Will I ever meet her, Chiron?"

The centaur shrugged, reaching for another piece of meat.

"If the gods think it prudent, then you will meet her, some day," he said.

Achilles fell asleep with dreams of his beautiful mother filling his head, and for many nights thereafter. But she never came and Achilles saw very few women other than the older ones who followed the centaurs. Every now and then he would catch glimpse of a young girl, trailing along behind the centaur women, but they were always so shy that they would dart behind their mothers the moment they saw him. And so, he gave little, if any, thought to women at all.

His days were filled with learning the art of weaponry and how to fight without them, hand to hand. Chiron taught him the basic skills of wrestling and of boxing. Achilles was not afraid to absorb a blow to the nose in order to get in his own blow, but he loved wrestling more than boxing. He enjoyed learning the art of tripping a foe to his back and of locking his arm under a foe's arm and sliding it up over his neck, to force the foe to his back, rendering him helpless. Most of all, he loved the trick Chiron taught him of trapping a man's arm at the elbow with your same arm, then pulling it back until either the foe screamed out in pain and surrendered, or the arm was broken. At first, he boxed and wrestled with Chiron, the old man on his knees, teaching him to feint and parry and how to set his foe up, then defeat him with a clever move. As his skills developed, there were several younger centaurs close to Achilles' size that he was allowed to spar with. It wasn't long before he could defeat them all in either wrestling or boxing.

Equally as important as the skills he offered, Chiron instructed his young pupil how to behave like a warrior. Chiron taught Achilles to ignore pain and discomfort and to regard them as only temporary distractions.

"Do not allow pain to rule your thoughts or your actions," Chiron advised him, over and over. "Make all your decisions independent of pain, for pain will quickly vanish but your actions will stay with you for as long as you live."

Achilles knew how to use the bow and arrow, yet he disdained them. He regarded them as weapons of a warrior who was not willing to fight face to face, with sword and spear. Chiron had stressed to him that the bow and arrows were an essential part of warfare, but he also conceded that the true warrior wanted his hand on the hilt of the sword…to face his foe head on, staring into his eyes, working his sword until once of them perished. Just the thought of such a struggle sent a hot tremor down the spine of Achilles; he ached for the day he could pit his skills against those of other warriors in the ultimate test.

"There is one true secret to winning such all-out battles," said Chiron, eyes narrow, peering into Achilles' face, "and it is this. Once you are in battle, your skill with the sword, your mind's willingness to endure pain, are very important. But often, the final measure of your success will rest solely with your ability to continue when other men are exhausted and willing to surrender…that is the quality that will determine how long you live. You must train both your body and your mind to never surrender to fatigue. Never!"

It was a lesson that Achilles took to heart. The words were always uppermost in his mind and he knew he would never surrender to fatigue. Chiron instructed his young pupil in more delicate matters, as well. The centaurs knew many ways of treating wounds. Chiron showed Achilles what herbs to place on open cuts and sores and then how to bind them to stop the flow of blood. Many warriors, he said, would die from the loss of blood as much as from the severity of the wound itself.

"Often," Chiron said, his voice low and solemn, "the life of a comrade can be saved merely by making certain that the wound is tightly bound and the blood flow is stopped. That is a trick not many know. Remember it, Peleusson. Blood is the essence of a man's life; he can not afford to lose it in great quantities."

Achilles quickly learned all the skills of the hunter. He knew at an early age how to trap smaller game and was instructed how to be wary of the larger animals, those that can kill a man. The mountain cats were dangerous and so were the small bears. But Chiron felt the most dangerous animal of all was the wild boar. Its long, curved tusks could rip a man apart. It also had a mean temper and was unpredictable. A wild boar could turn on a man at a moment's notice and split him from chin to belly button with one swipe of the tusks. It was an evil beast and one to be avoided, the centaur stressed.

Lastly, there was the lyre. Chiron loved the soothing sounds of the lyre and often would lay against the rough rock wall of his cave playing it gently, eyes shut, humming along with the instrument. Though Achilles was not interested in the beginning, Chiron convinced him that he needed the lyre to complete his education.

"Even great warriors like Theseus, Jason and your father, Peleus, had moments when they needed to reflect and to relax," said Chiron.

"How about Heracles?" asked Achilles, eager to know more about the most famous hero of all. Tales of his incredible feats of strength, called labors by some, were sung of in banquet halls from Ithaca to far-flung Crete and even to windy Troy. Achilles sensed that even the centaurs stood in awe of Heracles, as they often grew silent when his name was mentioned.

Chiron chuckled, fingering his stubby beard, at the suggestion of that powerful man playing the lyre.

"Heracles….now that's a different kettle of fish," said Chiron. "He was not a man that could be easily soothed. But, you should learn from your own father and Theseus, not Heracles. He was…." he paused, searching for the right words. "He was different from all the other heroes. Yes, very different."

Prod as he might, Achilles could not persuade Chiron to say any more about the mighty Heracles. Achilles ceased his questions, but he was resolved to press Chiron for more information, some day, on Heracles of Thebes.

There came a day when Achilles was given the chance to prove himself. Light from Helios' chariot filtered into the deep recesses of the cave through a tiny slit at the top and had been doing so for some time when Achilles walked to the entrance of the cave. There was something different in the air and he sensed it immediately. He saw Chiron walking toward him, talking excitedly with two other centaurs. Chiron stopped in front of him, a deep frown on his face.

"Have you eaten?" he asked.

"Yes," said Achilles.

"Good. Then grab your spear and dagger and come with me," said Chiron. "We are going hunting."

Achilles grabbed the weapons from the spot where he always kept them, next to his sleeping pad, and ran out to join the three centaurs who were already moving toward the tiny corral where they kept their horses. They gripped the manes of the short, stocky animals and swung easily onto the back, Chiron motioning for Achilles to do the same.

Soon, they were riding through a deep glen, sheltered with thick trees all around. Chiron moved his horse next to Achilles and learned toward him.

"A lion has turned killer," he said sternly. "Two women were in the forest searching for figs and berries when they were attacked." He paused. "The lion didn't leave much of them."

"We're going to find him and slay him," Chiron added solemnly.

Achilles nodded, hardly able to contain his excitement. It promised to be a grand adventure and he was very pleased that the centaurs had invited him to take part. A short time later, the centaur in the lead held up his hand, motioning for the others to halt. He slid off his horse in a fluid motion and bent to the ground, sniffing. The centaurs had lived all their lives in the woods and were expert hunters and trackers.

The other two came to his side and bent down, then stood and sniffed the air. Chiron took Achilles by the elbow.

"He is an old fellow, but still a formidable foe," he said. "We are going to spread out, going in four directions. Give the warning call if you see him and we will come running. If you hear another give the cry, move quickly to where it came from."

These were all techniques Achilles was familiar with, from nighttime discussions with Chiron to smaller hunts he had been on. He had never been after such a dangerous animal before and he gripped his spear as tightly as he could, glancing down at his waist to make sure the dagger was well sheathed and ready for a quick withdrawal if needed.

For some time, Achilles crept slowly through the dense foliage, all his senses at their keenest. He sniffed the air, like Chiron had taught him to do, searching for a strange smell of any kind; he bent down to look for broken twigs, or droppage of waste, or a regurgitation sign.

Just when he was beginning to feel a keen disappointment that he would be left out of the fight the hairs stood up on the back of his neck. He heard the crackling and turned...to face a snarling mountain cat. It was about as long as he was tall and its brown hide had patches of fur missing, from fights with other forest denizens. His weight was that of a full-grown man. His teeth were yellowed and long, though one of his front fangs was broken off halfway, probably causing him considerable discomfort. He was crouching and snarling, moving one paw after the other. He was in a foul mood.

Achilles made a quick decision on whether to throw his spear and risk a miss or hold it firm as the cat charged, trying to ram it into his chest. He had scant time to ponder his choices; the cat charged with a hideous growl. It took two bounds and then leaped for his throat. Achilles side-stepped the beast and drove his spear upward with both hands, with all the force he could manage.

The point of the spear caught the lion midway in its leap, going deep into the lower stomach, under the spot Achilles had aimed for; he had hoped to hit the heart and end the battle immediately. The cat flew into him, screaming in rage and pain, its talons raking the air. One swipe caught Achilles, and blood spurted from four different cuts on his chest.

The two sprawled in the grass and dirt, the lion twisting and jerking, trying to get at the man-thing that had wounded it. But the spear was deep in the cat, hindering his moves. He leaped wildly in the air, biting at the spear shaft, and then turned toward Achilles, who had scrambled to one knee and was pulling his dagger out. The lion slammed into him and Achilles threw his left hand at the furry face, staring into the blood red, narrowed eyes. His thumb slid into the open mouth and he smelled the terrible breath as the lion's weight forced him to the ground underneath it. Achilles threw his knees together, in the fashion Chiron had instructed him, so the lion could not rake his stomach and try and disembowel him with its claws.

Achilles gaped up, left hand half in the beast's mouth trying to hold the teeth at bay, his right hand driving the dagger into the furry hide. The lion screamed, trying to get at him; with a desperate lunge, Achilles slammed the dagger upward for the fourth time, into the beast's chest, finding its heart.

With a shudder, the animal fell to the side, its great body heaving, in a death spasm. Achilles jerked to a sitting position, wiping his bloody left hand over his face, staring at the cat as it died. Slowly, he pulled himself to his feet. He gaped at the lion and then the pain in his chest made him look at his own body. There were four deep scratches, with blood seeping out of them. He studied the wounds for a moment, then bent down over the lion and pulled his dagger free, wiping the blade clean on the furry hide. He sheathed the dagger and took a few steps, leaning against a big tree.

He remembered lifting his face and giving the centaur warning cry. And then he sagged against the tree, losing consciousness.

All three centaurs heard the war cry and raced through the dense forest, trying to find its location. They met, glancing around wildly, straining for more signs. They spread out again in a small circle, tense, knowing that their young comrade had most certainly met the mountain lion and that one of them, or possibly both, was dead or severely injured.

Chiron stumbled into the small clearing first. He knew at a glance what had transpired. He gave the war cry and ran to where Achilles was slumped against the tree, assessing his wounds. Moments later, the other two centaurs burst into the clearing and joined him, glancing at the cat.

"He is going to live, that much is sure," said Chiron at last, looking up at his comrades. "Let's get him back to the cave; bring the cat. Peleusson will want to see what he has done."

The moon chariot drove across the night sky twice while Achilles slept in the cave, with Chiron tending to his wounds with herbs and special waters. He chanted an age-old prayer and called upon Apollo, the great healer of Mount Olympus, to help in the recovery of "the son of Peleus." Achilles stirred several times and mumbled warnings and even gave a feeble war cry once, and then each time lapsed back into a deep sleep. But Chiron was not worried, for he knew his heart was strong and his recovery would eventually come.

On the third day, Chiron was sitting with his back to the heavy pile of animal skins that Achilles was sleeping on, playing his lyre and singing softly in his thick, low voice.

"I killed a lion today," said a shaky voice behind him. Chiron turned toward Achilles, a smile creeping over his face.

"You are only half correct, Peleusson," he said.

Achilles looked at him in surprise.

"You did indeed kill a lion…but it was not today. It was three days ago, and yet another half of day."

Achilles lay back down, lifting a hand to his head.

"He caught me off guard," said Achilles. "He should have killed me. One of the gods, Zeus, I suspect, must have been with me. Or…maybe it was Thetis."

"No, there were no gods or goddesses present that I saw," said Chiron. "Only one angry old mountain cat, and a tough, young warrior. That is all."

Achilles fell back asleep and then awoke half a day later to the delightful aroma of venison cooking. He sat up quickly. He peeled back some of the herbs on his stomach, and grimaced weakly, seeing that the healing process had taken hold. Then he was overwhelmed by a tremendous sense of hunger. He stood up and walked out into the fresh air of day. He saw Chiron sitting in front of a huge pit, with deer meat well roasted and ready for eating. He walked toward a small wooden table the centaur had set out, and saw bowls filled with vegetables and fruit. And even a piece of thick bread that Chiron had undoubtedly gotten from one of the women in the lower hills, who was adept at baking.

"I'm so hungry…I could eat a bear," said Achilles, sitting down at the table on a wooden stump. He winced at the pain in his chest but began to eat. Chiron pulled up a stump and sat with him, watching with delight as his young charge wolfed down the food.

"When can I see the lion?" asked Achilles, finally done eating and wiping a hand across his mouth.

"It's being cleaned by the women," said Chiron. "You will soon have a lion's robe to wear when you go out to hunt."

Achilles smiled.

"Just like Heracles," he said proudly.

The centaur nodded.

"Just like Heracles," he said.

It took a week for the women to finish the lion's skin. They skinned the cat and cooked the meat. Lion was tough eating, but acceptable for people who didn't have an overabundance of meat in their diet. On the eighth night after the death of the lion, a celebration was held for two reasons: to honor the great deed of Achilles and to celebrate the fact that the lion would no longer be stalking and killing human prey. Nearly thirty centaurs and almost as many women folk attended, and songs were sung into the night. One old man sat by the huge fire, talking about the adventures of Theseus and Heracles; Achilles was fascinated as he watched the firelight flicker on the old man's face while he spun his tales.

Everyone wanted to see the wounds the lion had left on Achilles' chest, and he proudly showed them all around. The wounds were scabbing up and healing, due to the herbs Chiron had used on them. Though the pain had largely departed, Chiron told him there would likely be scars there for the rest of his life. It was not something that bothered Achilles in the least.

"Some day, they will make a good story to tell my children, and my grandchildren," he said.

Several jokes were also offered and the best one came when an old centaur stood up and pointed a crooked finger at Achilles, saying, "The lion that once feasted on us is now being eaten by us." Everyone laughed heartily at the way the fates had turned on the old mountain lion.

Then, in front of everyone, Chiron presented to Achilles the lion skin robe. The head of the beast was still attached, though its eyes were gone. His mouth was open and the fangs seemed very small and much different to Achilles than when he was being attacked. But Achilles was proud of his deed, and when he saw Chiron smile at him, just before bed, he knew Chiron was proud of him, as well.

Achilles slept well that night, pleased by the excitement of the ceremony and warmed by the lion skin wrapped around him as he lay on his cot. Dreams came to him and filled him with contentment, for they were visions of victorious battles.

Patroclus

Two months after the great celebration, Chiron ambled over to where Achilles was wrestling with another young centaur. He watched for several long moments and then motioned Achilles to his side.

"Tomorrow will be a momentous day," said Chiron, choosing his words carefully. "We will be joined by….a guest. A very special guest." He paused to let the words sink in. Achilles merely nodded, waiting for him to continue. "His name is Patroclus, and he is a distant relative of yours. His mother was a cousin to your father; and his father, Menoetius, sailed with Peleus and Telamon on the Argo. Patroclus and Menoetius are staying with Peleus, as his guests."

Achilles showed no emotion, so Chiron continued.

"Patroclus is a year older than you and a fine, powerful young man. He will be a good….companion for you."

Achilles shrugged. "Why do I need a companion? I have all the other centaurs, and you, Chiron."

The centaur smiled faintly and nodded. "Yes, that is so, Peleusson. You have learned many things, and learned them well. But….have you learned how to interact with other men, other warriors your own age? Yes, this visit is a good thing."

With that, he ambled off, leaving Achilles alone with his thoughts. He had a difficult time sleeping that night. He pulled the lion skin snuggly around him and tried to visualize what the morning would bring, and how he would feel about sharing his private domain with this…trespasser. Achilles finally drifted off with unsettling thoughts working their way through his mind.

The day dawned bright and clear. Achilles leaped from his bedding and glanced about the cave. Chiron was gone already, which was unusual. On most days, Achilles was the first to rise and leave the cave, searching for food and adventure.

Achilles pulled on his brown chiton and walked to the entrance and glared out into the day. He saw six centaurs standing in a circle, their horses behind them. And in the center he saw two men, one old, one young. He recognized the older man as Phoenix, a friend of Peleus who had visited them on Mount Pelion on several occasions. He was very wise and told good stories, and Achilles liked him. But he frowned as he walked to the group and saw the younger one staring at him.

"Peleusson.....come meet Patroclus," said Chiron, extending a hand. The young man was dressed in a white tunic, drawn in at the waist by a thick cord, and wore dark sandals. Achilles stopped in his tracks, staring at him. It was almost like looking in the clear drinking pool behind Chiron's cave and seeing his own image staring back at him. The youth was his exact same height; he had long, blonde hair the same length as was the hair of Achilles. His face was angular and he had a long, straight nose, and thin lips, the same as Achilles. To top it all off, they were of nearly matching physiques.

"So...you notice the similarities between the two of you, as well," said Chiron. "From a distance, it would be difficult to tell you apart."

Patroclus stared at him with a bemused expression. Achilles felt a flush of anger swelling up from some unknown depths.

"No, it would not be difficult," he said, his voice low and even. "I would be the one who was winning whatever we were doing...whether it be running, or throwing the spear, or wrestling, or boxing."

Chiron could hardly repress a smile and Phoenix arched an eyebrow. The centaurs ambled closer at the words, sensing a contest. The smile left Patroclus's face and he stepped forward, confronting Achilles.

"We shall see about that, Achilles," he said.

Achilles felt the hair stand on the back of his neck. No one had ever dared call him Achilles before. He was always known as Peleusson....in honor of his father, not by the name his mother had bestowed upon him.

"Why do you call me Achilles?" he asked, his jaw tightening.

"Isn't that your name?" asked Patroclus perplexed, spreading his hands out. He turned to Phoenix, searching for support. "Is that not what you call him, Phoenix?"

Achilles was clearly upset and Chiron acted quickly to distract him.

"Yes, a contest between the lads would be good. Let's have a race."

He barked out some commands to several of the centaurs and two of them drifted off down the meadow, a good distance away. They raised their hands when they had positioned themselves. Chiron walked to the lads, who were assessing one another with critical expressions.

"Let's see who can reach the centaurs first," Chiron said.

"That is nothing," said Achilles. "We should run to them and all the way back."

Chiron raised an eyebrow and glanced at Phoenix. It was a long distance for men to run at full speed, let alone boys of this age.

"What do you think, Phoenix?" he asked. Phoenix held up a hand to block the sun from his eyes and then looked at the lads.

"Yes, both ways," he said. "It will be a good test. I think they are both up to the task."

Patroclus stripped off his tunic, exposing a lean, muscular frame. He was white skinned and obviously had not been in the sun as much as had Achilles. Achilles pulled off his shorter tunic and his dark skin was startling by contrast. Even Patroclus was taken aback by the beauty of Achilles' body; the muscles were long and lean, and rippled beneath his bronzed skin. He was an adonis in the making.

"Peleusson has matured quickly," said Phoenix, standing next to Chiron and keeping his words soft so as not to be overheard. "But Patroclus is a marvelous athlete, and a year older. He runs like the wind." The two lads stood next to each other, eyeing the centaurs a long ways off. Chiron lifted his hand high, calling for their attention. They turned to him. He shouted a word and lowered his arm in a rush.

The two were off, racing over the short grass. Patroclus spurted ahead and Achilles felt a sting of surprise. The young man was very quick and Achilles redoubled his efforts. They raced at full speed and reached the centaurs at exactly the same time. But Patroclus had thrown himself to the ground and somersaulted back to his feet at the turn.....a beautiful move that put him two strides ahead of Achilles on the return portion of the race.

"Oh, he has learned the rolling technique that the Cretans use. I wonder who taught him that," mused Chiron, turning to Phoenix. The tutor smiled. "Peleusson...will have a very difficult time making up for that."

Achilles was running like he had never run before but he could not make up the distance. He thought Patroclus would tire in the final steps, but he did not. They were almost neck and neck when they streamed past Chiron and Phoenix but Patroclus was just slightly ahead.

The boys walked in a tight circle, Achilles glaring at Patroclus. He felt an anger deep inside him that burned like a thunderbolt from Zeus. He fought for his breath, but not from the exertion, for the run had not tired him at all. It was the disgrace of not winning that was torturing him. The anger he felt was overwhelming. He felt the power coming to him again.

"We have to wrestle and box next!" Achilles growled, the words hard and cutting. Patroclus stood with hands on hips, staring at him. He nodded.

Chiron glanced at Phoenix. The teacher pondered the thought and nodded his agreement.

"Which will it be first?" asked Chiron. "Patroclus, you are the victor. The choice is yours. Which do you prefer?"

"Wrestling," he said.

Phoenix winced, glancing at his old friend.

"Patroclus is an excellent wrestler, Chiron," said Phoenix. "I fear this could go poorly for Achilles and then you will have a very angry Peleusson to deal with."

Chiron fingered his beard and called the contestants together.

"No biting, no groin blows and no gouging of the eyes," he said sternly. "Anything else is fair, under centaur rules. Is that acceptable to you, Patroclus?"

Patroclus nodded, staring hard at Achilles. He did not like the look that had come over Achilles's face; it was a mixture of pain and hate and was nothing like he had ever seen before. It was very unsettling.

Chiron knew the rules were acceptable to Achilles. He, too, had seen the look on his young charge's face, and understood what it meant. He was worried for Patroclus, but he also knew there was no way to call off the match. He motioned them together and barked out the command to start.

Patroclus was unprepared for what confronted him. Achilles charged into him like a wounded lion and threw his arms around his waist, locking his hands at Patroclus's back. Patroclus groaned, struggling to break the hold, but was immediately lifted off his feet. He was tilted and then slammed hard to the earth. Chiron and Phoenix winced as they heard the young body collide with the solid ground. Patroclus shook his head, dazed, and pushed up to all fours.....which was what Achilles wanted as he remained behind Patroclus, holding him at the waist, waiting for his moment to strike. Slowly, Patroclus struggled to his feet. Achilles lifted him off the ground and then slammed him to the earth again. Patroclus moaned loudly, stunned and hurt. Achilles hooked his right arm around Patroclus's right arm, and pulled it back, hard. Patroclus shrieked in pain. His arm was trapped in the fearsome arm lock that Achilles had learned from Chiron, and Achilles was applying terrible pressure.

A loud moan cut the air and Chiron leaped forward. He grabbed Achilles' arm and jerked it free from the arm of Patroclus, breaking his hold. Achilles stared up, eyes wide.

"Enough, Peleusson! Stop!" gasped the centaur. "It is over."

Chiron pulled him to his feet. Achilles' breast was heaving as he stared down at his helpless foe, writhing in pain in the thick grass. Patroclus could barely move his arm. He sat up, clutching it, tears streaming down his face.

"My arm…I think…it's broken," he gasped, looking up at Phoenix, who had come up to see how badly his charge was injured.

Achilles' heart was pounding like it had never pounded before. Chiron glanced at him and nodded toward the cave.

"Go and wait," he said sternly. "I will join you there shortly."

Achilles glanced about at the other centaurs. They were grinning and nodding at him, pleased with his efforts. He turned and walked to the cave without a word or a backward glance.

The sun had neared the midway point in its journey across the heavens before Chiron and Phoenix entered the cave. Achilles was sitting against the far wall, sharpening the point of his spear. He glanced up without expression. Chiron held a bowl of figs and berries in one hand and a pot of meat in the other, while Phoenix carried a bowl of thick goat's milk and also a long-handled vessel filled with wine. They both found a thick goat skin and sat down. They began to eat, offering Achilles a plate. He took it and nibbled at the food, glancing up at them.

"You are a very good wrestler," said Phoenix finally. "I don't think Patroclus has ever lost a wrestling match before."

"I have never lost a foot race," said Achilles.

Chiron nodded.

"I think his arm will mend," he said.

"It doesn't matter to me if it does or doesn't," said Achilles, his voice flat and without emotion.

"Well, it should matter, Peleusson," said Chiron. He fixed his gaze steadily on Achilles, who stared back defiantly.

"Why?" he said finally.

"Because Patroclus is a good young man. He will prove to be a good companion to you, and a good friend. He is not your enemy."

"I don't need friends," said Achilles.

There was a long pause.

"All men need a friend," said Chiron. "Phoenix here, we have been friends for many years. And your father…..do you not think Peleus and I are good friends? Why do you think that you are here, if not for friendship. What have I, an old man, to gain by having this impetuous, headstrong young boy living with me for so many years?

"Quality friendships do not come easily and they are not easily kept. They must be fed and nurtured, and must be able to survive long, tough ordeals. But a true friendship can sustain and nourish you through all the years of your life.

"Patroclus can be such a friend to you, Peleusson, if you will allow him to be."

There was another long silence before Achilles spoke.

"How do you know that, Chiron? Do you see what is in his heart, and in mine? Are we compatible, just because we look so much alike? Can not the outside deceive us as to what is lurking on the inside?"

"Those are all good questions, Peleusson," said Chiron. "But the answers were sought and found long before we brought Patroclus here. His father, Menoetius, and your father are close friends, and have been for many years, ever since they sailed to the Black Sea with the argonauts. Now, the fates have been unkind to Menoetius and his family. He was living in the village of Opus when Patroclus got into a fight with another young man, over a game of dice. The young man died and Menoetius and Patroclus were forced to flee for their lives. They have sought refuse in Phthia and your father has made them welcome. Patroclus has come here to Mount Pelion, at your father's request. He hopes a bond will grow between the two of you like exists between him and Menoetius."

He sighed, pausing for Achilles to digest his words.

"He is a good young man, with many of the same qualities that you value so highly," said Phoenix. "You are two of a kind, in nearly all ways."

Achilles pondered all that was said, still fiddling with the edge of his spear point.

"But you must allow yourself to accept his friendship," said Chiron.

They all continued nibbling at their food in silence. Chiron and Phoenix drank some wine, then fell to talking quietly between them. Achilles drank the goat's milk and wiped his hand over his mouth. He stood, finally, and glanced down at the two old men, both of whom he greatly admired.

"Is his arm broken?" he asked finally.

"No, we have mended it, and it will be fine, with time," said Phoenix. "He is strong and the arm survived."

"Has Patroclus eaten?" Achilles asked quietly.

Chiron glanced up.

"No, he has not eaten yet today," he replied.

Achilles grabbed a plate and filled it with meat and fruit, then found a cup and filled it with milk. He walked out of the cave, carrying the plate and cup as Chiron and Phoenix watched him go.

"He will be...a good friend, once he learns to control the rage that flows within him," said Chiron. "I have never seen a rage like his, except in one other person."

Phoenix nodded.

"Only in Heracles," he said.

"Yes," said Chiron. "Only in Heracles."

In the three months after Patroclus' arrival on Mount Pelion, he and Achilles became like brothers. They were inseparable, hunting together and competing in all types of athletic events. Patroclus showed Achilles the rolling turn he had used to win their race and Achilles explained to Patroclus the arm lock he had used to nearly destroy his elbow. They engaged in spear-throwing contests and in mock sword duels, with Achilles always coming out on top. He was simply too quick and too skilled for Patroclus.

The only sport they refrained from was boxing; they sparred just once and Achilles struck Patroclus so hard that he nearly broke his cheek-bone. As it was, his eye swelled shut almost immediately and it was several days before Patroclus could see clearly out of it again. From that day on, they decided they had grown so close that neither wanted to strike the other with hard blows to the face.

Also, Achilles was growing more accustomed to being called Achilles. It was the name that Peleus used in the palace when referring to his son and was therefore the name that Phoenix and Patroclus knew best. Only Chiron referred to him as Peleusson, and even he was starting to call him Achilles. It was the name that Thetis and Peleus had decided upon before he was born, and it meant god-like. Achilles liked the sound of his new name and he began thinking of himself as Achilles.

In the fourth month of Patroclus' stay, Chiron called them together and announced they would all be traveling to Phthia soon. Peleus had decided it was time for Achilles to leave Mount Pelion and begin learning how to live as the prince of a great city.

But there was something more important in the trip, Achilles suspected. He saw Chiron and Phoenix conferring on several occasions, with expressions of great concern on their faces. When he approached them and tried to involve himself in the conversation, they drew strangely quiet. The night before they were to depart for the Phthia, Chiron finally confided in him.

"There is another great adventure stirring in the winds, one that could even surpass the voyage of the Argo," Chiron told Achilles and Patroclus. They were all sitting around the fire and Achilles felt a chill down his spine, despite the warmth of the flames. There was something in Chiron's voice, a sense of urgency that was hidden deep. Achilles leaned forward, exchanging glances with Patroclus, eager to learn more.

"What is it, Chiron?" Achilles prodded. "Surely, we should know if there is trouble in Phthia and if my father needs us."

"No, it is not in Phthia," said Chiron. "But it could involve Phthia." He took a long sigh and glanced at Phoenix.

"You tell them, Phoenix. You understand these matters better than I do. It is has been far too long since I have sat at the long table of any of the great kings of Hellas."

Achilles leaned back, spellbound. Yes, it was a moment of tremendous importance if Chiron was talking about the other kings of Hellas. Achilles had heard of most of the great rulers, but they seemed so far away and their kingdoms so remote that he had scarcely any interest in them. But now, perhaps all of that was going to change.

"What we heard, from a messenger that Peleus sent yesterday, was that a terrible calamity has befallen the house of Atreus." Phoenix paused, glancing about the fire.

"The house of Atreus?" asked Patroclus. "I have heard of it."

"Agamemnon is the son of Atreus and is the ruler of Mycenae, the most powerful city in all of Hellas," continued Phoenix. "The citadel is said to be made of gold and the fortification walls that surround the citadel were built by the race of Titans, eons ago. There are two massive lions chained to the main gate, past which all visitors must go to enter the city. And Mycenae has a treasury that knows no limits.

"Menelaus, another son of Atreus, is the ruler of Sparta, the second greatest city in all Hellas. He is married to Helen, who some say is the most beautiful woman in all the world. Maybe the most beautiful woman who has ever lived.

"Recently, Sparta was visited by an emissary from far-flung Troy, the city that lies on the Hellespont, the guardian of the route to the Black Sea. It is also a very rich city, as it is able to extract a handsome fee from all ships that sail past to trade in the Black Sea regions."

Phoenix paused to take a long drink of wine. Achilles could hardly wait for him to continue. Phoenix wiped the wine from his lips with the back of his hand and his eyes narrowed.

"This emissary to Sparta was led by a young prince from Troy. His name is Alexandros and he is, by all accounts, a bit of a rogue. But, a handsome rogue. They say he is the rival of Apollo himself when it comes to good looks, and his way with women.

"While in the palace of Menelaus, and under the protection of the time-honored rules of hospitality, he apparently became infatuated with the queen. And he abducted Helen, taking her back to Troy as his concubine."

The cave was silent as the two old men and the two young warriors pondered the ramifications of such an incredible and audacious act.

"He violated the sacred rules of hospitality that govern all civilized men," mumbled Patroclus.

"What is the Spartan king planning to do about it?" asked Achilles.

"There is talk of a united army, bringing together the finest soldiers in all Hellas," said Phoenix, his voice trembling with emotion. "It would be an army like which the world has never been seen before. And, an assault would be launched against Troy itself."

"How would they get Hellas to unite? It has never happened before," asked Chiron, his brow wrinkled in thought.

"There are two ways," said Phoenix. "One is the lure of gold from Troy. There are tales of the treasury that would stagger even a king like Agamemnon. Aside from the tribute they collect from passing ships, the Trojans are skilled traders in their own right. It is also a city renown for the building of chariots and the taming of horses. There would be riches enough for everyone. It is a great adventure, a fabulous expedition. That in itself would entice many of the kings.

"And then there is the covenant that is being rumored. There is talk that when King Tyndareus offered Helen as a wife, and the riches of Sparta, as well, that he was fearful the rejected suitors, in their jealousy, might want to harm the new king and queen of Sparta. So, Tyndareus arranged for all the suitors to sign a pact declaring that if anything happened to Helen they would all unite to seek revenge."

"Very interesting," said Chiron, stroking his beard once again. "Whose idea was that?"

"They say it came from Odysseus, king of Ithaca," said Phoenix. "He didn't really court Helen, but he wanted her cousin, Penelope, for a wife. And Tyndareus gave Penelope to Odysseus as a reward for coming up with the grand idea of the pact."

"This Odysseus sounds like a cunning man," said Chiron. "Where did you say he hails from?"

"The rocky island of Ithaca, far to the east, is where Odysseus rules," said Phoenix. "It is a small kingdom, but a prosperous one."

Chiron turned to Achilles and Patroclus, who were hanging on every word.

"We leave at daybreak for Phthia, which is a hard ride of three or four days. Best get some rest."

They stood to go to their beds. Achilles glanced back down at his mentor, a gleam of adventure in his eyes.

"Don't get too excited just yet, Achilles," said Chiron, looking up at his charge. "Peleus and Phthia were not part of the pact. Peleus was not a suitor and you were too young to be one. There is no obligation for a prince of Phthia to take up arms in this war, even if it should happen."

The palace of Peleus

For the average traveler, moving by ox-drawn cart or even chariot, the journey from the land of the centaurs on the northern slope of Mount Pelion all the way to the palace of Peleus in the southern part of the kingdom took the better part of six days. But a group on horseback could cut the trip by a good margin. The first two days, they saw no one as they moved through dense forest and open glen. Only Helios, pulling his fiery chariot overhead, and the vast variety of birds that filled the air kept them company. On the third day, they began to encounter very small villages, comprised of mud huts; often, the villages looked deserted but the still-burning campfires and meat left hanging on outside racks gave away the fact that the occupants of the huts were merely hiding, afraid the travelers may be hostile.

On the fourth day, topping a small crest, they saw the walls of the palace and the surrounding town several leagues before them, sprawling over the next hill. Phthia had not changed since Achilles had last seen it as a very young boy; in fact, it had changed little in the last two hundred years. The walls of the city were composed of huge rocks and stones. Wooden beams were used to support the walls, which were not near as high as Achilles recalled. In several spots, he could see where the wall had crumbled away, making them more vulnerable to an invading army.

"It is not how I remembered it," said Achilles to Chiron, a touch of disappointment in his voice. The man-horse looked over at him and shrugged.

"It is enough," he said plainly. "Certainly more than you are accustomed to, both in size and comfort."

"But the walls aren't very large," said Achilles. "How could they keep out an invading army?"

"They are adequate," replied Chiron. "It is the reputation of the man who rules behind the walls of a city that deters enemies, more so than the size of the walls. Remember that, Achilles."

As they approached the town, Achilles was struck by the number of people living outside the walls in small huts and raising animals. They passed numerous little farms, and the men stopped their work to stand and stare as they rode by. The men were garbed in tattered chitons and most were barefoot. They pointed at Chiron, gesturing and whispering. Many times Achilles heard the word "centaur" spoken, in a hushed tone of deep respect. Glancing at his mentor, who rode tall and majestically, looking straight ahead, Achilles felt a sense of pride at being with him.

Several of the young boys walked briskly alongside the horses, then fell back as the horses disappeared from view. Achilles noticed several young girls staring at him and Patroclus, and pointing at them to others.

They entered the city's walls, riding past a solitary lookout. The soldier nodded at them as they passed, recognizing both Phoenix and Chiron. The huts inside the walls, in which most of the people lived, were composed of clay bricks, baked hard in the hot sun of summer, and reeds formed the make-shift roofs. They rode past a few scattered shops where workers toiled at their tasks. They saw a blacksmith hammering on a sword blade in a tiny, open-air workplace, and then a chariot maker, weavers and several potters. There was even a small winery, where women were stomping on grapes in a huge open vat. Achilles had the feeling that the city was not in prosperous times, but was struggling to even exist. It wasn't, he noted, as grand a place as he had dreamed it was. The city had a small agora, where citizens met to exchange their wares and to barter for food and other necessities. Figs, olives, barley and animals, especially oxen, were used as money in communities such as this all over the mainland.

The palace itself was modest, sitting on the crest of the small hill. It housed just the royal family of Peleus and the royal servants. A total of fifty people lived inside the palace and the once brightly-painted exterior walls were showing considerable signs of wear and neglect.

They stopped in front of the small palace. Just as Achilles slipped from the back of his horse, he saw a powerful-looking man stride out onto the top step and stare down at them, hands on hips. He wore a handsome purple cloak, tightly belted at the waist, the belt secured by a golden buckle, and leather sandals. His long, brown hair was tied behind his head in a bun and he sported a short, well-trimmed beard. Achilles recognized him immediately as his father, the king of Phthia.

"Chiron...old friend!" Peleus shouted as he bounded down the steps, taking three at a time. He embraced Chiron, hugging him tightly and slapping him on the back. He saluted Phoenix with a firm grip on the forearms. Then he turned toward Achilles.

"Son....how you've matured!" he said, his voice thick with the accent of the southern people. He walked to Achilles, who was now as tall as his father, and embraced him. Achilles could smell the sweat coming through the heavy perfume Peleus had obviously just recently thrown on. He embraced his father stiffly, then pulled back. Peleus noticed the withdrawal and let him go, smiling faintly at Chiron.

"Achilles!" Peleus continued. "You are quite a wrestler these days, I understand. "We must arrange a tournament for you, so we can all see your skills."

"You won't be disappointed," said Chiron, "I assure you that." He turned and smiled faintly at Patroclus for emphasis.

"Just make sure I don't have to wrestle him," said Patroclus, and all laughed; all save Achilles. He stood straight as a spear, unable to take his eyes off his father. He was fascinated by the long scar that ran down the left side of his face, back near the ear. He wondered why he had never noticed it before.

"How did you get your scar, sir?" he asked suddenly.

Peleus reeled back in mock surprise, then turned toward Chiron and Phoenix, throwing his arms out wide.

"Did you hear that? Did you hear the very first question the son asked his father? A warrior's mind, I see." He turned back toward Achilles, a twinkle in his eye, placing an arm around his son's shoulders.

"That is something I will have to tell you, boy," he said, winking. "That and many other tales. We have lots to talk about, you and me."

Inside the palace, Menoetius and a young girl were waiting for them. The girl's name was Polymele. She arrived several years after Achilles, born to a woman whose name no one knew. Some said the woman was a goddess who visited Peleus in the dark of night, but very few really believed that. More likely, she was the daughter of a woman who had caught the king's eye after Thetis left him, but who was not invited to stay after giving birth to a daughter. Polymele was pretty but shy; she was more interested in flirting with Patroclus than in seeing Achilles for the first time in many years.

The palace consisted of twenty separate rooms. There was the throne room, where the king would meet citizens to discuss important issues of the day, and where he would settle petty disputes and serious arguments. There was a banquet room, reserved for large gatherings, and a smaller eating room for the king and his family, and nearly a dozen sleeping rooms for members of the royal family and the many guests who were constantly coming and going. There was also a large bathing area and an enclosed garden area with benches, where casual discussions could be held amid a pleasant setting.

Of the many paintings on the walls, most were of hunting and battle scenes. One that caught the attention of Achilles depicted a group of centaurs chasing women and he looked carefully at the faces of the centaurs to see if any bore a resemblance to Chiron. He thought several of them did and the realization made him smile faintly.

The first night in the palace was devoted to considerable eating and drinking in the large banquet room. Peleus told Achilles how he had received the scar, in a great battle on the seashore on the voyage with the argonauts. It came during a fierce sword fight, but he was attacked from the side while fighting a warrior in front of him.

"The fellow who did this...he paid dearly for it," said Peleus, leaning forward, staring at Achilles. "I lost some blood, but he lost an entire head. And what's more, it came at Troy. Yes, indeed, we actually stopped at Troy on our way to the Black Sea. We were on shore at night with a little raiding party when we were attacked by a sizable group of Trojans.

"They had us outnumbered three to one, and I thought we were going to be destroyed....until Heracles showed up with that damn club of his, and started swinging it wildly, sending those accursed Trojans fleeing for their lives."

Everyone laughed at that story and others that followed quickly. Eventually, the talk turned to the matter between Sparta and Troy. Chiron was the first to broach the topic.

"Peleus, what do you hear from Sparta?" he asked. Peleus had been laying back on his large recliner, two hunting hounds sprawled out beside him. He immediately sat up, wiping his hands with a cloth provided by a servant. He wore a very serious expression.

"A month ago, Agamemnon called upon all the kings of Hellas to gather at Mycenae for a counsel," said Peleus solemnly. "I have just returned. Agamemnon feels that Troy must be punished for its intolerable actions. He is, as you can imagine, an angry man. Not only was his brother wronged, but he feels the entire house of Atreus, and all of Hellas, for that matter, was insulted by this pup from across the sea."

Chiron, Phoenix and Menoetius all nodded in recognition of the terrible insult that had been dealt out by the prince of Troy.

"I understand there is a pact between many of the princes, those who were suitors of Helen," said Phoenix. He paused for a sip of wine. "If that is the case, then surely they will all feel honor-bound to participate in an expedition against Troy. That is certainly understandable. What I fail to see is how Phthia should be involved. There was no suitor from this land for the hand of Helen, if I recall correctly."

Peleus nodded. He cleared his throat, as though suddenly anxious.

"True enough, Phoenix," he said. "However, there seems to be – should I say, a request, an urgent request – that Phthia get involved." He paused for a long drink of wine as the others waited for him to continue.

"Apparently, the seer, Calchas, has proclaimed that Troy cannot be conquered unless Achilles fights against the Trojans."

The room grew silent. Achilles felt the hairs stand up on the back of his neck as all eyes turned on him. Chiron assessed him long and carefully, then leaned back in his chair, almost in a slump.

"Why Achilles?" ventured Phoenix. "Has his fame spread so far from Mount Pelion, at such a tender age, that the great kings and princes of all Hellas would be loath to go into this grand adventure without the help of such a youth?"

There was another long pause.

"Perhaps," said Peleus, "it is because of the prophecy that surrounds his mother."

The words silenced them all. Then Peleus sighed and stood to his full height, glancing around the room. "Friends, this is a great night for Phthia. The prince has come home and has brought with him great friends of the throne. Let's retire, for we have grueling contests planned for tomorrow."

Each of them was shown to their sleeping rooms. Patroclus and Achilles shared a room with two large cots in it. They both stripped off their tunics, shaking the dust from the long trip, and laid down wearily. A torch provided scant light from its resting place on one of the walls. Neither had spoken, but Patroclus was about to when Chiron entered the room. He walked over to Achilles, gazing down at his young pupil.

"Your world is going to begin changing rapidly, like a lightning bolt from Zeus," he said gently. "Are you ready for it, Achilles?"

Achilles propped himself up on one elbow, staring up at the best friend he had ever known. He felt a stirring in his heart, knowing his days with the great centaur were numbered and would soon end. He nodded.

"Good," said Chiron. "Tomorrow, there are four contests in honor of your homecoming. I have told your father you will enter only the wrestling, nothing more. And Patroclus," he continued, glancing at the other young man, "you will enter the foot race."

Achilles frowned.

"Enter me in the javelin throw and the boxing, as well," he told Chiron.

The centaur nodded. He stood and started to walk away. Then he came back, and stared down at Achilles.

"Soon, you will see your mother."

Achilles was stunned.

"Thetis…is here?" he asked.

Chiron nodded.

"She knew you were coming and she has asked Peleus for permission to see you. He has granted it."

Achilles sat up, suddenly every muscle tense.

"Chiron….what did Peleus mean when he talked of my mother's prophecy coming true?"

"That is something you may ask her yourself," said Chiron. He turned and left the two young men alone with wild thoughts whirling in their minds.

The athletic contests were to be held on an open field outside of the walls, next to a thick grove of trees. There were several hundred spectators present, scattered along the sides of the competition area, some sitting and drinking from wine vessels and eating chunks of thick bread. All of them were looking forward to a pleasant diversion from their monotonous routine of toil from dawn to dark.

When Achilles and Patroclus arrived with Chiron and Phoenix, all of them on horseback, a murmur ran through the crowd. Achilles heard the words "centaur" and "man-horse" several times and knew they were spoken with a feeling akin to awe. To the village people, a centaur was a rare sight and was something of a mythical character.

Peleus, Polymele and their attendants sat on thick chairs on an elevated platform, high enough that the king had a good view of the entire field. There were a number of young men milling about. But they did not appear of the athletic nature.

"I don't see much in the way of competition," said Patroclus, turning to Phoenix. "Is this the best that Phthia has to offer?"

"Hardly," said his mentor. "Look there…"

He pointed to the edge of the trees, where nearly one hundred well-muscled young men were congregated near several large tents. Patroclus had not noticed them before and gave them a hard look.

"They are the Myrmidons, special troops of Peleus," said Phoenix. "They are great warriors, seasoned fighters, raised since boys to be warriors. They are men to be greatly respected, in all areas of competition."

Chiron and Achilles had already spotted the troops and were watching them as they began to assemble. They wore black tunics, with the sleeves cut off at the shoulder, and they were large and muscular. They formed ranks, with one man in charge barking orders, and then they marched toward the field. The peasants stood tall as the elite corps marched past them and stopped in front of Peleus. The king stood and saluted them.

"This is going to be quite a day," whispered Chiron to Phoenix. "Peleus has decided to see what his young son is really made of."

A herald addressed the crowd, offering greetings from the king. He declared there would be four sports contested, beginning with the spear throw, then the foot race, followed by the wrestling and, lastly, the boxing. He added that there were twenty entries each in the first two events and only two entries in both the wrestling and the boxing. He quickly called the spear contestants together.

Achilles moved to the group, jostling the spear he had used for years on Mount Pelion. Each man was given just one toss and he was listed last of the twenty. One after the other, the men stepped to a line and threw. The weather was perfect and the tosses were very good. One man in particular, Automedon, had the longest throw of the lot. After watching his spear strike ground, he walked past Achilles and smirked.

"Beat that, if you can!" he said. Achilles paid him no heed but walked quickly to the line, pulled his arm back and let fly. The crowd gasped as his spear took wings. It soared high into the crisp air and sailed beyond Automedon's effort by the length of two men. He turned and walked to Chiron without a word.

There was a murmur from the crowd as Achilles was declared the winner. He glanced at Automedon, who was glaring at him. The man was many years older than Achilles, and taller. He had a short scar cutting across his cheek and a long, nasty scar on the inside of his thigh. Achilles judged him as a wily warrior, one who had seen many battles and would rather die than lose, in anything.

The runners lined up, twenty in all. They were told of the course and where the turn-around point was located. When the herald dropped his arm, they took off running at a great pace. Achilles leaned forward, eagerly watching Patroclus. He wondered if he would try his special somersault turn and smiled when he did. The crowd roared in delight at the maneuver but several of the Myrmidon warriors shouted derisive comments. Automedon stepped forward, watching intently as Patroclus crossed the finish line well ahead of the others.

The announcement of Patroclus' victory brought another great cheer from the crowd… and from Polymele, who leaped up from her seat, clapping her hands together joyously. Achilles glanced up at his father, who sat rigid and without expression on his chair. Achilles wondered if he and Patroclus were bringing pride to Peleus, or were causing him embarrassment by defeating his best Myrmidon warriors.

Chiron placed a hand on Achilles' shoulder and squeezed hard for emphasis on what he was about to say.

"You have a very worthy adversary in the wrestling," he said. "Phoenix has seen this warrior compete before. He has great experience and is much larger than you. I want you to be cautious, to move him around and tire him out before you try the arm lock. Do you hear me, Achilles?"

The warrior was announced as Memnes; he was taller than Achilles and far wider in the shoulders. He was many years older and gave the appearance of having been in many brawls. The announcement of his name brought a loud roar from the spectators, while Achilles' name caused only a smattering of shouts. Polymele stood and clapped her hands together as she watched her half-brother prepare to wrestle.

A large circle was drawn and the two men stepped into it. The herald gave some instructions, telling them that biting, eye gouging and kicks to the groin were outlawed.

"This is a civilized contest," he remarked, bringing laughter from the Myrmidons who had lined the circle, anxious to see their comrade score a resounding victory and restore some lost pride.

Achilles stood motionless as Memnes circled him. The warrior wore a heavy scowl and when he grinned Achilles saw that half his teeth were broken off.

"I'm going to break you in half, little boy," Memnes muttered, swinging his arms back and forth across his massive chest. "You may be the son of the king, but I am the greatest wrestler among the Myrmidons. We are the finest warriors in all of Hellas. I will defeat you, but I may spare you some broken bones if you cry out for mercy quickly enough."

Achilles felt the power starting to move through his body. It was an uncontrollable force and he knew it came directly from Zeus. He began to move, too..... weaving up and down in a manner that Memnes had never seen before. He stopped, staring at Achilles.

"What style is this, boy?" he mumbled, perplexed. Then Memnes charged, arms outstretched.

Achilles moved deftly aside; he caught Memnes by a wrist and twisted it hard, dropping low as he did so. The large man flew over him and fell heavily to his back. He rolled twice and stood up, grass sticking out of his hair and mouth. He spat and charged again. Achilles tried the same move, but Memnes swerved into him, blocking the attempt, and swung his right elbow wildly. It crashed against Achilles' face and sent him flying to the ground. He rolled quickly and stood up. He heard Patroclus gasp as he felt the blood pouring down his face.

"Foul!" cried Phoenix, stepping forward. "That was a blow!"

Chiron grabbed his friend's arm and pulled him back, a wild look in his eye.

"Never mind the foul," he said, voice low. "Injuring Peleusson is the worst thing any man can do."

Memnes smiled at the sight of blood running down Achilles' face. He motioned for Achilles to come closer and wrestle more. Achilles moved toward him slowly. He lifted his hands quickly, as though he was going to deliver a punch. Memnes raised his hands to ward off the expected blow and Achilles dove at him, hooking both arms around Memnes legs and tumbling him to the ground. Memnes shouted in surprise and rolled over to his stomach, scrambling on all fours. He shook his head, feeling Achilles behind him, on top of him. Then the older warrior pushed off the ground and began to stand... just as Achilles knew he would. As the large man came to his feet, Achilles gripped him hard, one arm around his waist the other between his legs. With a loud grunting sound, Achilles lifted him high into the air, then titled him and drove him hard into the ground.

There was a sickening thud as Memnes collided with the earth. He groaned loudly, dazed. He shook his head and struggled slowly to his hands and knees again, his face now bleeding, too. When he reached back with his right arm, Achilles was waiting. He trapped the arm in his favorite move and jerked it hard. Memnes gasped, sensing that he was in terrible trouble. He fought to jerk his arm free, but to no avail; Achilles had it locked tight. The two men struggled, one trying to desperately free his arm, the other trying to break it. There was a sharp crack; Memnes screamed in pain. Achilles released the arm and stood. He stared down at the warrior writhing on the ground, moaning loudly.

The Myrmidons gaped at Achilles in silent admiration. The match had taken less time than the race. Achilles had beaten their finest wrestler with little effort, it seemed to them. He walked back to Chiron and Patroclus and heard his name shouted by the herald, and by the crowd. He glanced up at the king's platform and saw Peleus standing, hands on hips, smiling.

"I am ready to box now," said Achilles to Chiron. The centaur nodded and used a linen strip to wipe the blood from Achilles' face. The herald shouted out the rules of the boxing contest, motioning the athletes to the area where he stood.

Automedon was the foe in the boxing and he strode into the circle with his fists raised high, acknowledging the cheers of the Myrmidons. Achilles was given a short rest, then the two warriors faced each other. Automedon sneered at Achilles; when the time came to touch fists, Achilles could feel the rage again. He wanted to do more than defeat Automedon....he wanted to humiliate him.

They circled each other cautiously. Automedon offered a few light feints with his left fist, then he threw a right hand aimed at the chin of Achilles. Achilles slipped under the blow and sank his knuckles into Automedon's face. The soldier groaned heavily and backed off, blood running from his mouth. His eyes narrowed with anger as he charged back in, swinging both hands. Achilles ducked beneath the blows and delivered a wicked punch to the man's heart. Automedon stiffened as though he had been shot by an arrow and then sank to the ground, bent over and helpless, gasping desperately for his breath.

When it became obvious that Automedon could not continue, the herald declared Achilles the victor. The crowd swarmed around him. The peasants ran up, smiling through broken teeth, bowing and offering their congratulations. Then Peleus pushed through the crowd and offered his handshake.

"Chiron has taught you well, my son," said Peleus, beaming with pride. "You are the finest wrestler I have ever seen. And your boxing skill is suitable, as well."

The Myrmidons gathered around Automedon, helping him to his feet. He shook his head as Memnes slid an arm around him. Together, they hobbled over to where Achilles stood. He saw them and tensed, perplexed. He could not fathom why they had come to him.

"We want to offer our praise," said Automedon, staring at Achilles. "We are Myrmidons and proud of it. We will follow you, son of Peleus, wherever you lead us. We will be honored to fight with you at Troy."

Achilles was stunned. He had not expected such tribute from these men. But he knew instinctively that what they said was from the heart, that he had indeed won their loyalty. He glanced at Chiron and then at Peleus, who were watching intently, smiles of pride on their faces.

"We had to test you, son….to see if all that Chiron and Phoenix were telling us was true," said Peleus. "Automedon and Memnes are two of the finest men I have ever had fight at my side. They will obey you and honor you….at Troy!"

"Troy!" gasped Achilles. "Is it a certainty, then? We will be going on this great expedition, Patroclus and I….with the Myrmidons?"

Peleus nodded, throwing an arm about his son's shoulders.

"Come with me," he said. "We have much to discuss."

They sat and talked late into the night, all of them. Peleus invited Automedon and Memnes to join them and Achilles found himself warming to the two warriors. They were battle-hardened soldiers who had worked their way up the ranks among the Myrmidons. They had seen action on a number of smaller fronts but had never been involved with anything like the proposed expedition to the land of the Trojans.

Peleus told them more of the latest developments regarding Troy. All the Achaean kings had agreed to unite for a war against the sons of Priam. They selected a place called Aulis, a little island just off the coast of Athens, as the gathering point. Peleus had committed fifty ships from Phthia and five hundred fighting men, half of his entire corps of Myrmidons. In return, he expected a sizable share of the booty take from Troy.

The next day, Peleus took Achilles and Patroclus to the armory to select swords, breastplates, helmets and greaves. They also took shields, both opting for the smaller shields over the larger eight-shaped shield. They cared less about the protection and more about the mobility, as the large shields were difficult to carry and to maneuver with.

They selected thick swords with stout handles, ones that handled well. But when it came time to take their spears, Peleus pulled Achilles away. He led him down a short corridor and into a very small room where his own battle gear was hanging. He stood and gazed at the armor he had worn in numerous battles, his son by his side.

"This is for you," he said, his voice thick with emotion. He walked to the wall and took down a long spear. He hefted it, moving it around with obvious affection, and then handed it to Achilles, who was surprised at its weight.

"It was crafted many years ago, on Mount Pelion, by the very best of the spearmakers of the centaurs," he said. "This spearmaker was Heracles' friend; he found the perfect tree. He made just two spears from the tree – Pelion ash spears. One he gave to Heracles, before the voyage with Argo to the Black Sea. The other he gave to me, on my wedding day. It takes a special brand of man, a very powerful man, to wield it. I give it now to you, Achilles. But leave it here on the wall until you depart, and then it is yours to take."

They returned to the banquet hall to join the others. The night had been so special that Achilles was reluctant to have it end. He and Patroclus finally left for their rooms, discussing quietly the great adventure that lay ahead of them. They clasped arms, vowing to protect one another at all costs, and then embraced. They took to their cots and were soon fast asleep.

It was around midnight when Achilles was awakened by a rustling on the cot next to him. He strained to hear and turned slightly to try and see what was happening. There were two figures on the cot and he could hear the soft murmurs of a woman. He lay breathless as he saw the form of Patroclus moving on top, and the woman begin to breathe heavily. He watched for a long time as they made love and he gasped slightly when he saw the woman finally get up to leave, long after they began. And then he smiled.

In the banquet room, Peleus leaned hard on the table and stared at Chiron. The light from the hearth fire cast deep and grotesque shadows on the walls. Several empty wineskins now lay on the floor, next to the hunting dogs, sprawled out and sleeping.

"Tell me what kind of a son I have," said Peleus, staring at Chiron. He lifted a hand and wiped away the red wine and leaned forward anxiously. Between these two old friends there could be no deceptions; it was time for true talk.

"The best," said Chiron.

"How so?" said Peleus. "In what ways?"

"As you saw today, in all ways," said Chiron. When he said no more, Peleus leaned back in his chair, eyeing his companion. He was determined to wait him out if it took until dawn. After all, there was plenty more wine.

"He is not so strong as Heracles, of course," began Chiron finally. "But he is much quicker than he was, with both his body and his mind. As for Theseus and Jason, two of my other finest pupils, he exceeds them both in every way you can measure: he is stronger, faster, smarter. And Peleus, he has much of you in him, as well. He is, in spite of himself, very compassionate and capable of great tenderness. He is deeply sincere. But, he has one major weakness."

"And what is that?" said Peleus, his eyes narrowing.

"He can't control the power that he feels comes from Zeus," said Chiron slowly, carefully choosing his words. "He is very sensitive to what he perceives as injustice. Right and wrong have no middle ground for Achilles. He sees things with startling clarity. What is right is right, and what is wrong is wrong. And he would die defending his values. This spirit becomes a rage within and gives him great power, but it also makes him vulnerable to his own emotions."

Peleus leaned back, head in his palms, reflecting on all that Chiron had told him.

"I want my son to be a warrior, the greatest warrior the world has ever known," he said, his words thick with emotion. "He needs to know what it means to be a warrior. But, there is more to it than physical might, as we both know. That is why I sent him to you, old friend. There is no better teacher than you."

Chiron nodded, accepting the compliment for what it was; he knew that Peleus meant it with all his being.

"He will be my last pupil, this Achilles," said Chiron.

Peleus understood why, but he still needed to ask.

"It is not easy to give them up, you know," said Chiron. "I have led twenty, maybe more, young men on the path to being a warrior. They were all special, some more than others...but all special. But I have never had one like this one, Peleus. When they all leave, something of me leaves with them. Maybe it is because I am now so old."

They sat in silence, enjoying their wine and their friendship. Several times they lifted their wine cups and drank before Peleus spoke again.

"Maybe the prophecy is true, then," said Peleus.

"What prophecy?" asked Chiron, raising an eyebrow.

"You remember the wedding day, when Thetis and I were united," said Peleus. "When the seer rose up and said it was prophesized that the son of Thetis should be a far better man than her husband."

"I remember," said Chiron. "But I thought that perhaps you had not."

He knew that such a prophecy could deeply wound a proud man and he knew that Peleus was a proud man.

Peleus shrugged: "Who wouldn't want their son to be greater than he?"

"Many men, even most men," said Chiron.

"Well, I've had my days and my glories, old friend," said Peleus. "I've lived hard. I have known great men, shared in great deeds. I've known a few great women, too," he said with a chuckle. "I regret nothing, begrudge my son nothing. Whatever fame he earns, will it not also attach itself to me, in some way?"

Chiron nodded.

"Well said, Peleus. But great men need great adventures. Will there be a golden fleece for Achilles to rescue, or stupendous labors to perform, or a monster to slay in the labyrinth of Knossus? Jason, Heracles and Theseus were fortunate that the Fates gave them wonderful adventures to pursue."

Peleus slammed a fist on the thick table.

"By Hades, there wasn't any such adventures for me, but I found them anyway," he shouted. "If there were no monsters left in the world, then I created them."

He stood and paced along the wall, running his thick hand over the rough stone, as if relishing the feel of cold rock against his mortal flesh. He moved to the large cabinet and pulled out another wineskin. He opened it, returning to the table. He poured another cup for both of them and sank into his large chair, lifting his feet up to the table.

"Did Jason really have a golden fleece to find, or did he invent one so that he might justify his lust for adventure and gold? You and I know that Jason was nothing more than a pirate, eager to loot and take what he could. Was there a monstrous dragon protecting the fleece? Let the story-tellers believe that, Chiron....you and I, we know better.

"But I will tell you this; we fought many great battles in a strange land far, far away. We came back with fame and fortune, more than I could have ever dreamed of. When we returned, all Achaeans were eager to greet us, to show their hospitality.

"Why, some even call us gods now, if you can believe that. All because we were successful pirates."

Peleus leaned back in his chair laughing and Chiron chuckled with him.

There was another long silence before Chiron spoke.

"Have you see Jason or the fabled strongman in recent years?"

"They say Jason lives in Egypt, where he is treated like a god," said Peleus. "And Heracles — I have not seen him since we were at Troy. He got off the Argo at a small island before we returned to the mainland. I have not seen him since, and that's been twenty years now."

"They say he's dead, killed by a poison arrow," said Chiron taking another long drink of the wine, wiping his mouth with his sleeve.

"Yes, I've heard that tale and I suspect it may be true," said Peleus. "I don't know if he's dead or not, but I never expect to see him again, not in this life. They talk of him now as if he were already a god."

"Gone to Mount Olympus to join his father, Zeus Cloudgatherer," said Chiron, taking another swig of wine. They paused again to savor both the wine and the memories of days long gone.

"And what of Telamon?" said Chiron. "Is your brother a friend again, or an enemy?'

"With Telamon one never knows," mumbled Peleus. "He was always so anxious to compete with me, at every turn of the road. He was so much larger, as you know, but was never able to best me in anything. He still rules over Salamis. He has a giant of a son, named Ajax, and I hear he is destined to be a great warrior. You can bet that if there is a war at Troy, the kingdom of Salamis will be well represented."

They decided to drink a toast to the memory of Heracles, the greatest of heroes. They toasted him many times, well into the night.

The following days were a blur of activity as Achilles and Patroclus trained for hours on end with their new weapons and feasted at night with Peleus. Well past midnight of their sixth day in Phthia, Achilles was startled awake by a rough hand on his shoulder. He sat up quickly, rubbing the sleep from his eyes, blinking. Peleus's face was directly in front of him.

"Shhhhh," Peleus whispered, placing a thick finger on his lips. "Follow me."

He straightened and walked softly out of the room, into the hallway. Achilles climbed off the cot and moved after him, startled by the appearance of the king in the early morning hours. The king was wearing a fur piece across his chest and a furry loin cloth, with thick sandals. He clutched a fur top piece and sandals in his hand and tossed them at Achilles.

"There's a chill in the air," he said. "Put these on."

Achilles quickly slipped them on and faced Peleus.

"Here," he said, handing Achilles a spear. "We're going on a hunting trip."

"Should I call Patroclus and Chiron?" asked Achilles, clutching the spear.

"No, it's just you and me, son," he said.

He turned and hurried down the empty hallway, Achilles close behind. They broke into the clearing and Achilles was further surprised to see a chariot, with two magnificent black steeds, waiting for them. He recognized Automedon as the driver. They climbed in. Automedon nodded solemnly at him.

"To the camp," said Peleus.

Achilles felt a shiver down his back. Chiron had told him that the Myrmidons lived by themselves outside the village and to the north. The chariot clattered through the empty streets. There was no activity at all and Achilles glanced up at Diana to see where the moon was. It was still an hour until dawn, he guessed by the moon's position in the sky. Chiron had taught him how to read the time of day by watching the sun, and the time of night by the stars and the moon.

Achilles gripped the handrail as the chariot sped over the rough trail. Peleus peered into the dark and mumbled to Automedon, who nodded. Achilles wondered what was so urgent that they would steal out of the palace in the dark of early morning, like common thieves departing from a crime.

"What is the reason for this trip, father?" he asked Peleus, leaning next to the king.

"It is time you met the Myrmidons," he said. That was all.

They drove for a long time through the sparse forest and then broke into a small clearing, filled with small huts. The first light of day was now upon them. There were a few men stirring in front of the huts, talking quietly and cleaning weapons. A few women were walking to the river with vases, for morning water. No children were up and about yet, as it was too early for them.

When the men saw it was the king approaching, they walked quickly to the center of the village, where they knew the chariot was heading. Men saluted Peleus and he returned the salute, snapping his arm out straight, his fingers knotted in a tight fist. Achilles noted with pride the great respect that showed in the mannerisms of the men.

Automedon reined the horses in and Peleus dismounted, motioning for Achilles to follow. Within moments, there were two hundred men gathered around a large bonfire, burning bright in the center, the smoke spiraling upwards toward the morning sky. Peleus whirled around, smiling at the men. He walked over to several and exchanged an arm embrace. Then he motioned Achilles to his side.

"Myrmidons!" he began, pausing to give the word its due respect. "This is my son, Achilles. He has come home to Phthia and I am rightly proud."

The sound began softly, a humming….and then it grew into a loud, throbbing noise. It took a moment for Achilles to realize it was coming from the mouths of the Myrmidons, a clucking noise he had never heard before. It filled him with a sense of awe; he knew if he was a warrior opposing them, it would quickly become much more – a sense of fear!

"Alilia…alilia….alilia…..alilia….alilia….."

The Myrmidons stared at Achilles, clucking, and then began to hold their spears out toward him. He stared back at them, his temples pounding, running his eyes over the face of every man there. They were like men he had never seen before…faces taut and drawn, almost chiseled. They all wore black tunics and boasted of long, lean arm muscles, perfect for slinging a spear or for swinging a sword for hours on end.

Peleus leaned close to him.

"They are paying tribute to you; they have heard of your victories. Most of them were there. They know you are now, truly, the son of Peleus."

The Myrmidons began dancing around the fire in a wild scene, tunics hugging their bodies. They rammed their spears high overhead, shaking them, screaming the war cry. Peleus gaped at them, then grabbed his own spear and leaped into their midst. Achilles watched with total fascination as his father danced around the fire, head jerking up and down, eyes nearly shut, lost in a trance. Achilles felt movement at his side and he turned to see Automedon standing next to him with a wild look in his eyes.

"Dance, Peleusson!" he shouted. "Dance with your warriors. Dance with the Myrmidons!"

Achilles turned back to the fire and felt the spell coming over him. He clutched his spear and ran to the circle, falling in behind his father. He threw his head back and screamed.

"Alilia…alilia….alilia…..alilia….alilia….."

On and on they went, until pure exhaustion overtook them all. When it was over, Achilles slumped to the ground, sitting next to his father, amid the Myrmidons. He knew he was one of them now, for all time.

The following days passed quickly. Achilles and Patroclus were greeted warmly everywhere they went in the city and there were several court women who wanted to have the handsome princes meet their daughters. Though they both enjoyed the attention, Achilles hung back while Patroclus took the lead, flirting with the girls, hugging the prettier ones who came too close. Achilles was eagerly awaiting the opportunity to talk to Patroclus about the woman on his cot. It came when they were walking through the palace after a strenuous day of wrestling and sword work.

They came across Polymele and several of her attendants. Achilles nodded to his half sister and smiled at her. She returned the smile, but could not take her eyes off Patroclus as they passed one another.

"Polymele is a pretty lass," said Achilles.

"Yes," said Patroclus.

"And she seems to like you," Achilles said, looking at his friend.

"You can not tell much from a glance," said Patroclus, gazing straight ahead.

"Perhaps not. But you can tell a lot by watching from the neighboring cot," said Achilles.

Patroclus frowned and stopped abruptly, facing him.

"We thought you were asleep, and our desire overcame us," he said defensively. "It was the work of Aphrodite, I swear."

Achilles tried his best to look upset, but could not. When Patroclus saw his mood was not one of anger, he was relieved.

"She is a sweet girl," Patroclus said. "But, I fear she will be sad shortly, when we sail away." He paused and then continued: "But until that day, I plan to get to know her even better. And she has a friend who would very much like to meet you."

Achilles shook his head.

"I am interested only in the adventure that lays ahead," said Achilles. "Troy is all that Zeus will allow me to think about."

"Ah, don't blame your lack of interest in girls on the gods," laughed Patroclus, slapping him on the shoulder. "The goddess Aphrodite can work miracles, if you will just give her half a chance, Achilles."

Try as they might, Patroclus and Polymele could not persuade Achilles to meet any of her friends. All his energy was consumed with honing his fighting skills in long, demanding workouts with the Myrmidons. He visited their camp daily, looking for anyone willing to work with him in sword practice or wrestling. Even his nights were filled with dreams of battles; he was being consumed by his love of war. Peleus watched from afar, talking to Chiron and Phoenix as he watched his son overwhelm foe after foe, in everything he tried.

"Maybe he is not my son after all, but the son of Zeus," shrugged Peleus one day. "He is like no warrior I have ever seen."

On the twentieth night of their stay in the palace, Achilles retired early and had been asleep for a long while when he jerked suddenly awake. He glanced about the room, sensing a presence. He sat up and stared into a corner. A figure was standing in the shadows. He stood slowly, blinking away the sleep, wondering if Zeus Cloudgatherer had at last come to acknowledge him.

But it was a soft, sweet voice that called out to him; a woman's voice.

"Achilles," she said sweetly.

He moved slowly to where the woman waited. She wore a light gown and he could see through some of it. She was small and very trim. He gaped down at her. He was aware of a mist in the air and suddenly he had difficulty breathing. Her hands slid into his.

"Come with me, Achilles," she said in a voice that was like a song. He wanted to resist and to pull his hands away, but he did not. Somehow, he felt she had a strange power over him.

They walked out of the room and down the dark hallway, then turned and moved through a small doorway, out into the patio area. The moon was shining brightly overhead and she led him to a long bench. She turned and faced him, dropping his hand, and he saw her clearly for the first time. She was much older than he was, but was beautiful. Very beautiful. She had light colored hair, like his, and it was braided in a fashion he had never seen before. She smiled up at him, the mist still clinging to her.

"I am your mother," she said.

"Thetis!" he gasped. He could find no other words.

"Yes," she said. And then she hugged him. He could smell her perfume and it was intoxicating. Slowly, he embraced her and they stood together for a very long time, until at last she released him and slid her sweet hands over his arms.

"You are sooooo powerful," she said. "Watching you fight the day after you arrived, I was very proud."

"You....were there?" he gasped.

"Oohh, yes!" she smiled. She sat down on the bench and motioned for him to join her. He sat next to her, still mesmerized by her. No wonder she had charmed Peleus, he thought and even had the great god Zeus contemplating a romance. He had not seen many beautiful women in his life, but she was the most beautiful woman he had yet known.

"You were magnificent. The centaur has taught you well."

"You and Chiron are not friends," he stammered, not knowing what else to say. "He has told me the story of my birth and of the River Styx."

She sighed, hands folded in her lap.

"Chiron is a man of many talents," she said. "Highly intelligent, fiercely loyal, at least to your father; a seducer of women; a teacher of boys and mentor of heroes." She tensed and stared at him.

"Do you want to be a hero, my Achilles?" she said, her voice low and soothing. She placed a soft hand again on his bare arm and caressed it. "Is that what your heart yearns for, to be like your father, only greater?"

Achilles was uncomfortable. He felt like he was being seduced by his own mother, not in a sexual way but in a way in which she would draw him closer to her and try and bend him to her will, whatever that may be. He pulled back slightly and her hand dropped from his arm.

"Where have you been all of my life?" he asked. "Why have I never seen you before this moment?"

Thetis glanced at the moon, darting behind the scudding clouds.

"Do you believe in the gods?" she asked him, returning her gaze to his.

He nodded.

"Yes, doesn't everyone believe in the gods?" he responded.

"And, what do you believe, my Achilles? Do you believe that they watch our every move and plot for and against us...that the gods determine our victories and our defeats? Do you believe that the gods really care about poor mortals playing out their pitiful lives down here on this lonely, tired piece of ground we call earth?"

He ran his eyes over her, trying to understand what she was talking about. She stood and walked to the edge of the garden. She moved so gracefully that at one point he thought she seemed to be floating. He had to wipe his eyes with his hand and look again. Perhaps it was because he was so tired, he told himself. She returned to the bench, smiling down at him. She sat again, very close to him, her breast touching his arm. There was a slight but very pleasant aroma in the air.

"Zeus has a very special plan for you, Achilles," she whispered up at him, her dark eyes boring into his. "You are not like other men. No, not like any other men at all. Do not allow yourself to get caught up in the mortal world and the mortal way of living. There is something far more wonderful awaiting the son of Thetis. I am a goddess, you know, and I can give you a life you can not even imagine, here and now."

She paused, and Achilles stared into her eyes, spellbound.

"Will you come away with me tonight?" she whispered.

He felt weaker than he had ever felt in his life. Was she working some magic on him, he wondered. He longed to be with her, close to her.

"Where...why?" he muttered.

She took his hand and stood, tugging gently. He stood, looking down at her. She walked out of the agora, holding his hand tight. He moved beside her, tall and proud. The street was deserted and they walked quickly out of the palace area and down a side street, to the gate. The sentry was dozing and didn't even look up as Thetis and her son slipped out into the night.

There was a covered cart waiting for them. The driver wore a long, black tunic with a hood that covered his features. He stared at them hard and nodded as Thetis gave a nod in return. Two heads peered out from the back of the cart. Thetis climbed swiftly into the back and reached for Achilles. Without hesitating, he climbed in behind her. The cart moved slowly away from Phthia, with Diana the moon goddess watching from far above.

The Kingdom of Skyros

Peleus ran through the halls, filled with rage. "Damn that witch!" he shouted, his words bouncing off the stone walls. "Why was I foolish enough to let her come? How could I not see through it all!"

Chiron met him in the room in which Achilles stayed, with Patroclus and Phoenix at his side.

"She apparently cast a spell on everyone," said Chiron with a shrug of disgust. "She has learned a great deal of mind control from Nereus in the years she has been away, Peleus."

Peleus stomped around the sleeping room and turned in a small circle, the others watching him. He came back and faced Patroclus.

"You saw nothing? You heard nothing? How is that possible?" he shouted, waving his arms in the air.

Patroclus shrugged sheepishly.

"I was exhausted from the day's activities," he said weakly. "And so was Achilles. At least, so I thought. We hardly spoke. We laid down and I was fast asleep. I don't know if she came into the room, or if he left on his own."

"She came into the room, you can wager that," said Chiron. "I have talked to the sentry outside the palace throne room. He saw nothing and remembers nothing. He was obviously under her spell. She must have hypnotized him. And the same with the sentry at the main gate."

"They are no match for a goddess," said Phoenix.

"A goddess, my horse's hind end," sputtered Peleus. "She's no goddess and you know it as well as I do, Phoenix. She's a witch. Nereus has had her under his spell for many years and has taught her the potions that seduce and the hypnotism that works like magic. A witch's magic. She is nothing but a sea nymph who can work spells on weak and unsophisticated minds."

He turned to Chiron.

"Is that not true, Chiron?" he demanded. The centaur nodded.

"True enough, Peleus. But….she is very good, I fear. Remember how she once convinced you that she was different animals and you kept letting her go from your grip, thinking you were fighting a snake, and then a lioness, and then…."

Peleus cut him short with a flip of the hand.

"Yes, yes! I remember, damn it. And she had me under a spell again when she came here three nights ago and asked to visit Achilles. I must have been under a spell; why else would I have agreed to such a stupid thing?"

He slapped his hand against his forehead and then turned to Chiron. He shrugged.

"Who knows where Achilles is right now, and what wild thoughts she is putting into his young mind?"

Achilles had never been on a ship before. He stood tall at the bow, staring out over the wine-dark sea ahead, the stiff breeze stirring his long locks. Thetis moved to his side and took his arm in her white hand. She looked up at him, the tremendous pride in her son showing on her features once again.

"There is Skyros," she said, pointing to a small piece of land jutting out of the water. "It is a beautiful island. You will fall in love with it and the people who live in the palace, Achilles. I promise. It is my gift to you – the island of Skyros and all its wonders."

They had ridden in the cart for two days, stopping often for long breaks in the countryside. The wagon was full of food of all types and wine. There were four others along, two men and two women. Achilles had never been able to sit still for very long, but for some reason the journey did not bother him. He spent a lot of time sleeping, somehow able to ignore the bumping and the jostling. He had several long conversations with his mother and finally was able to ask her the one question he wanted most to ask.

"What is the prophecy about me that bothered my father?" he asked when they had stopped for the third time on the last day and they were off by themselves in a small grove of trees. She sighed and turned to face him, looking up at him with the powerful stare that seemed to transfix him.

"Peleus knew the prophecy that was sent to me when I was still a young girl," she said. "But he chose to ignore it. I had other suitors, very powerful suitors, mind you, all who chose to accept the prophecy. They were wise in doing so; Peleus, it turns out, was not so wise."

Achilles was not pleased that she spoke lightly of Peleus.

"Did you ever love him?" he asked his mother.

"Oh, I did, once upon a time," she said. "He was very handsome and very powerful. He was a great warrior. But, he did not know how to appreciate a goddess. He did not give me the respect he should have."

"Did you kill my older brothers?" Achilles said, feeling a wave of anger moving through him. "And did not my father save me from a drowning death?"

She turned her eyes on him again and his anger quickly departed.

"The prophecy is what you asked about," she said sweetly. "And it was this – that my son would be far greater than his father."

Achilles was silent as he pondered the meaning of the words.

"Peleus believes the prophecy?" he asked finally.

"Yes, he does now, I'm sure, after seeing you in action. Why do you think he threw you against his finest Myrmidon wrestler and boxer, at such a tender age? He wanted to see you beaten, so he could say the prophecy is false. But you showed to everyone, including Peleus, that the prophecy is indeed true."

Achilles sat heavily on a tree stump. He placed his elbows on his knees, his head dropping into his hands.

"The prophecy is not yet true," he said softly. "Winning a wrestling match and a boxing match does not make a man a great hero. I have much to do before anyone can say I am as great as my father. He sailed on the Argo, with Heracles and Jason. He has fought in many campaigns. He is a great warrior and a great king. I am nothing but a pup from Mount Pelion, raised on wild boar meat, goat's milk and figs."

She saw that he needed time alone with his thoughts and walked lightly through the trees, admiring the beauty of the place. When she came back, he was standing by a giant oak, waiting for her. She could see at a glance that he was changing back to the old Achilles and she knew she needed to seduce him again. She moved to his side, catching his arms. He stared down at her, about to speak, but she used her eyes and perfume in the manner Nereus had so skillfully taught her. He said nothing and she led him back to the cart.

She had told him of their destiny and now he was eager to see the island. She had urged him to forget about Chiron, Mount Pelion, Patroclus, Phoenix, Peleus and, most of all, talk of war with Troy.

"It is not your concern," she told him, stroking his arms tenderly. "Troy is not your destiny, Achilles. We will go to Skyros, where you will pick a wife and become king some day. You will have a long, wonderful life and be content, with many children and grandchildren to tend to. I will be at your side through the years. That is your true destiny, my son."

The rocky outline of Skyros was now straight ahead. Achilles felt at peace.

They received a grand welcome at the little palace of King Lycomedes. There was much dancing and celebrating. The court was delighted to welcome a sea goddess and her young, handsome son. They ate a huge meal and drank much wine, Lycomedes and his queen, Leta, showering lavish gifts on them. Achilles was presented a stunning purple robe, with a gold trimmed belt and a silver belt buckle. He was attended to by servants, who washed his feet and fit them with sandals. He was waited on in royal fashion.

Just when he thought it could get no better, there was a soft sound of flutes and the gentle singing of women. And then Deidamia, princess of Skyros, entered the banquet hall. She was breath-takingly beautiful, very small and sultry. Her raven hair was pulled back in a tight bun, with long strands dangling down each side of her face, in the style made fashionable by the Minoans. Everyone stood when she entered, including Achilles. He was stunned as she walked straight to him and sat down at his couch, looking up at him. She patted the couch gently and he sat beside her, unable to look away from her rosy cheeks and painted lips.

"You are the great Achilles?" she asked demurely. "I have heard so much about you. They say you are the most wonderful warrior in all of Hellas."

He wanted to be humble, but he could think of nothing to say other than, "Yes, it is true, I am Achilles."

Thetis watched from the other side of the room, sitting on a huge cushioned chair and smiling coyly. She glanced at Lycomedes and Leta, and saw how happy they were that their daughter was to be united with such a handsome young man. Her dreams were coming true, Thetis told herself. Peleus had thought he was going to win Achilles over, but she had stolen him away, right from under Peleus' nose, just as he had stolen Achilles from her in the cave of Nereus, some sixteen years earlier. And now that she had her son, she would never let him go. Between her spells and Deidamia's charms, Achilles now belonged to her!

But she had not considered the man from Ithaca in her planning.

The reputation of Odysseus was known far and wide. No man, the bards said, was as clever as the wily king of Ithaca. From his fertile mind had sprouted the concept of the pact among the suitors of Helen and from his mind had come the early plans for the battle against Troy. While honored for his courage and valor, he was far more respected for his wit and cunning.

And so Peleus was comforted to see the stocky Ithacan walking toward him in the Phthian throne room. He wore a boar's tusk helmet, different from the full-face helmets worn on the mainland, and a furry breast plate and leggings. He looked more like a wild man from the hills of Thessaly than the lord of an island kingdom.

If anyone could find Achilles, Peleus reasoned, it would be Odysseus.

They exchanged greetings and arm embraces and Odysseus said he had been sent as an envoy from the high king Agamemnon, who was to be in command of all the troops in the assault on Troy. It was a right bestowed on him because Agamemnon ruled the largest and most wealthy city, Mycenae, and also because he was the brother of the injured party, Menelaus.

After a brief show of hospitality from Peleus in front of royal guests, the men retired to a private room, with just Chiron and Phoenix present. They all sat quickly and took their wine vessels in hand.

"So tell me, Peleus, where do you think your son has flown to?" said Odysseus, his brows wrinkling as he sipped his wine.

Peleus carefully regarded the man with the stout physique and long scar on the inside of his thigh. Odysseus was shorter than he was and weighed considerably less. But Peleus judged him as a man you would not want on the other side of the battle line. He had a pleasant demeanor, but it was for show, Peleus knew. The real man was constantly studying and analyzing the situation before him. Yes, Odysseus was a very different kind of king and hero, thought Peleus. He wasn't certain he trusted this Ithacan, but he knew that he respected him.

"Tell me first about the fight with the wild boar," said Peleus, pointing to the long scar. Odysseus feigned surprise, straightening out the leg and glancing down at the ugly scar, which ran from below his right knee to under his loincloth. He tapped the scar with thick fingers, then glanced up at the others.

"It happened when I was a pup, off in the woods by myself. It was a huge boar, and it had been causing havoc with the farmers. I got separated from my father, Laertes, and the other hunters. The boar came roaring out of the bush without me seeing it. I heard the damn beast and whirled just as his tusk ripped me open. If the goddess Athena had not been with me, I would have died at age twelve – and I would not be able to find Achilles for you, and for Agamemnon."

They all laughed at the story, then fell to serious business.

"I do not know where she took him for certain," said Peleus, his eyes narrowing. "I know she has him under her spell. She is an enchantress!"

"A witch?" interrupted Odysseus, raising an eyebrow.

Peleus shrugged. "Either one....witch....or enchantress."

"She understands potions of all sorts and herbs that cause one to take leave of his senses," said Chiron. "She has studied for years under Nereus, that scrawny sea bastard. He is a worthless old man who attracts young women to his clan and casts a spell over them. But, admittedly, he has knowledge in seductions that have been handed down for generations. He has taught her well. She could have Achilles under a hypnotic spell, or a potion of some sort. He is very pure and would be susceptible to such tricks."

"Either way, the lad is not himself," said Peleus.

"And, what is he like when he is himself?" asked Odysseus. "I have heard stories that he is already, at age sixteen, a skilled warrior, with a temperament for battle that is similar to that of the great Heracles."

There was along pause as the men searched each other's eyes.

Odysseus continued: "You know that Calchas has spoken a prophecy that Troy cannot fall without the prince of Phthia in the field. Now, I don't worry too much about such utterances, but Agamemnon and Menelaus swear by them. They won't make a damn move unless they have consulted some seer or prophet somewhere to see how the gods view their enterprise."

Peleus threw a hand up in frustration.

"The gods! They are always meddling in our affairs. Don't they have enough on Mt. Olympus to keep them busy? Why must they always be so interested in what we mere mortals are doing?"

Odysseus shrugged.

"Are we not fascinating, we mortals, always brewing up some great new adventure, some trouble to get ourselves into? The gods love us because we are so prone to ruin everything and then they have to come save us....from ourselves."

"How do they save us?" asked Chiron, taking a swig of wine. He enjoyed this man Odysseus. He recognized in him a very clever mind and knew that he was a rarity among the princes of Hellas.

"Well, we need Ares for courage to fight and Aphrodite for the power to love," said Odysseus, relishing the opportunity to share his thoughts. "We need Zeus to overcome all the evils of the world. We need Hades to warn us of the dangers of overstepping our boundaries, and finding ourselves in his dreaded land of the dead."

He paused, then continued: "Poseidon warns of us drifting too far from our home, whether it be here (he tapped his heart) or here (he tapped his head)." He winked and they smiled.

"And Athena?" asked Phoenix.

"Aha!" said Odysseus, raising a finger to emphasize the point. "In Ithaca, Athena is the most revered of all the gods and goddesses. She provides wisdom. Athena gives the reasonable man the power to think through his mistakes and to correct them before they cause his doom. Athena is the one to whom Odysseus prays the most."

Chiron nodded and glanced at Phoenix, who was staring at Odysseus. They knew full well that this was a man that required watching, at all times.

"And it is Athena who will guide you to Achilles?" asked Chiron.

Odysseus glanced quickly at the man-horse, a hard look on his features. And then he smiled, recognizing in Chiron a man who thought as he did.

"Yes, Athena will guide the way," he said.

Much later, Odysseus, Peleus and Chiron sat in the garden outside the palace, deep in conversation.

"She must have someone she can count on," said Odysseus, searching Peleus's eyes with his own. "Over the years, where has she gone to be worshipped as a goddess? Surely, nowhere near here, where Nereus is well known."

Peleus swayed gently to and fro, feeling the effects of the large quantities of wine he had consumed and the strong emotion of the moment. He was furious that he had been duped by Thetis and that she had been able to steal his son from beneath his very nose. But the fury had quickly given way to grave concerns. Both he and Chiron knew the dangers Thetis posed if she was able to get young Achilles under her spell and keep him filled him with the drug of forgetfulness.

"Peleus," said Chiron suddenly, straightening up. "What of Lycomedes, in far-off Skyros?"

Peleus stiffened. A slow smile worked its way over his face as he turned toward his lifelong friend.

"Chiron, you just may have it," he grunted. "That miserable old king. He has never liked me since the Argo sailed past and we drank all his wine and seduced his women," He glanced at Odysseus. "It was mostly Heracles, of course."

"Of course," said Odysseus, with another wink. Everyone knew that the fabled strongman, no longer around to defend his honor, was the perfect dumping ground for all their misdeeds.

"Thetis went to Skyros years ago, in an effort to anger me," said Peleus. "They formed a bond, a friendship of sorts that I have never been able to understand. He must lust for her. That I could understand."

The three men huddled close, discussing strategy. When they broke several hours before dawn, they had settled on a plan. After a long sleep,

Odysseus was soon on his way to the island of Lycomedes.

The king's long, purple robe swirled around him as he hurried along the stone walkway. Four officials of the court were behind him, struggling to keep up with the older man. Lycomedes stopped when he reached the outermost section and stood next to two sentries, who glanced at him nervously. Both were in full armor, with dancing headcrests. They peered at their king through the narrow eye slits.

"It is not a big procession," said the first sentry, "and I see no weapons."

Lycomedes squinted into the glare of the setting sun and held his hand up to block the bright rays. His long, graying beard bounced as he nodded in agreement.

"I see no weapons," he repeated. "No more than forty or so men. There are pack animals and five carts, but this is not an assault troop. That is certain."

He sighed and motioned for the sentries down below to allow the small caravan to enter once it had reached the gates.

Odysseus and his company moved slowly through the gates of the small citadel, smiling and waving at the citizens who stood and watched them roll past. They were dressed as sea merchants, men who sailed from port to port in the spirit of trade.

"This is a small garrison, one that would be easily taken," muttered his right-hand man, Ariside. "A handful of Ithacans could rule this citadel in a day."

Odysseus nodded.

"If we were so inclined," he said. "But today, we are merely merchants, intent upon displaying our goods and making some trades." He paused. "And finding the key to Troy, with all its incredible riches."

Ariside nodded grimly, his thoughts already on the treasure trove of Priam.

The procession halted in front of Lycomedes's modest palace and the king walked down the steps to greet them. He approached Odysseus, who wore a short brown tunic, tied tight at the waist, and was sporting a green cap.

"Greetings to a welcome traveler," said Lycomedes. "Where do you come from and what is your business in the city of Lycomedes, king of Skyros?"

Odysseus nodded a greeting, keenly aware that he was being closely observed by the king and several officials standing behind him. In the world of the open sea, all travelers were treated with suspicion until the host was totally satisfied they meant no harm. Hospitality came later.

"We are from the island kingdom of Ithaca, on a journey to Troy. My name is Telemachus," he said, taking the name of his infant son back on Ithaca, so he would be sure not to forget what name he had made up. His mentioning the fabled city at the mouth of the Hellespont drew some collective gasps. "And we wanted to trade with Lycomedes before we set sail for the city of Priam."

"You don't seem like a merchant to me," said Lycomedes, raising an eyebrow. "You look like you may have fought many a battle," his eyes wandering over Odysseus hard-muscled limbs.

"That was indeed the case in my youth, noble king," said Odysseus with a sly grin. "Now, I am a man who prefers to trade rather than to try and take. There is far less risk to it."

Lycomedes smiled faintly and glanced past him, to the carts.

"What have you brought?" he asked. "We don't have much to offer in trade."

Odysseus grinned and walked to the carts, turning back the top to display a vast array of items Peleus had supplied for the trip. There were rolls of fine linens and thick vases, brightly painted in a style that was popular in Mycenae, so as to not suggest they may have come from Phthia. There were thick jars of olives, rare on Skyros, and jars full of honey and wine. Lycomedes and his officials wandered past, glancing into the carts, nodding and talking lightly among themselves.

"Come and make yourselves comfortable in the palace," said Lycomedes, finally. "We have room for ten of you. The rest will have to find sleeping places outside the walls."

Odysseus nodded and returned to his group, giving orders as Lycomedes and the others walked back up the steps and disappeared into the palace.

The first night was filled with drinking, eating and storytelling. Lycomedes and Leta were at the head table and invited Odysseus and Ariside to join them. There were acrobats skilled in the art of bull dancing from Crete, and lyre playing by two sweet women. Odysseus glanced around the hall, looking for young men and women, but saw few. Finally, he ventured a question to his host.

"I have heard that King Lycomedes has two beautiful daughters," he said, wiping the wine from his lips with the back of his hand. "Are they with us tonight?"

"No," said Lycomedes. "The oldest, Deidamia, has just been married. Her sister is with her as is our custom until she finds a husband of her own."

Odysseus sat up, sensing an opening.

"Surely, a princess of Skyros would bring a host of suitors," he said. "What is the name of the fortunate prince?"

Lycomedes glanced at Odysseus, assessing him once again.

Odysseus was gambling that Lycomedes' pride, nurtured by the wine, would get the best of him and that if Achilles was indeed the husband, he would not be able to keep from boasting. He waited as Lycomedes took a long swig of wine and wiped his mouth with the sleeve of his tunic. He was getting drunk, Odysseus knew.

"He is from a very noble lineage," the king said, leaning forward to stare at Odysseus. "Very noble, indeed." Odysseus nodded and bit into the thick bread, tearing away a large piece with his teeth.

"He wouldn't be from the house of Priam, would he?" asked Odysseus.

Lycomedes drew back, glaring at his guest. He turned and whispered to his wife, Leta, who nodded faintly. Then he turned back to Odysseus.

"There are rumors that the mainland chiefs are plotting a war against Troy," said Lycomedes. "You say you are a merchant; but I wonder if you are not on some form of spying mission, Telemachus."

"Not me," said Odysseus, leaning away and stretching his arms above his head. "I am, as I told you, a merchant these days. I'll leave the warring to other men."

He stood, bowed and announced it was time to retire. He and Ariside walked to their room and laid down on their beds. Soon, they were both fast asleep.

For three more days, there was no sign of young people at the palace other than glimpses Odysseus would catch from time to time. On the third night, he thought he saw two young women walking in the second garden, further from the main house. He crept along the outer wall, flat against it, hiding in the shadows, for a better look. The two sat down close to him and began embracing. Soon, they were kissing and he smiled, thinking he had stumbled upon a pair of women who loved the same sex. He shook his head, never understanding how a man could love another man, or a woman another woman and was about to leave when he saw one of the women stand. He gaped, and then gasped. It was not a woman at all, but a handsome young man dressed in a woman's cloth.

He shrank down further into the shadows so he could observe more. The young man was talking softly and the young woman was staring up at him in adoration. And then a word was spoken that Odysseus could hear clearly and it sent a chill down his back. The young woman had called her companion Pyrrha. Odysseus recognized that name as one that Peleus had said Thetis loved and had used on occasion when referring to her son.

It was some time before they left the garden. When they were gone from sight, Odysseus hurried back to his room. Ariside saw his expression and sat up on his cot.

"What is it, Odysseus?" he asked.

"I have found Achilles," he said. "Now, the trick is to make him show himself."

The following day was a hectic one in the square. Word had spread of the new merchants in the city and local dealers had arrived from all around the countryside to show their goods. Men and women busied themselves in the marketplace, with children darting in and out between the small tables stacked with goods. Odysseus took time to study the shops where swords were being hammered out, and inspected the thick shields. Many were so large they would conceal a man's entire body, providing good protection but also limiting his movements. Odysseus smirked when he saw others inspecting the shields and murmuring their approval, knowing they valued the ability to protect themselves higher than they valued their ability to fight aggressively. It was a style of fighting that he rejected. He was also interested in the shops of the chariot makers; chariots had always fascinated him as there were very few of them in rocky Ithaca. But his mind was constantly preoccupied with the trap he was setting.

He had told the king he would leave in the morning and so this was the king's final chance to see his finest wares. Lycomedes had invited him into the palace at dusk to show his linens and fabrics to the household of the king. Lycomedes even hinted that his daughters might be present, drawn out by the lure of seeing the finest materials from the mainland. It was that hope which Odysseus was clinging to.

When they arrived in the palace, the main room in front was filled with nearly one hundred men and women of all ages. It was the private gathering spot for the royal family and close friends; in the back sat two large statues, one of Cloudgathering Zeus and the other of his wife, Hera, queen of the gods. Odysseus glanced about to see if he recognized the young man and woman from the garden, but he did not. All of the women were wearing heavy veils over their faces and were clustered together in the far corner.

"The Fates have smiled on you all today," Odysseus announced loudly as he walked into the center of the large open room, with Ariside and several others following behind. Odysseus spun around, spreading his arms, smiling widely, a style he had learned from traveling bards who visited Ithaca. "We have saved the very best for last. Please come and see what we have to offer to the house of Lycomedes."

The men unfolded the large sacks full of merchandise and spread the items on the floor, in large piles. The women moved forward, chattering easily, eyes locked on the fine linens and cloth before them. Odysseus noticed several hanging back, then he saw a larger figure wrapped tightly in a long robe start to turn away and leave. Odysseus turned and nodded at Ariside, who had moved to the center of the room.

"What have we here?" announced Ariside loudly, reaching down into the pile of cloths and pulling out a magnificent sword. "Telemachus, did you mean to leave this sword here among the items to be traded?"

Immediately, the figure Odysseus was watching stopped and turned slightly toward Ariside. Odysseus moved toward Ariside, his eyes peeled on the figure across the room.

"Yes, that sword is for sell or for trade. It was given to me by a famous warrior who sailed on the Argo many years ago," he said, loudly enough for all to hear.

The figure leaned forward, watching intently. The other women giggled at Odysseus' bravado and returned to their clothing. Ariside, as prearranged, laid the sword back down in the pile and walked away.

Odysseus turned his back on the figure at the rear of the room and pretended to take an interest in the other customers. He chatted briefly with the women, all the while his eyes darting back to the solitary figure hovering in the rear. He could sense the person was torn between the decision of whether to stay or leave. Finally, the figure moved over to the pile, then bent down and reached slowly for the sword. The figure kept the cloak tightly around it and gripped the sword, turned it over several times, then laid it back. Odysseus knew it was Achilles.

As Achilles began to move away, Odysseus nodded to Ariside and held up two fingers, the prearranged signal. Ariside ran to the entrance, peered outside, and then turned back toward the assemblage.

"Attack!" he shouted. "We are being attacked!"

Women shrieked and began running from the room. Lycomedes had been at a table chatting with two officials and glanced up startled.

"What... who...attacks?" he bellowed.

Ariside ran into the center of the room as twenty of Odysseus' men barged into the room, brandishing swords and yelling wildly. Lycomedes shrank back and shouted for the guard. Five soldiers came running down the hallway.

Odysseus smiled at what he saw. The figure he had been observing moved away several steps, then stopped and ran back to the pile of cloths. He reached into the stack and pulled out the sword and strode to the center of the room, ready to confront all twenty men by himself.

"Peleusson!" shouted Odysseus loudly. The name echoed off the walls.

The room came to a dead halt. The men who had rushed into the room backed away, grinning, looking at their commander, Odysseus. Lycomedes gaped unbelieving, beginning to comprehend what was transpiring. Achilles stood tall and alert, eyes locked on Odysseus. His garment had fallen to the floor, revealing a torso with striking muscularity. His arms rippled with lean muscles as he held the sword chest high.

Odysseus walked over to the young warrior, smiling.

"I am Odysseus, king of Ithaca," he said evenly. "Your father has sent me to find you, Achilles. There is to be a great expedition against Troy, and you are needed to lead the Myrmidons into battle."

Achilles stared at the sagacious man standing before him, an expression of utter confusion on his features.

"Why do you call me Peleusson?" he mumbled. "And....who is Achilles? I am Pyrrha, the husband of Deidamia. I am a prince here. I do not know you."

He tilted the sword as if he might strike. Odysseus stepped back, his hand moving quickly to his dagger hilt. He had no desire to engage this powerful young man in any sort of battle. No, he intended to win this engagement with his wits, not try to depend on weapons.

"You are the son of Peleus, ruler of Phthia, a mountain kingdom on the mainland," said Odysseus in a low, even voice. "Your given name is Achilles and you are a mighty warrior, not a weak prince of a toothless kingdom."

Lycomedes bellowed again and was now surrounded by twenty guards. He motioned them forward, to take Odysseus by force. Odysseus' men moved quickly to the their king, and the two sides faced off. Suddenly, one of the guards charged Odysseus, striking at him with a spear. Like a cat, Odysseus leaped aside and pulled his dagger, burying it deep in the soldier's stomach. The soldier pivoted and screamed, clutching the blade. He fell heavily to the floor, jerking in terrible pain.

"Stay where you are, or my soldiers will cut you down like dogs!" growled Odysseus to Lycomedes. "Your men are no match for my warriors!"

Achilles stared at the dying soldier on the floor and then back at Odysseus. He glanced over at Lycomedes and behind him at the beautiful young woman clinging to her father's arm.

"It is...coming back to me now," mumbled Achilles, one hand clutching the sword, the other moving to his head, palm flat against the side. "My mother....Peleus...."

"And Chiron," said Odysseus.

"Chiron," croaked Achilles. "And Patroclus!"

"They are all waiting for you," said Odysseus, knowing he had won.

The young woman slipped out from behind Lycomedes, dashing to Achilles, staring up at him with wide, blue eyes. She wore a long, ashen tunic, and removed her veil. Her long, dark hair hung to her shoulders and her lips were painted with the juice of the wild berry. She was beautiful and Odysseus knew she could hardly be more than fourteen years. She placed her small hands on the arms of Achilles, her eyes devouring him.

"You must not go," she whispered to him. "Thetis has warned us that you will never return from Troy. You will die there, and be buried there!"

Achilles shrugged.

"It is my desire to fight at Troy. And my destiny," he said simply.

She flung herself into his arms and he dropped the sword to the stone floor, where it made a terrible clattering noise. She clung to him, weeping, pushing her thin, taut body into his. He held her tight, staring down at her, one hand winding its way into her long, dark hair. He kissed her lips softly, then looked up at Odysseus.

"I will come, soon," he said.

Odysseus was about to respond when he heard the murmuring. It started softly and slow, but grew louder quickly. He turned slightly and saw all heads turned in the direction of the back of the large room. There, between the large statues of Zeus and Hera, a figure emerged from the shadows.

"The goddess comes," mumbled one of the women. They shrank back as the lithe figure moved past them. She was thin and walked as though her feet barely touched the stone floor. Her brown hair was wound tight around her head and tied in a knot at the back, with long strands of hair dangling down each side of her face. She wore a thin white robe that was very revealing, open down to the waist, just barely covering her small but perfectly shaped breasts. She was so beautiful that even Odysseus had to blink away his first glimpse.

"Thetis!" gasped Lycomedes. "You have come just in time to save your son."

She walked straight up to Odysseus, confronting him with a hard look. He smiled faintly, eyeing the woman without giving an inch.

"So, you are the wily Odysseus, king of Ithaca, and you have come to steal my son away from me," said Thetis, her voice sweet and almost musical. Immediately, he recognized her style of speech and her gaze as that of the wood nymphs he had met on an island south of Ithaca. The style was meant to seduce and beguile others, and Odysseus had to fight to regain his composure.

"Not to steal your son, nymph, but to restore him," said Odysseus.

"You have deluded him into believing he is something he is not. You have tried to kill him once again, only in a different way."

Thetis was surprised at his knowledge. She moved to Achilles, clutching an arm. Deidamia stood transfixed, staring at Thetis.

"He will not sail to Troy," she said defiantly. "He has a wife here and has a duty to stay with her. She is carrying his child."

Achilles stiffened at the words and glanced at Deidamia.

"There is a larger duty that calls to him, and I do not think he will shirk from it," said Odysseus. "He is, I am told, a fighting man at heart. He knows that he cannot avoid the call to arms and that he must fight at Troy, if there is to be a war at all. All of Hellas is counting on him."

Thetis threw herself at her son, gripping his arms desperately. She stared wildly up into his gray eyes.

"Achilles, you must choose now, for all to hear, even the gods. I can protect you, and see that you live a long, happy life, with many wonderful children and grandchildren to love and adore you. Or...." her voice turned deep and sorrowful, "you can gain a fame that will endure forever, as long as men gather around the fire and sing their hymns of valor and of heroes. But, that life will be short, my son. Very short."

He studied his mother and then his wife. His gaze turned to the piercing eyes of Odysseus. He lifted a clenched fist to his chest.

"Ever since I was a pup on Mount Pelion with Chiron, racing against the wind, fighting lions and bear and wild boar, I have dreamed of being a great warrior," he said. "Day and night, it is what occupies my thoughts, always. That is what I would choose, first and foremost, above all things."

Thetis threw her head back and began to chant, eyes closed. Her voice was high pitched and sweet and then she opened her eyes and stared up at her son. She held a small container in her hand and moved it to his face. Odysseus knew she was trying to seduce him with the intoxicating herbs of the wood nymph and ran to her, pulling her roughly away. She turned into Odysseus, cursing at him, squirming, and trying to kick her way free.

"No, nymph, you will not work your magic here any longer," grunted Odysseus, squeezing her arms so hard she squealed in pain. He motioned to his men to escort Achilles, now partially seduced, from the temple.

Achilles walked slowly with the warriors surrounding him as Odysseus forced the struggling woman from the building out into the clear sunlight. He ran down the steps, jerking her with him. All of his troops, forty strong, were lined up, in the animal skin battle gear the Ithacans were known for.

"Well done, Ariside," Odysseus said, nodding at his captain. "It is time to leave this bewitched kingdom."

He released Thetis and she stood where he had left her, with Lycomedes and Deidamia at her side. Helplessly, they watched the Ithacans, and Achilles, march away. They moved quickly down the dirt-packed street, men and women peering at them from their little huts and shops. No one attempted to block their way.

"Odysseus, beware!" screamed Thetis, clenching her small fist and shaking it at him. "My father, Poseidon, will seek revenge for the way you have treated his daughter. Beware the wrath of the sea god, man of Ithaca!"

Odysseus merely grinned as he continued marching down the street, Achilles at his side. He had no cares at all for the empty words of a seductive nymph who thought she was a goddess. None at all.

Aulis and Ajax

It didn't take long for Achilles to come to his senses. When he first did so, he was too embarrassed to speak with Odysseus. But the wily Ithacan was highly skilled at getting others to talk and expose their feelings, and he treated Achilles like a son. By the time they had made the trip back to Phthia, Achilles had told Odysseus how his mother had seduced him, first with sweet talking and the hypnotic eyes and later with herbs and perfumes. They were techniques she had learned as a member of the Nereid, the women of Nereus.

"It is a form of hypnosis that only the most skilled nymphs have learned from their mystic mentors," said Odysseus, sitting next to Achilles on the bumpy ride in the lead cart headed toward Peleus' palace. "And you need not feel ashamed for falling under the spell of such a woman, even if she is your own mother. You are such a tender age, Achilles. I hear that you run like the wind and can catch a spear you've thrown even before it touches the ground. Chiron says your courage is equal to that of the fabled Heracles. Still, you are young, and can fall prey to the tricks of women like Thetis."

Odysseus also told Achilles of the troubles that led to the planned war with Troy.

"It all began when a scoundrel from Troy, Alexandros, one of many sons of their king, Priam, decided he needed a wild adventure. He came to the mainland to hunt and to find sport. While visiting King Menelaus at Sparta he fell under the spell of Aphrodite, and of Helen, the king's wife."

Odysseus paused and leaned back, clapping his fingers together behind his head. A slow smile came across his lips as he reflected back on some previous moment in his life, when he was young like a stallion and full of pride and spirit.

"She is a beauty; Helen is perhaps the finest woman these eyes have ever seen. When Menelaus left for his own planned hunting trip, he invited Alexandros to come along. But Alexandros, already smitten with Helen, feigned illness and stayed behind. When Menelaus returned five days later, Alexandros was gone...and so was Helen." Odysseus paused to shake his head. "Imagine a man leaving a woman like that home alone with a handsome, love-starved young man." He shook his head again and then continued. "And for what? To hunt wild pigs?

"Well, of course Menelaus was in a rage. He ran straight to Mycenae, where his brother, Agamemnon, rules supreme. Mycenae is the richest city in all the mainland and Agamemnon could sense a real adventure brewing here. Together, the brothers planned this grand war, and then set out to enlist the aide of the other princes."

"How did they do that?" asked Achilles. "How is it that the princes of Hellas are willing to leave their palaces to bring back the wife of the Spartan king, who was foolish enough to lose her in the first place?"

"That is an excellent question, young Achilles," said Odysseus. "The answer has its roots in the wooing of Helen, many years earlier. Her father, King Tyndareus of Sparta, saw the lineup of suitors, many princes eager to land such a beauty and to become king some day of rich Sparta, as well. So Tyndareus, in his wisdom, hatched a plan – with my assistance, actually – that all the suitors must swear an oath to protect Helen and her new husband if anything evil should ever happen to them.

"We sealed the bargain with a solemn sacrifice. We sacrificed a beautiful stallion and cut it up, making each of the suitors stand on a bloody portion and swear an oath of loyalty to Helen and her new husband. That way, all of the suitors were dedicated by blood to whoever became her choice.

"Oh, I have to thank Athena for the wisdom of that one," he said, slapping his thigh and chuckling hard. "Men may worship Aphrodite when it comes to matters of the heart, but Athena is the goddess for me."

"What did you stand to gain with such a plan?" asked Achilles after a pause.

Odysseus looked at his young companion with an arched eyebrow.

"You are a wise one, Achilles, to see that there is always something to be gained in such a bargain. What I wanted was not Helen but her fair cousin, Penelope. She was far more to my liking. And I told Tyndareus that if he accepted my plan, all I wanted in return was the hand of Penelope in marriage.

"Everyone was pleased," he said. "Menelaus got his beautiful wife, Helen got a husband from a famous lineage, Tyndareus got his alliance and protection for Helen and I got Penelope. She is the mother of my son,

Telemachus, and is a wife of great patience and understanding, which are great virtues for women of men like you and me, Achilles."

They were silent for a spell.

"My father was not a suitor of Helen," said Achilles. "So, why is Phthia bound to such an agreement with Sparta?"

"No, Peleus was not a suitor, already having Thetis for a wife. But his brother, Telamon, was a suitor and Peleus took an oath on his behalf, hoping to strengthen his case." Odysseus laughed again. "Peleus is a handsome man, but Telamon is not, more of a brutish type. His son, Ajax, is your cousin and he, I am told, is a giant of a man, like your uncle. Ajax has a fierce pride and a wild temper and will undoubtedly be among the chiefs going to Troy. You and he will have some fun trying to decide who is the greatest warrior – the son of Peleus or the son of Telamon."

Achilles nodded grimly at the words. He was already looking forward to meeting Ajax and resolving the issue.

At the palace, it was a joyous reunion for all. Peleus thanked Odysseus for his efforts in locating Achilles and bringing him back, rewarding him with a beautiful shield of thick ox hides and a bronze-edged sword that only the strongest of heroes could wield effectively. And then Odysseus departed immediately for the long trip to Ithaca. He had his own family to see and affairs to tend to before marshalling his troops for the long trip to Troy.

Peleus, Chiron, Achilles, Patroclus and Phoenix sat up long into the night, eating sweet meats and sipping the barley drink, as well as some wine. They all told stories and then the others fell deathly quiet while Achilles began describing how his mother had drugged him and beguiled him into going to Skyros. When he talked about Deidamia, Peleus watched carefully, nodding gently, sensing that his son was truly enamored of the young princess.

"She is going to have my son, and we have agreed on the name of Neoptolemus," said Achilles, with pride.

Finally, Peleus spoke again.

"What matters is that Achilles is back in Phthia and ready to take over the command of the Myrmidons. I will send fifty ships and nearly three hundred fighting men to Troy," he said. "There will also be many others that will have to go… charioteers, servants and the like. It will be a great armada that the Argives send to seek vengeance on the House of Priam.

"The host will gather at Aulis, an island off the Athenian coast, and very soon. Achilles, you must be prepared to leave in seven days. This will be a very costly expedition, one that will nearly exhaust our small treasury. I will count on you to bring back a goodly share of the spoils to

Phthia. You must be aware of Agamemnon and Menelaus; I know little of them except that they are greedy men."

Chiron nodded at all Peleus said.

"Phoenix will go as your mentor," continued Peleus. "He knows my heart in all matters and knows how Chiron has trained you. Patroclus, of course, will be your confidant and second in command. He is as trustworthy as a friend can be."

Patroclus beamed with the compliment and nodded at Achilles. They had become fast friends ever since their wrestling match on the distant hills of Mount Pelion, and Achilles loved him like a brother.

"You talked to the messenger from Mycenae," said Peleus, turning to Phoenix. "Can you give us the list of the war chieftans who will be at Aulis?"

The aged friend of the king nodded.

"Of course, the army will be led by Agamemnon, king of Mycenae. He comes by that right due to his blood relationship with the aggrieved, and by the fact that Mycenae is the richest city on the mainland. He will command the largest army. He is said to be bringing a hundred warriors times ten and will command nearly one hundred ships.

"Idomeneus of Crete will be his second in command and will be bringing nearly as large a force. He is fine warrior, known far and wide for his great looks. He is so handsome that many were surprised that Helen did not choose him as her husband, but there is a suspicion that Tyndareus would not let her do so, for Idomeneus would have taken her from Sparta back to Crete, and left Sparta without an heir to the throne.

"Nestor of Pylos is getting well along in years, but he is still a man of great courage and knows more about fighting on horseback than any of the other chiefs and will be in charge of the cavalry. In fact, he is so good with horses that he could be a centaur," he added, winking at Chiron, who snorted his doubt of such a bold statement.

"Menthesus will lead the Athenians and Diomedes will lead the troops from Argos. This Diomedes is a warrior of vast repute and reportedly fell in love with Helen at first sight, and takes the kidnapping as a grave affront to him personally. He has a boiling temper and will be a formidable foe for any Trojan.

"And then we have, of course, the two Ajaxes." He paused, glancing at Peleus, who nodded for him to continue.

"The one they are calling the Lesser, because he is the smaller of the two, is a Locrian. He is a swift runner, perhaps the equal of Achilles and Patroclus in a race, and deadly with the spear. They say his aim is remarkable, even at great distances. He is, they say, a strange man, often not in total control of his mind. And, he always has a tame serpent with him – a snake longer than a tall man, that slithers along behind him wherever he goes. He worships Ares, the god of war. He also is a formidable warrior.

"The other Ajax, whom they are calling the Greater due to his immense size, is the son of Telamon. We have heard tales of his prodigious strength, and of his prodigious vanity." He glanced at Achilles, who was listening intently to every word.

"He comes from the island kingdom of Salamis, of course, where Telamon rules supreme. He carries an immense shield made from at least twelve bulls' hides. He is proud of the fact that few other men can even lift the shield, while he swings it about in battle as a weapon, knocking warriors to the ground with it and then ripping them with his sword.

"And he is very proud of his wrestling abilities, we are told."

Chiron snorted again and then glanced at Peleus.

"Telamon always fancied himself quite a wrestler too, I recall, until the funeral games of Eumaus, when he ran into Peleus."

Peleus leaned back in his heavy chair, digesting all that was said. He looked over at Achilles and then at Chiron.

"Telamon is a good wrestler, but he always relies too much on brute strength. That has always been his way; and I suspect that is his son's way, as well." He turned his gaze on his son. "Bear that in mind, Achilles, if the time comes, and I think it will, that you and Ajax will be forced into a wrestling match. If he is like his father, Ajax will quickly throw skill to the wind and try to overpower you with brute strength."

Phoenix ran through the names of more princes and chiefs and told what little he knew of them. Diana was about to take her chariot to the stables for the coming of the dawn when they all at last gave way to Sleep, the most irresistible of all the gods and goddesses, the one no man can long deny.

The following day was a blur of activity as Peleus and Achilles returned to the armory to pick up the armor they had previously selected. Then he took the Pelian ash spear from its resting place on the hallowed wall where Peleus had hung it years before, after using it in battle for the final time.

Automedon approached Achilles, asking to be his driver. Not only was Automedon making a sacrifice in not becoming a war chief, but he knew it was a very dangerous profession in warfare. Most warriors knew that the fastest way to cause havoc with an army was to kill the driver of the lead chariot, making the war leader take the reins in order to keep the horses in check. Automedon would become, therefore, the primary target for enemy swords, lances and arrows. Achilles accepted the offer and gripped his one-time wrestling foe at the forearms to show his respect for his decision.

"I will not let you down, lord Achilles," said Automedon. "My life's mission will be to direct your chariot safely in and out of battle, so that you may earn great fame for Peleus and for Phthia."

Five days later, Achilles and Peleus rode into the camp of the Myrmidons with Automedon at the helm, so that Achilles could meet with the other warlords. They had been alerted long ago to be ready for the great adventure and all had made their goodbyes to their wives and off-spring.

Achilles saw that many of them were sitting in front of their huts, naked to the waist, painting their shields and breastplates with a thick form of pitch, dark black in color. He remembered then what Chiron had told him years ago on Pelion, but had forgotten: the Myrmidons always painted their shields and armor black, to try and inject fear into the hearts of their foes. Black was a forbidding color and made most men think of the darkness of the Underworld, which is where the Myrmidons wanted to send their foes. Achilles nodded at the warriors as he walked past and they nodded back, a few of them even smiling faintly. He met with the war leaders and told them to assemble in front of the palace of Peleus in the morning, that he would meet them there.

When it came time to depart the following morning, at the crack of dawn, the street in front of the palace was packed with warriors in black armor, twenty war chariots and dozens of horses. Achilles stood before Peleus and Chiron, fathers both of them, each in his own way.

"Never forget, you are the son of a king, the son of Peleus," said his true father, a stern look in his eyes. "I know you look to no god, but trust to your own limbs and heart to give you victory. Chiron has told me that. Your courage will carry the day, even when the day looks darkest. Remember your choice in life, Achilles, and do us all proud, yourself foremost....and return home in victory to assume the kingship which I will leave to you."

They stood motionless for a moment and then clasped forearms. Achilles was surprised when the older man had to look away quickly.

"Now, I have something special for you," said Peleus, motioning for two servants to come forward. They were carrying a large chest between them. It was ornately decorated in gold and silver trim, with scenes of fighting men all around it. They set it down in front of Peleus and backed away, smiling at Achilles, knowing what was in the chest.

"Open this with me," said Peleus, bending down, his tunic trailing on the ground. He worked one of the latches quickly and Achilles did the same on the other side. Together, they opened the chest and Peleus stood up, smiling down at his son. Achilles gaped into the chest. It was full of the most marvelous armor he had ever seen in his life, a brilliant gold in color.

"This was given to me by Heracles, as a special gift on the day of my wedding to Thetis," said Peleus, his voice thick with pride. "He would never say where he got it, but I believe it was made for him by Hephaestus, the blacksmith of the gods himself. It is so heavy that a normal man can not wear it. Only a very powerful man, like Heracles....or you....can wear it, Achilles. It is too heavy for you now, but you will grow into it. Some time, on a very special day, you will wear it into battle. When you do, think of me, think of home in Phthia."

Achilles stood up, eyes riveted on his father, his heart pounding. He had never seen such magnificent armor. Knowing that his father wanted him to have it made Achilles as proud as he had ever been in his life!

Chiron stepped up to Achilles and ran his eyes down his lean body, covered only by a short tunic. The long, golden hair hung limp, almost to his shoulders. Chiron glanced over at Patroclus, standing tall and straight beside him, yet two steps back. He admired Patroclus for his devotion to Achilles, and for knowing his place. There was not a touch of envy in Patroclus for his friend, only unswerving admiration and loyalty.

"You have a great friend at your side and the finest fighting men ever known at your disposal," said Chiron, his voice barely audible. "Peleus has trained them to wage war like no others, with boundless skill and energy. They will follow you even into Hades." He paused, his eyes boring into his pupil's eyes.

"I have tried to instruct you in all ways of life...how to be a warrior, and how to be a friend. Carry these lessons with you, from Mount Pelion to the plain of Troy. You must never forget that you are Achilles, the pride of Phthia. And Peleusson!"

He too gripped Achilles' forearms and then stepped back, looking away.

Achilles backed up, his eyes wet with emotion, his heart swelling with pride. He loved these two old men and he would die trying to make them proud of him. Without another word, he turned and strode to the chariot that was waiting for him. He stepped up onto it as Patroclus took the next chariot. Achilles nodded to Automedon.

"Go!" he commanded. "We are done here."

Automedon cracked the whip and the two horses jerked, then pranced quickly away. The chariot carrying Achilles turned abruptly and rolled slowly down the wide street in front of the palace. The procession then slipped through the streets of Phthia as men, women and children stood at their doors, watching.

"The Myrmidons are off to Troy, to fight a great war," Achilles heard one man shouting to his children. "That is Achilles, son of Peleus...

there in the lead chariot."

Again, Achilles felt the stirring in his breast. Then they were through the small gates, out into the farming village that lay in front of the walls of the citadel. Farmers were walking slowly into the fields, hoes over their backs, staring at them in curiosity. It was not every day that they saw the Myrmidons marching off to war. Halfway through the village, Achilles glanced back once over his shoulder, but he could no longer see Peleus and Chiron standing on the steps of the palace, far, far away – and he had no way of knowing that he would never rest eyes on either of them ever again.

Achilles looked up at the chariot of the sun and saw it was starting to go behind a cloud.

"Go and hide if you will, Helios," he said softly, staring up. "I am gone to Troy and no one will stand before me. No one!"

It took ten days to reach Aulis, most of it by land and the last short leg on ships that Peleus had arranged, through Phoenix, to be purchased. The small island just a mile off the Argive coast was a beehive of activity when Achilles and the Myrmidons arrived. It was selected by Agamemnon as the most logical site for the entire host to gather and develop the plans for the final move to Troy.

The Myrmidons marched into the large sprawling camp with Achilles and Patroclus at the lead, side by side, in their chariots. They were stunned by the size of the encampment, having never seen so many people in one spot before. The soldiers of the various cities stopped their work and athletic competitions to watch them go past. Most of the men were naked except for brief loincloths and were sweating profusely in the blazing sun. Some were working on chariot wheels broken by the long trip, while others were sharpening swords and spear points. Many were wrestling and boxing, while others were engaged in races and spear-throwing contests. Some merely strolled down by the water's edge and then collapsed on the thick sand, hoping to relax before setting sail. There were plenty of women in the camp, too, some workers, but many simply there to provide pleasure for the warriors. Many of them took long looks at Achilles and Patroclus as they rode past, admiring their handsome faces and lean bodies.

While most of the Achaean soldiers wore beards of various lengths, the Myrmidons were clean shaven. Peleus had instilled in his men a desire to look different than other warriors and to act different. They were proud of their appearance and ignored the comments thrown their way by the other soldiers, with regard to their shaven faces and black armor. But the Myrmidons couldn't understand much of what was being said; there were so many dialects and accents that it was difficult for men from varying sections of the mainland to communicate effectively. Much of the talking was done through hand signals and gesturing, though many of the important words were common from tribe to tribe, and city to city.

As soon as the Myrmidon ships were first spotted off shore, the word was sent through the camp. Heralds took the message to Agamemnon, where he was in a large tent meeting with the other chieftans. The great king had leaned back in his huge throne chair, which he insisted on bringing with him from the throne room at Mycenae, and glanced over at his brother, and at Nestor.

"So, the great Achilles will honor us with his presence after all," said Agamemnon. "I am most anxious to meet this young lion – and to see if he does indeed eat the marrow of bears, and can run down wild boar and kill them with his own hands."

The other chieftans laughed at Agamemnon's words, all except Ajax the Greater. He sat rigidly in his chair, towering over the table, a stern expression playing on his features. He was more anxious to meet his cousin than any of the others, of that he was most certain. In fact, he had been praying nightly to Ares, his patron god, that Achilles would show up and that the two of them would have the opportunity to test one another. His father, Telamon, had talked many a night of how Peleus always seemed to have the upper hand and gain the lion's share of the credit during all their many adventures; Ajax was determined that this unfortunate cycle of circumstances be broken once and for all.

As Achilles rode through the camp, heralds came to his side, peering up into the chariot, asking him to halt. He did and they gave him directions on where to take his troops. They marched to the outer flank of the large camp and found a resting place near a large cliff, overlooking the sea. Achilles and Patroclus dismounted and helped the Myrmidons erect their tents, an occurrence that shocked the other troops who came by to watch. Never before had they seen princes take a hand in such affairs.

Phoenix strolled over to where the two were toiling, sweat pouring down their brows, their muscular bodies glistening in the sun.

"So, this is how princes prepare themselves for combat," he said with a smile. "Such work is very rewarding, Achilles. It will endear you to your troops all the more."

He walked away, Achilles watching him go. He knew Phoenix was right; what surprised him was that Phoenix knew what was in his mind. He had indeed joined into the work for two reasons: he was bored from the long trip and anxious to use his muscles, and he realized the Myrmidons would see that he was one of them, and not a chieftan who sat and sipped the barley drink while they worked.

Achilles and Patroclus worked all day long and when their tent, with the insignia of Phthia etched deeply on all four sides, was up and standing tall and proud, they retired into the tent. Phoenix joined them and six servant women brought their food, which was composed of roast pig, bread, olives, beans and, to finish off the meal, grapes and figs. There was also plenty of the barley drink and watered wine for washing it all down. Phoenix was glad for the wine, but Achilles and Patroclus both preferred water carried in by vases from a nearby brook.

They ate quietly, all tired form the long trip and the day's events. Achilles and Patroclus were clad only in loins cloths, the heat still hanging high in the night sky. Phoenix had on a short chiton, unbelted at the waist. They were reclining on cots covered with thick furs from Mount Pelion and Achilles was playing his lyre when the heralds arrived.

The two men stood ramrod straight at the opening to the tent while a servant announced them to Achilles. He motioned for them to enter and the two men, slender and with shortly cropped beards, bowed slightly as they walked inside the tent.

"The high king Agamemnon welcomes Achilles and his Myrmidons to the camp," said the taller man. "He bids you to join him at dawn's passing in his tent, for breakfast, and to meet the other chieftans."

Achilles nodded.

"Tell the high king that Achilles, Patroclus and Phoenix will join him in the morning," he said.

The second herald stiffened a bit.

"The invitation extends only to lord Achilles," he said.

Achilles smiled faintly.

"Tell the high king that Achilles, Patroclus and Phoenix will happily meet him in the morning," he repeated. The first herald was about to respond, then saw the look in Achilles' eyes. He nodded and the two men departed.

"Tomorrow should be an interesting day," said Phoenix as he laid down on his cot. "I think I will need a good night's sleep."

Agamemnon marched out of his tent and strutted through the camp of the Mycenaens, his long, purple robe fluttering behind him as he hurried along. He stroked his pointed black beard, his long, black locks jostling with his movement. He was a large, powerful man, with thick forearms and a heavy face. He was not a handsome man, but he was a man who looked important.

And he was important, very important. As was his custom, he carried with him the mighty scepter of the king of Mycenae, a symbol of the most powerful city in all the Achaean mainland. The heavy bronze and wooden beam, trimmed with gold, was reputedly forged by the god Hephaestus himself, the resident blacksmith of Mount Olympus. According to Mycenaen lore, it was given to King Pelops by Zeus Cloudgatherer, and was handed down from king to king – from Pelops to Atreus to Thyestes and, finally, to Agamemnon.

The citadel of Mycenae sat tall and proud overlooking the Argive plain, guarded by two fierce lions, chained to the main gate. Its walls were massive, the largest in all of the mainland, larger even than the fabled walls of Tyrins. Reputedly built by the race of giants known as Cyclops, the walls even had a name of their own – the Cyclopean Walls. Mycenae was inhabited by nearly six thousand citizens, including the out-lying regions, and Agamemnon ruled supreme.

He came to an open spot and saw the other warlords already assem-bled under a large tent. There were half a hundred there and that many more servants attending to them. There was a loud chatter; obviously, they were excited about something.

Agamemnon was upset that his arrival did not warrant more than just a few nods of recognition. He glanced about for either Nestor or his brother, and at last spotted Menelaus standing with Idomeneus of Crete and Diomedes of Argos. They were heavy in discussion when Menelaus glanced up and saw his brother striding toward him.

"Greetings, Agamemnon," Menelaus said stiffly.

"What is going on? Why wasn't I notified earlier?" Agamemnon said, staring hard at his younger brother. Menelaus looked remarkably like Agamemnon, being just three years younger and somewhat lighter. But one would not have a hard time understanding the two were offspring from the same parents.

"We sent heralds, but you were deep in sleep and your servants refused to awaken you," said Nestor. Thirty years older than Agamemnon, he was thin and wiry, with a long, white beard. He was king of rocky Pylos and had been a warrior of strong reputation in his earlier days. He was well past his prime but was held in high regard by all for his wisdom and his counsel was often sought by Agamemnon.

"Or, deep in some other activity," said Menelaus, soft enough that none but Agamemnon heard. The Mycenaen king glared at his brother, then turned back to Nestor.

"I understand the prince of Phthia has finally arrived," he said.

Nestor nodded across the open way, toward where Achilles was standing with Phoenix and Patroclus. They were talking with another group of men, which was led by a veritable giant of a man, who was towering over Achilles and speaking loudly to him.

"That is Peleusson there...the one with the golden mane," he said. "The other young man is his companion, Patroclus, who looks remarkably like him. The older man is Phoenix, his mentor, sent by Peleus."

"Hmmmmm," said Agamemnon. "This Achilles looks very young and untested."

"It seems his cousin, Ajax, thinks so, too," said Diomedes with a smirk of anticipation. "I sense a fight brewing here."

Agamemnon was immediately intrigued. He strode over to the group and all eyes turned his way, the bantering coming to a halt. Nestor was at his side, with Menelaus and Diomedes close behind.

"Allow me to make the introductions, since I am the oldest here," said Nestor. He looked at Achilles straight on, to get his attention, and then turned toward Agamemnon, who had drawn himself up to his full height. He noticed he was a bit shorter than Achilles and he did not like that fact.

"Agamemnon, high king of Mycenae of the famed Lion Gate," said Nestor, loudly for all to hear. "Commander of the united forces by acclamation!"

Agamemnon smiled stiffly, facing Achilles.

"And this, my lord, is Prince Achilles, son of Peleus, king of Phthia."

Achilles offered his arm and Agamemnon clasped it and felt the strength. Achilles' forearm was like a staff of pure oak, Agamemnon thought.

"We have heard much of your prowess, young Achilles," said Agamemnon. "Your presence, and that of the mighty Myrmidons, is greatly appreciated by me and my brother, Menelaus." He half turned and nodded toward Menelaus, who stepped forward. Agamemnon introduced Achilles to him and then to Nestor, and to Diomedes. Achilles, in turn, introduced Phoenix and Patroclus.

"This is my mentor, Phoenix, and my good friend and cousin, Patroclus," said Achilles in a low voice. "We have come to provide what assistance we can in righting this terrible wrong done to your family. The royal house of Priam will pay dearly for this great affront, not only to your brother and house but to the golden rule of hospitality."

Phoenix had coached Achilles on what to say and how to say it when meeting the high king and the other warlords. He smiled faintly, pleased at how well his pupil had performed. Making reference to the rules of hospitality helped to justify the war to Achilles. He wasn't as angered about the affront to the two kings, who he did not know, as he was about the Prince of Troy savaging the rules of hospitality. Guests were to be treated with the utmost respect, Chiron had told him, unless and until they violated that trust with some misdeed. What Alexandros had done to Menelaus was the worst offense of all – taking a man's hospitality and then stealing his most coveted possession, his wife.

Agamemnon nodded, pleased with what Achilles had said. Then he glanced over at Ajax, who was glaring at them. The man was at least a head taller than anyone present and weighed far more. He had thick, unruly reddish hair, with a beard that covered most of his face and upper lip, all of the same color. He wore a brown tunic, trimmed at the shoulders, where from sprouted two massive arms. There were some in the camp who thought he was larger than Heracles, and perhaps almost as strong.

"I see you have met Ajax already; is he not your cousin, by way of your fathers?"

Achilles nodded and Ajax grunted.

"We have met," said Achilles stiffly.

Ajax seized the opportunity, storming up to Agamemnon and fixing him with a deadly glare from his brown eyes. Even Agamemnon felt the urge to take a step backward when confronted by the huge warrior.

"Yes, our fathers are brothers," Ajax spat out. "But that is nothing to boast of, at least on my part."

There had been a murmuring among the warlords when Ajax came forward, but it ceased like a fire that had been suddenly drenched by a tidal wave of water. All eyes were on Achilles as he turned to squarely face the giant. There was a burning in his gray eyes that matched the fire in Ajax's.

"I don't know what I have done to anger you so much, Ajax, but you have just spat on my father's name," said Achilles. "He is not only worthy of being the brother of Telamon, he is superior to Telamon in any way you cut it. He has been favored by Zeus, from birth to marriage to his kingdom. You need to watch your tongue when speaking about my father."

Ajax sneered at his words.

"Or what, little prince?" he asked in a mocking manner.

"Or I will make you swallow them," said Achilles, standing directly before the giant.

A deathly silence fell over the group; no one moved a muscle. Later, Phoenix was to say that even the gods and goddesses on Olympus drew quiet, staring down at the scene playing out before them on earth, between the two mightiest warriors in the entire camp of the Achaeans.

"I hear your mother is a goddess, from the sea," said Ajax with a sneer. "And that you tried to avoid this war by dressing as a girl."

Chuckles broke out all around the group and Achilles felt the rage swelling inside him. He stared up at his cousin, his temples pounding....just like they had on Mount Pelion when facing the lion and wrestling Patroclus for the first time.

"And I hear that you pride yourself on your wrestling," said Achilles, his words measured. "I would like to test your skills, son of Telamon."

There was along silence as the challenge took root in the minds of all the warlords. Ajax was taken by surprise and then a grin spread across his lips. He lifted his arms and shrugged off his tunic, displaying large, bulging muscles that any blacksmith would be proud of. He turned to a smaller man at his side, who carried a bow and a quiver of arrows on his back. Teucer, his half brother and constant companion and a warrior well known for his shooting skills, took the tunic from Ajax.

"You have bitten off more than you can chew, Peleusson," Ajax said, loudly. He swung his massive arms quickly across his chest, to loosen up his muscles, and stood ready, facing Achilles. The others backed up quickly, eagerly awaiting a match they could have only dreamed of – the son of Peleus wrestling the son of Telamon, the offspring of two of the greatest heroes who had sailed with Jason and Heracles on the legendary voyage to the land of the golden fleece.

"Who will judge this match?" Ajax said, turning around to glance over the crowd. "Who has the stomach for it?"

Nestor stepped quickly forward, smiling faintly.

"I will do the honors," he said. Both Ajax and Achilles nodded their consent.

Achilles eased off his tunic, exposing his much leaner physique. Ajax flexed his muscles again, drawing gasps of admiration from the crowd. Agamemnon glanced at Menelaus, offering a chuckle.

"This should not take long," he said quietly. Menelaus nodded his agreement.

"What are the rules?" asked Nestor, standing between the two warriors.

"It makes no difference to me," said Achilles, his voice low and even. "Let Ajax decide."

"No biting and no eye gouging" said the giant. "Anything else goes."

Nestor looked at the two warriors and raised his scepter, much smaller than the one Agamemnon carried. He held it high as the two men stared at one another, then let it fall.

Ajax advanced quickly, a sneer on his lips. He held his fists up high, each half the size of a man's head, it seemed to Patroclus, watching closely. He felt a stab of anxiety in his stomach, but he had no doubt of the outcome. None at all.

Achilles moved slowly, hands held halfway up, expecting the giant to throw a punch. Ajax feinted with two left-hand punches then threw a right that, had it connected, would have ended the match immediately. But Achilles was nowhere near the punch. He ducked easily and moved away, showing no emotion. Ajax pursued him and threw two more ponderous punches, neither connecting.

"Stop moving....come exchange blows and fight," mumbled Ajax. "Is this how Peleus teaches his son to wrestle?"

Ajax advanced again and threw another left feint. Achilles slid under the fist and, instead of moving away again, threw a hard punch into the left side of the giant's chest. Ajax grunted heavily, eyes wide, and stumbled backwards. He felt a numbness where the blow had landed and had to gasp for breath. He stood motionless for a moment, a surprised look on his face, and then held up his hands again. He stepped forward cautiously. Achilles charged hard into him and Ajax grunted loudly as his cousin's arms flew around his waist. Ajax felt the amazing strength of Achilles as his feet left the ground momentarily. He gasped and planted his feet solidly on the earth. He threw his palms to Achilles' chin, pushing it back with all his might.

The two men were locked tight, motionless. Achilles held Ajax around the waist, trying to hoist him again but Ajax was so tall that his feet were still on the ground. He pushed Achilles' head back farther and farther, and grinned wickedly as he heard the much smaller man gasp for breath.

Ajax was preparing to throw a fist to Achilles' throat when Achilles disappeared. He had ducked under Ajax's right arm with a lightning move and slipped behind him. Ajax tried to twist around to look for his foe; then he felt his left leg being blocked by Achilles' foot and he was hurled to the earth, landing heavily on his side. The breath was knocked from him. He shook his head wildly, the long hair swirling, and gasped for air. Slowly, he struggled up to his hands and knees, Achilles solidly behind him.

Patroclus leaned back, arms folded across his chest, and smiled. Phoenix glanced at Patroclus, a thin smile working its way across his face as well. Teucer leaned forward, eyes wide. The other warlords stared at the two wrestlers, not sure what was happening. They only knew that the great strength and size of Ajax seemed to be adding very little to his advantage.

Ajax shook his head again, angry from the fall, and started to rise, pushing off the ground with his hands, coming unsteadily to his feet. As Ajax stood upright, Achilles lifted him high, titled his massive body and slammed him viciously to the ground. Ajax groaned loudly, his left arm trapped beneath him and badly damaged. Again, slowly, he struggled to his feet... and again he was lifted and flung wildly to the ground.

This time, the giant lay prone, unable to move. Blood gurgled out of his mouth. Achilles gripped his arm and tried to jerk it back in the arm lock he had been taught on the hills of Mount Pelion, by the man-horse. But to his surprise, he could not budge the mighty arm of Ajax, who was fighting to keep it from Achilles' grasp. Apparently, Telamon had told his son about Peleus's ability with the arm lock and Ajax, although hurt and dazed, was determined to not fall into the trap.

Achilles shifted immediately, sliding both hands under the arms of Ajax, and locking his fingers on the thick neck of the giant. In desperation, Ajax pushed up to his hands and knees, grunting heavily and perspiring, the sweat dripping off him. He tried to stand and to hold his head erect, but Achilles' hands were forcing his neck downward. The two warriors struggled mightily – Achilles on top, keeping Ajax's head bowed by exerting terrible pressure on his neck, Ajax struggling to keep his head erect.

The Achaean chieftans stood transfixed as they watched with disbelieving eyes. The smaller warrior was winning the contest of strength over the giant. Achilles slowly forced Ajax's chin downward. Ajax groaned loudly, his face buried in his own chest, hardly able to breathe. With a might surge and scream, he jerked his head upright, his eyes wide, gasping and uttering an oath.

And then, his head was forced back down. Slowly, he sagged to his stomach, defeated and helpless. His face was pushed into the ground, dirt and grass filling his mouth. He could not breathe. He began jerking and coughing.

Achilles released his hold and stood, staring down at the quaking body, then looked at Nestor, who was regarding him with a sense of wonder. He lifted the hand of Achilles and the chieftans began cheering.

"Achilles is the winner!" declared Nestor. The other warlords gathered around Achilles, slapping his back and offering praise. Slowly, Ajax sat up, staring at Achilles with a stunned expression. Teucer and two of his men helped him to his feet; he wiped his hand over his mouth, and spat. He watched Achilles receiving congratulations and then turned and staggered slowly away, the others straggling along behind him.

Patroclus and Phoenix were sitting outside the large Myrmidon tent in the growing dark, discussing the day's events and the great wrestling match over and over, when they saw a huge figure moving toward them. Patroclus squinted and then turned to Phoenix.

"It's Ajax!" he said. He stood and watched the giant approach. Ajax was wearing a short tunic, belted at the waist, and the scowl was gone. He halted in front of the two men, looking past them into the tent, lit by oil lamps in each corner.

"Is Achilles here?" he asked, his voice low. He stared straight at Patroclus.

"Yes," said Patroclus, moving away. "Let me announce you."

He slipped into the tent and found Achilles sitting on a chair in the far corner of the large tent, his tunic wrapped around him, strumming softly on the lyre. He glanced up at Patroclus.

"Who were you talking to? I heard a strange voice."

"Ajax has come to see you," Patroclus said.

Achilles laid down the lyre and pondered the situation for several moments. Then he stood and squared his shoulders.

"Send him in," he said.

Moments later, the giant walked through the opening and Patroclus shut the flap behind him, remaining on the outside. Phoenix glanced up at him and he merely shrugged. They both tried to listen to what was being said inside the tent.

Ajax stood before Achilles, their eyes locked. Then, he sighed and held out his arm in friendship.

"I was wrong to accuse you of being less than you are," Ajax said gruffly. "I was also wrong to say anything about your father, or mother, that may have offended you. Surely, your mother must be a goddess for you to have such strength and skill." He paused. "You are….a great warrior. I am proud to be of the same lineage as you."

Achilles felt the tension flow out of him and a slow smile came over his features. He recalled the words Chiron had spoken to him months earlier concerning the value of having friends and comrades. He respected Ajax and felt he could even learn to like him.

"We have much in common, Ajax," he said. "I have heard stories of your strength and courage many times, from both Chiron and Peleus. I am glad that we have finally met and I hope we can be friends. And comrades in arms, once we land at Troy."

"Never have I lost a wrestling match," said Ajax, his voice thick. "I acknowledge you are the better man. I have never seen quickness like you possess, nor felt strength like yours. They can not be from mere mortals."

Achilles smiled and took the extended arm. They sat through much of the night, exchanging stories of their youth, talking of their fathers. When Ajax finally left, Achilles felt he had at least one, hard-earned friend outside of the Myrmidon camp that he could count on, other than Odysseus.

Iphigenia

The days stretched into weeks at the camp, which grew in size as new arrivals came on a daily basis. The warlords met in Agamemnon's great tent for counsel and to devise strategy for the assault on Troy, while the common soldiers hunted, worked on their spears, swords and arrows, and engaged in a variety of spirited athletic contests. There were two forms of athletic contests going on, one for the common soldier and another for the princes and kings. In the latter, Achilles showed himself to be the greatest in all endeavors. He won another wrestling contest, as only one other dared to even enter it after seeing his bout with Ajax. He also won the spear throwing and the long race, with Patroclus finishing third, behind the swift-footed Ajax the Lesser, who nipped him for second place right at the end.

Agamemnon announced the departure date for Troy, but suddenly the winds died away and they could not sail from the island. For weeks after announcing the plans to leave, the huge army was landlocked on Aulis and their supplies began to dwindle. Tempers grew hotter with the weather and several of the warlords began talking about going home.

Matters grew worse when the prophet Calchas arrived and asked for lodging while he assessed the situation. Calchas, who had lived well beyond sixty years and was very feeble, had been a priest of Apollo, living on Mount Ida behind the walls of Troy. When Alexandros arrived in Troy with his stolen queen from Sparta, Priam sent Calchas to consult with the Oracle at Delphi as to the fate of the city.

When Agamemnon learned of Calchas and his mission to Delphi, he had him brought to Mycenae to see what he had learned from the Oracle. It was then that Calchas had told Agamemnon and the other chieftans that Troy would be taken only if the son of Peleus joined the expedition.

The Achaean leaders did not want Calchas in their camp, but feared to turn him away since he was close to Apollo, and no one wanted to anger the powerful god. When he first appeared, wearing a long, white robe and leaning heavily on his staff, only Achilles made him welcome. He was given a tent in the camp of the Myrmidons and spent several days talking with Phoenix and Achilles. But he took long walks along the seashore, gazing up at the sun and chanting to Apollo for guidance. At last, he asked for a meeting of the warlords. Achilles agreed to arrange it.

Agamemnon was not pleased with all that was going on. He had not wanted to hear from Calchas, but did not have the courage to send him from camp or to ignore his request for a meeting. And so he agreed to have all the warlords assemble at his tent when Calchas arrived, with Achilles, Phoenix and Patroclus escorting him.

What transpired was devastating to Agamemnon.

"I have spent considerable time praying to Lord Apollo about the death of the wind," said Calchas in a strong and steady voice that belied his age. He did not look at the other warlords, but kept his gaze locked on Agamemnon, who sat at the head of the huge table, ringed with thirty other warlords.

"You were on the hunt when you came across a stag that was loved by Apollo and Artemis," said Calchas. "You ran it down and shot it with your arrows, and it died an agonizing death, crying out to Artemis for revenge."

Calchas paused for effect. The room was deathly quiet. Agamemnon leaned back in his chair, his hand, rich with rings of power, gripping his drinking cup so tightly that the figures on the cup left an imprint in his palm. His lips twitched and his pointed beard seemed to sway gently. His dark eyes were locked on Calchas.

"Artemis, through her brother Apollo, the most glorious of the gods, demands a tribute in trade for her favorite stag," continued Calchas, undeterred by Agamemnon's menacing countenance. "A magnificent tribute, one that only a great king can make."

There was another long pause as all eyes shifted to the king of Mycenae.

"And....how much gold does Artemis require?" Agamemnon said, his voice low and thick with anger.

"It is not gold she wishes," said Calchas. "Gold does not breathe and run, and love, like a beautiful stag. Artemis demands....a living sacrifice." He paused.

"She demands the life of the daughter of Agamemnon."

A gasp ran through the tent as the warlords turned to one another, eyes wide with disbelief. Then, they all turned back to Agamemnon.

The high king said nothing, his face red with anger. He ran his eyes over the men he had assembled for this meeting, and they lingered on Achilles for a moment, who stared back without betraying his feelings. Then Agamemnon rose to his full height, the long, purple robe hanging below his knees. He looked suddenly larger and stronger than he had ever seemed before.

"What you ask, seer, is impossible," he said, voice low and thick. "Are you mad, to think that a king would kill his daughter, even for such a noble cause as to seek vengeance on Troy?"

He paused, and then slammed both fists down hard on the table.

"Are you mad, I ask you?" he shouted, the veins standing out in his neck.

Calchas merely nodded faintly.

"Some may say so, great king," he said. "But I only tell you what Apollo has told me to say. These are not my words, mighty Agamemnon. These are the words of Apollo himself."

He stood, much smaller, and faced the high king from the opposite end of the long table.

"I can only tell you that the winds will not come until you have paid your debt."

With that, he turned and walked out of the tent. Achilles, Phoenix and Patroclus departed with him, leaving the warlords stunned and silent in their seats.

For three long days, there was no further discussion on the matter. Calchas stayed close to Achilles, fearing to venture too near to Agamemnon or the others. But the high king did not leave his tent, often sitting up until the moon goddess was high in the sky, drinking wine and yelling at anyone within earshot, mostly Menelaus and Nestor. He was greatly relieved when Odysseus finally showed up, the last of the warlords to arrive. After leaving Phthia, Odysseus had journeyed all the way to Ithaca to make sure he was leaving his island kingdom in good hands before venturing to Troy. He had told his queen, Penelope, that he may be gone for as long as a year, and he was very sad to leave his young son, Telemachus, who had just passed the first year of his life.

Upon arriving in camp with his small band of troops, Odysseus was immediately summoned to the tent of Agamemnon to hear the terrible news. There were only five warlords there, besides Agamemnon – Menelaus, Nestor, Idomeneus of Crete, Diomedes of Argos and Ajax the Greater.

"I do not like this Calchas," sputtered Agamemnon, pacing the room, stopping to lean on the thick table, glaring at Odysseus. "He has brought evil words to us. What does he, or anyone, expect me to do when faced with such an impossible choice? Give up the assault on Troy, or give up the life of my eldest daughter?

"As for Achilles, I do not like this man, either. He has given safe harbor to this prophet and, hence, put me in this terrible spot. Achilles....is too perfect. He is the best wrestler, the fastest runner, throws the spear the farthest. And, damn it to Zeus, is even the most hand-some man in the entire camp."

"Then, he gives lodging to Calchas, and makes us all listen to his ranting. And look where that has gotten us!"

He sank into his huge chair, head in hands, staring at the empty cup. They continued drinking for hours, exchanging ideas and angry shouts as each offered his opinions. At long last, Agamemnon stood shakily and looked around the tent at the others.

"Even if I did agree to such a scheme – to sacrifice my daughter – how would I get her to come here? The queen is always suspicious of anything I do. How could I possibly entice Clytaemnestra to bring her daughter to Aulis? There is no chance of that. None at all. We are doomed men, it seems."

There was a long silence as Agamemnon slumped back into his chair. Odysseus then stood, hands on hip, looking at the king of Mycenae.

"Maybe we can use all of that to our advantage," said Odysseus.

Agamemnon and the others looked at him.

"Go on," said the high king. "We're listening."

"Calchas has said the winds will not come until Apollo is appeased by a great sacrifice," said Odysseus. "Your daughter." He paused for dra-matic effect as the warlords stared at him.

"Well, if you are determined to get Iphigenia here, if you have made the decision in your heart to sacrifice your daughter for this great cause, there is one sure way that Clytaemnestra will oblige you."

"And how is that, great Ithacan?" said Agamemnon, derisively. "Even your nimble wit can't find a way to do that, I'll wager."

Odysseus smiled.

"What mother wouldn't want her daughter to have Achilles as a hus-band?" asked Odysseus, arching an eyebrow.

Agamemnon suddenly sat up, staring at Odysseus as the words sunk in. Menelaus leaned back in his chair, studying his brother. Nestor and Idomeneus shook their heads in wonder at the plan and at the audacity it would require. All eyes were locked on Agamemnon.

"It....might work," the high king said slowly, his eyes narrowing in an evil stare. "It just might work." He looked over at Odysseus. "Athena must truly love you the best of all the kings and warlords, to give you such a scheming mind."

Ajax stood, towering over the others, a glum expression on his features.

"I am not a part of this plan," he said firmly. "Achilles will be furious unless he is consulted. And, if consulted, he will not give his consent."

Odysseus stared up at the son of Telamon.

"How do you know that?" he asked. "Are you and Achilles suddenly friends after your wrestling match that I have heard about?"

Ajax glared at Odysseus.

"We are cousins, and we are friends," he said.

Agamemnon looked up at Ajax.

"We respect your new-found admiration for Achilles," he said sternly. "But you must give an oath that you will not speak of this plan to anyone, most of all Achilles. The entire fate of the expedition could rest on our plan and it must not leave this tent."

Ajax placed his hands on the table, palms down. He was clearly in anguish over the decision. Finally, he lifted his gaze.

"For the sake of the expedition, I will say nothing," he said, and marched out of the tent into the dark night.

Menelaus turned to Agamemnon.

"Does this mean... you accept the plan?"

"What choice have I?" croaked Agamemnon, pain in his voice. He stalked around the room, his robe swirling with each step. "Do I give up the greatest adventure in the history of man. Or do I give up my daughter?"

"We need revenge for the atrocity that has befallen all Achaeans, brought on by the prince of Troy," shouted Menelaus, rising to his feet and slamming a fist on the table.

"You have been greatly wronged," said Nestor, looking up at Menelaus, "and so to has your brother. This can not go unanswered." He turned to Diomedes, who was leaning back in his chair, saying nothing.

"What say you, Diomedes?" asked Nestor. "You have brought nearly five hundred men and you have shown yourself to be highly skilled in the arts of war, second only to Achilles in many respects. What are your thoughts?"

Diomedes, dark haired and handsome, leaned forward slightly, one hand resting on the hilt of his dagger.

"I came for just two reasons," he said. "To test myself and my warriors in battle. And to gain glory. I am ready to fight at a moment's notice. I am eager to proceed, at all costs."

"Then, we have little choice," said Idomeneus, nodding at the words of Diomedes. "The Fates call to all of us. But still, it is up to Agamemnon.

He has the greatest choice to make. We must hear him out."

Agamemnon glanced around at the warlords.

"I will give my decision tomorrow," he said weakly. "Now, I need to be left alone."

He retired into his second tent, leaving the other warlords to talk quietly into the night. They discussed the huge decision that lay before the high king, and all admitted it was not a decision they would want to contend with.

"He will make the sacrifice," said Nestor at last. "His duty demands it. The cause is too noble to resist."

Odysseus smiled wryly.

"And so is the treasure trove of old Priam," said Odysseus.

The camp was in a state of high anxiety, with thousands of soldiers, aides and camp workers meandering about, or lying in the blazing sun by the water's edge. It had been six weeks since the winds had disappeared and the food supply was almost exhausted. Tempers were running short and everyone was eager to see an end to the waiting. And then word came that they were to have a special visitor from Mycenae.

Nerves had gotten the best of Agamemnon ever since he sent word to his wife, Clytaemnestra, that her beloved daughter was to be married to the prince of Phthia, the finest of all the Achaeans. The fame of Achilles had spread all across the mainland and his father's reputation was of the highest regard. Even the queen of Mycenae would be pleased to have her daughter become the bride of Achilles. Agamemnon sulked in his tent, consuming more of the barley drink than ever before. Even Menelaus was loath to enter the tent and engage his brother with conversation of any sort, for fear that it would quickly turn into a tirade against either Calchas or Achilles.

At last, the day arrived that he had been both desperately needing and dreading at the same time. Heralds brought word to Agamemnon that the procession from Mycenae was approaching. Agamemnon rose from his great chair and threw his purple robe about him, and walked slowly out into the bright daylight. Menelaus, Odysseus and Nestor were there waiting for him, all wearing grim expressions. Agamemnon nodded faintly at them, then moved to greet his wife and daughter.

The two women rode next to the driver in the chariot that Agamemnon had sent to pick them up from the ship. Behind them were two more chariots and a cart pulled by oxen, with their servants and ladies in waiting.

Clytaemnestra was older than her sister, Helen, and not nearly as beautiful. She was darker skinned and shorter than Helen. Yet, she had a regal bearing, standing proud and straight. Her thin lips seldom formed a smile and her hair, much darker than Helen's, was pulled around her head in a tight embrace. She wore a light yellow chiton, which showed her ample breasts to good advantage.

Unlike her mother, Iphigenia was fair skinned and tall. She wore a chiton that exposed her trim arms, untouched by sunlight, fair and light. She also had brownish hair, but a very pretty face, much like that of her aunt Helen. She had an innocence about her that was beguiling; though just twelve years of age, she was already a beautiful young woman, with a trim figure.

Agamemnon shifted nervously as his wife and daughter stepped down from the chariot to greet him. Clytaemnestra embraced him briefly and then Iphigenia flew into his arms.

"Oh, father, I am so happy to see you," she said, then finally pulling back and staring up into the stern face of Agamemnon. "This is such a wonderful day."

Odysseus and Nestor stood stiffly by, immersed in their own thoughts. Odysseus glanced at Clytaemnestra, wondering if she had any suspicion as to what was transpiring. He had met the woman briefly when he was in line as a suitor for the hand of Helen, and found her to be charming but wise and calculating. She was a woman who observed all that went on around her and would not be easily deceived, he reasoned.

Agamemnon quickly took the women back to his tent. Menelaus, Nestor and Odysseus retreated to Menelaus's tent nearby, where they sat anxiously waiting developments.

"What is the schedule?" asked Odysseus of Menelaus.

"To carry it out as quickly as possible," said Menelaus. "My brother knows what must be done and that any delay will not be helpful. It will not be long."

Within moments, they were startled by a terrible scream. They rushed out of the tent to see Clytaemnestra running from Agamemnon's tent, hands gripping her hair, screaming hysterically. Behind her came Iphigenia, walking slowly with two large soldiers on each side. Iphigenia wore a stunned expression, staring straight ahead. She stumbled after several steps, and the soldiers gripped her arms and held her erect. Behind them came Agamemnon, wearing his war helmet pulled down tight over his face, the tall, crimson crest standing tall.

Clytaemnestra stopped abruptly, then swiveled to face Agamemnon and the soldiers.

"You beast!" she screamed at Agamemnon. "What kind of a man surrenders his daughter in any fashion, let alone the way you have done?

Have you no sense of shame? Are you no longer a man....a husband....a father?"

She ran at the soldiers and tried to pry their fingers from Iphigenia's arms. Two more soldiers came up and gripped her by the arms, pulling her away.

She jerked free, gasping, breasts heaving. Then she changed. Standing tall, she ran her hands slowly through her dark hair, composing herself. She looked around the gathering host of warlords and soldiers, her shouts having attracted considerable attention. The soldiers with Iphigenia had halted, as had Agamemnon. All eyes were riveted on her.

"Where is lord Achilles?" she asked, her voice thick.

No one answered her.

"Where is lord Achilles?" she shouted, turning to look at the faces of the hundreds of warriors around her. "Does the prince of Phthia know what evil is being done with the use of his name? Does Achilles, who men acknowledge as the finest of all Achaeans, know that the princess of Mycenae was lured here by a false promise of marriage to him....and now she has been betrayed by her own father?

"Does Achilles know that before the day is out, my beautiful Iphigenia will be sacrificed....in his name?" she wailed.

A deathly silence hung over the host. No one moved, until at last Agamemnon walked to the guards and motioned for them to follow him. Slowly, the procession wound through the wide array of tents, headed toward a high mound on the outskirts of the camp, where sacrifices had been made on a regular basis to the various gods and goddesses. All the previous sacrifices had been goats and sheep; now, the altar would taste human blood for the first time.

Clytaemnestra watched the procession slip away, until she was alone with her four personal servants. They gaped at her, tears streaming down their faces, wringing their hands, waiting for her to collapse. Instead, she marched over to where two young soldiers were standing, attired in chitons.

"Where is the tent of Achilles?" she asked, her dark eyes stabbing into their eyes. Both of them backed away, until she screamed at them.

"Where is the tent of Achilles? Can you not even give a simple answer to a mother who has lost her child?"

The first soldier pointed.

"It is that way, at the very end," he said.

Without another word, she turned and began marching toward the camp of the Myrmidons, her handmaidens straggling along behind her. But she did not have to go far. She stopped abruptly, her heart pounding. She saw striding quickly toward her two golden-haired young men, both naked from the waist up, bodies gleaming with sweat from the hot day, and behind them a small group of ten warriors dressed in black armor.

"I know it must be him," she muttered.

Achilles hurried to meet her, Patroclus at his side. The two warriors stopped in front of Clytaemnestra, towering over her. And she saw the anguish in their faces.

"You are Achilles!" she gasped.

"Yes," he said, lips drawn tight. "I have just heard what has happened. One of my Myrmidons was there, and ran to bring me the message… of how my name and honor has been misused. And how your daughter….has been cruelly cheated."

Clytaemnestra gripped his hard arms in her hands, her nails pressing in. She stared up at him with eyes that reminded him of Thetis's eyes, at the moment when he told her he was leaving for Troy. His heart grew heavy with grief, and then strong with anger.

"Save her, Achilles," she mumbled. "Please….save her!"

Achilles nodded and eased himself from her grip.

"I will… or I will die trying," he said in a half growl.

He was off and running, Patroclus at his side. She staggered back, watching the Myrmidons race past her.

And then she heard a shrill noise she had never heard before. It filled her heart with both fear and wonder at the same time. She gasped, hands to her mouth. For the first time, Clytaemnestra heard the war cry of the Myrmidons.

The sacrificial priests and attendants were waiting for Iphigenia. Two priests and ten assistants stood in long, white robes, looking to the skies and chanting heavily as the procession neared them. Behind them was a huge stone altar that had been on the island for eons. It was used by the current residents for sacrifices to appease angry gods and to plea for help from those same gods and goddesses when times were hard. It was a heavy stone slab laid on three legs of stone, roughly hewn from the small quarry in the center of the island. There were dark red stains all over the stone.

Iphigenia trembled and sobbed softly as she was led to the front of the altar. Agamemnon stood ramrod straight behind her, staring impassively ahead, unable to look again on the daughter he had seen go from an infant to a lovely young woman, growing up secure behind the lion gates of mighty Mycenae. Many of the warlords were present but several were absent, including Ajax and Diomedes. Neither of them was interested in seeing a young woman sacrificed, even if it did mean the launching of the assault on Troy was at last imminent.

The priests began their ritual, daggers gleaming in the sunlight as they held them aloft, praying to Apollo and Artemis, asking their for-giveness for wrongs that had been done to them. At last, the soldiers escorting Iphigenia led her to the altar, then stood back, releasing her. She stood reeling, eyes shut, arms crossed in front of her. In a stunningly small amount of time, she had gone from expectant bride to sacrificial lamb. She was whispering a prayer, the words too soft to be heard. Finally, Agamemnon stared over at her.

And then the war cry of the Myrmidons split the air.

"Alilia…alilia….alilia…..alilia….alilia….."

The priests stopped praying, lowering their daggers, glancing about, angry that anyone would dare interrupt their services. The soldiers tensed, gripping their swords, glancing nervously at Agamemnon. The warlords stood confused and puzzled, not knowing what was happening.

There was a short silence and then the war cry cut the air again. Achilles and Patroclus burst into view, running up the slight slope, the ten Myrmidons behind them.

Agamemnon spit out an oath and motioned for his soldiers to sur-round him and the altar. He had one hundred men at his disposal and he sent one of the heralds racing down the hill to summon even more Mycenaens. He drew the short sword hanging at his side and moved in front of the altar as Achilles approached him, wearing a deep scowl.

"This is not your business, prince," said Agamemnon, his voice heavy with anger. "What brings you here on the run, shouting your war cry against fellow Achaeans?"

"What brings me here is the ugly rumor that you have used my name in the most vile of ways," said Achilles, facing Agamemnon, but not drawing his sword.

"What do you mean by that charge?" said the high king, his face flush with anger.

"I mean… that I have been told you brought your daughter here from Mycenae with the promise that I would marry her," Achilles said. There was a long pause as the two powerful men regarded each other in the most solemn manner. "Is there truth in that story, or is it a rumor only?"

Iphigenia stared at Achilles with wide eyes, her heart pounding. She was seeing for the first time the man she was thought to be marrying soon, but now seeing him in a situation she could have never imagined while in her bed chambers in far-off Mycenae. She marveled at the young prince, numb with a combination of fear and admiration.

The Mycenaen troops moved in tighter around Agamemnon. They outnumbered the Myrmidons by ten-fold, but the Myrmidons moved up to flank Achilles, ready to charge at his word. They would die for their young prince without a moment's hesitation.

Achilles frowned deeply, and for the first time his hand fell on his sword hilt as he stared at the high king.

"Your silence gives me my answer," he said grimly. "Move aside, or I will cut you down where you stand."

The words hung in the air like a sharp sword ready to descend. Agamemnon could hardly breathe for the fury he felt. Not only was he being challenged by a man half his age to a duel he knew in his heart he could not win, but his very position as high king of the Achaean host was in total danger of being overthrown. If he rushed Achilles, he knew he would be killed by the young Phthian. If he backed away, he would be seen as a coward by his warlords, and by his own troops.

He was trapped by his own scheme in a manner he could have never imagined. He felt his throat tighten and his stomach churning. There was no escape. Even though his troops far outnumbered the Myrmidons, he had been challenged man to man by Achilles and honor would demand that he engage him.

"You risk....the entire venture to Troy, and angering Apollo and Artemis, as well," growled Agamemnon. "How dare you!"

As the Myrmidons and Mycenaens faced one another, ready to fight to the death for their prince and king, Agamemnon's salvation came from a source none of them could have ever imagined, least of all the king himself.

"Lord Achilles....father...please....come to me, both of you" said the voice, soft and beautiful. All were stunned and turned toward Iphigenia.

Achilles gaped at Iphigenia, unsure of what he had just heard. Agamemnon gawked at his daughter.

"Come to me, please, both of you," she said again, just as softly.

Agamemnon stumbled toward her, sword hanging at his side. Achilles hesitated, and then walked to her, as well.

She hugged her father, then turned toward Achilles.

"I have longed to lay eyes on you since I first heard your name, prince," she said, her blue eyes penetrating his. "You are... so handsome, as I had been told."

He stood before her, perplexed and unsure of what was coming.

"And when I saw you rushing to my defense, my heart was moved," she continued. "I know it is to protect your honor, but I suspect it is also to protect my life. I am not wrong to feel that, am I prince?"

"No, you are not wrong," Achilles said. "I would die to protect you, now that I have seen you, princess." He glanced over at Agamemnon. "How a father could sacrifice his daughter is beyond my understanding."

Agamemnon bristled, but Iphigenia stepped in between them.

"Father, I have made my decision." She paused. "So many soldiers will die on this expedition to Troy that you have planned. Trojans will die, too. Many women will weep; children will be left without fathers, mothers will lose sons. Sisters will lose brothers. Wives will lose husbands, and lovers." She paused and smiled faintly at the two men in front of her, men who were as different in temperament as they were in age.

"I have decided that I am ready to give my life to this cause," she said, her voice in a whisper. "I have decided I will accept my death as part of this great adventure."

Agamemnon was struck dumb. His face sagged and he tried to speak to her, but he didn't know what words to use. She turned to Achilles.

"I will die with the thought that the greatest warrior in all of the land was ready to die for me. But I can not allow that, prince Achilles. It has been foretold already that Troy can never be conquered without you in the field. The Achaeans need your sword and they need your courage, if they are to be successful."

"I only ask… that I be allowed to die in private," she said. "I want you both to leave and to take your warriors with you. I want no Achaean blood shed this day, but mine."

Achilles grimaced, struggling with his inner turmoil. Here was a woman who understood the decision he had made back on Skyros, a very young woman who had the same type of courage that he possessed. He admired her immensely. He knew she was a woman he could have learned to love.

He backed slowly away and waved Patroclus and the Myrmidons to follow him. He walked several steps away, then turned to face Iphigenia once again.

"I salute your courage, princess," he said. "It is rare to find a warrior with as much courage as you have. Even kings."

With that, Achilles turned and strode away, the Myrmidons falling in behind him. In moments, they were gone, and Iphigenia faced her father for the last time.

"Leave, great king," she said. "This is my time. You….will have many occasions to remember me in the years ahead."

Agamemnon was as moved by her courage as was Achilles. He sheathed his sword and backed away, staring at his daughter.

"You are wise far, far beyond your years, Iphigenia," he said. "May the gods welcome you to the Elysian Fields… and may they forgive me for this act."

"May your wife forgive you, too," she said softly. With that, she turned and walked to the priests, who surrounded her. Agamemnon and the other warlords walked slowly down the hill, back toward their tents.

It took four days for the winds to come, but when they arrived the ships were ready. There were nearly a thousand of them in all, painted with black pitch to keep them water tight. They had ten oars to a side and large sails ready to catch the swirling winds. The troops marched to the seashore and climbed aboard, each soldier responsible for his own armor, swords, shields and several days worth of food, which was carried at their sides in thick pouches.

Clytaemnestra had refused to stay in the camp of the Achaeans and had slept with her servants on the gentle slope of the hill where her daughter had given her life. Before leaving on the sorrow-filled trip back to Mycenae, Clytaemnestra visited Achilles in his tent. They sat together and talked quietly, she holding his hands and peering deep into his eyes. She spoke of his mother, Thetis, and how proud she must be of him. When she stood to leave, she hugged him.

"I will never forget the manner in which you showed your great respect for my daughter, prince of Phthia," she said softly. "I will pray to Zeus for your safe return from Troy so that your father and mother can see what a fine man they have brought into this world of ours, a world which offers so much treachery and pain to mothers like me." She drew a deep breath and her eyes narrowed.

"And I will also pray for the safe return of Agamemnon to golden Mycenae, so he can reap his reward, as well."

The City of Priam

Agamemnon and Achilles had not seen one another since the sacrifice and all the warlords knew there was bad blood between them. Phoenix met with Nestor twice to talk, two old men who held the other's wisdom in high regard, and they resolved to work with each other to bring the two leaders together, as much as was possible.

Achilles walked down to the ships with Patroclus at his side. His fifty ships were ready. The armada would sail along the mainland as much as possible, trying to keep the land in sight. The Aegean Sea could turn terrifyingly dangerous at a moment's notice, and all mainlanders knew that the sea god Poseidon was not sympathetic when ships ventured too far from land. But Achilles felt safer than most, due to that fact this mother was a sea goddess, and she understood the ways of Poseidon and would help protect his ships.

As soon as the strong winds began blowing, the armada set sail. Each ship's crew pulled up its stone anchor and laid it on the hard wood deck, with the thick rope coiled neatly beside it. Oarsmen took their positions as men scurried over the deck, letting the sails out so they could catch the wind. Each ship held about forty men and a few women servants.

The ships headed for sea with the land to the west and made it to the island of Lesbos in just three days, with some strong oar work, as well as the winds helping them along. The warlords disembarked there and were greeted hospitably by the king, one Philomelides, who threw a banquet in their honor. He was hopeful of not incurring their wrath and tried his best to be hospitable, knowing he could be seen as an ally to Troy and could be killed easily and his small kingdom overrun. Proud of his wrestling ability, he offered to wrestle any of the warlords, excepting Achilles, saying he had already heard of his wonderful skills and knew he would be no match. Odysseus accepted his challenge, and was smart enough to not eat at the banquet. Philomelides stuffed himself and when he entered the arena late that night, he was bloated and easily worn out. Odysseus defeated him quickly, much to the delight of the Achaeans, who looked upon the victory as a good sign for the invasion of the Troad.

They sailed next to Tenedos, a larger island that was actually visible from the highest point of the Trojan walls. The kingdom was ruled by a huge man named Tenes, who stood at the edge of the island with his army behind him, hurling insults at the invaders. The ships of the Myrmidons were the first to put into the tiny harbor and Tenes then directed his stinging tirade toward Achilles, who stood on the bow of his lead ship listening.

"This king needs to be taught a lesson," said Achilles grimly. He and Patroclus and a handful of Myrmidons went ashore. Tenes, adorned in thick armor and brandishing a long spear, was waiting for them. He stepped forward, singling out Achilles for combat. He was a head taller than Achilles and much heavier; but Achilles knew at a glance that the man's bulk would also make him move slowly. He donned his golden war helmet for the first time and, Pelion ash in hand, advanced toward the huge king.

"So, this is the great Achilles, son of a sea goddess," said Tenes. "I heard that you were hiding in Skyros with women, until found out. What makes you think you can make war with a man like me, foolish youth?"

Achilles grimaced and hoisted his spear. This was his first test in mortal combat and he could hardly contain his eagerness. Tenes closed ranks with him quickly and then fired his spear. He gasped with surprise when Achilles batted it aside easily with his Pelion ash.

"What a feeble cast, old man," said Achilles. "See how well you evade my spear." He cocked his arm and threw with one fluid motion, so quickly that Tenes managed to only half avoid the heavy spear. He threw up his ox-hide shield as the spear collided with it, the force of the throw knocking him off his feet. He rolled heavily in the thick grass and clamored to his feet, shaken. He saw Achilles running at him and drew his short sword.

"Come on!" he yelled in a voice thick with trepidation.

Achilles felt the power coming over him and began pouring blows on the king. Tenes backed up, stumbling under the attack. He had never felt such force in the strokes of a warrior before and a great terror took hold of him. He was about to plead for quarter when Achilles's sword broke through his armor and ran deep into his abdomen.

Tenes fell with a clatter to the ground, clutching the sword in two bloody hands, staring up helplessly. Achilles bent over him and pulled the sword free, nearly disemboweling him. Tenes jerked wildly once, then died immediately. Achilles unstrapped the war helmet from the dead king and rammed it overhead and screamed the war cry of the Myrmidons. Patroclus and the others broke after the soldiers of the slain king and they turned and ran for their lives, dropping their weapons as they fled.

Achilles stood triumphant, gazing over the land before him. He had made his first kill in battle... and he felt a hot tremor racing through his veins. His body quivered once, the muscles rolling as on a great lion standing to stretch.

The Myrmidons returned within a matter of minutes, laughing at the way the islanders had scattered. Patroclus stood before Achilles, looking into his eyes.

"Victory is sweet, my friend," he said quietly.

Achilles nodded.

"Let's go to Troy," he said, turning back toward the ships.

Phoenix came next to Patroclus and together they watched Achilles striding toward the ship.

"Don't forget what Peleus and Chiron told you that last night," said Phoenix. "We are both charged with watching young Achilles. Remember what they both fear in him."

Patroclus nodded.

"I remember well, friend," the young prince said, placing a hand on Phoenix's shoulder. "I remember well."

They returned to their ships and heard the cheers of the other warlords as their ships sailed past, straight to Troy. Suddenly, Achilles slammed Tenes' war helmet on the wooden deck and turned toward Patroclus.

"I have made a grave error!" he said bitterly. "By stopping here to fight this foolish king, we will not be the first ships to land at Troy!" He bounced a palm off his forehead in anger. "What was I thinking of, Patroclus. I have dreamed of being the first to leap from my ship onto the Trojan grass for weeks... and now I have lost that honor, for both myself and for Peleus."

"There will be honor enough when we land," said Patroclus. "You do not always need to be the first, Achilles. Not in everything."

Achilles glanced at his friend and smiled, nodding.

"You are right," he said. "There will be glory enough for all at windy Troy."

The city that guarded the Hellespont offered a magnificent view as the Achaean ships drew near to the plain of the Trojans. The warlords stood at the head of their ships with their warriors gathered around them, gazing at the sprawling city. They could see the impressive walls and the high-topped buildings nestled securely behind them. This dwelling by the sea had a long and illustrious past that few cities anywhere could match. Although no one knew for sure the exact time, Troy had been founded centuries earlier and was originally peopled by three different tribes – Trojans, Ilians and Dardanians. Eventually, they all merged together and became known by the name of the largest group, Trojans.

Troy was situated in a perfect spot to control all the major trade routes of the day. It was perched on a hill only one mile from the water's edge. Any ship master wishing to move his cargo past the city on its way up the Hellespont to the Black Sea could easily be attacked by Trojans; hence, all ships going past Troy had for centuries paid a high bounty to the Trojans, making their royal family extremely wealthy. Ships carrying gold, silver, iron, cinnabar, linens of all sorts, fish, oil and even Chinese jade were forced to pay a tribute to use the narrow shipping lanes that Troy controlled.

Troy was also well known for its herds of beautiful horses. The Trojan plain was full of high grass and ideal for raising horses. The city had hundreds of skilled horse tamers and prided itself for its well-made chariots. No chariots anywhere were of better design and durability than the chariots that came from Troy, not even those of far-flung Assyria.

Massive walls, much larger than Achilles had seen at Phthia and even larger than those of Mycenae, protected the denizens of the city. There were a series of watch towers which sprouted up along the walls, giving the fortification a truly majestic look. Inside the walls the Achaeans could see scores of rooftops of houses and temples, and up on the hill near the backside of the city sat the royal palace of King Priam. It was said that the old king had fathered nearly fifty sons, including ten by his queen, Hecuba. All of them and their spouses and offspring lived in the sprawling palace, so large was it.

The Trojans had long known of the enterprise planned against them; Agamemnon had sent an envoy to Priam even before calling the warlords to Aulis, demanding the return of Helen. Of course, Agamemnon didn't really think that Priam would return Helen with an apology and a huge sum of gold, as he had insisted; in fact, he would have been disappointed had the old king agreed to his terms. This war was going to be about far more than the return of a queen of Sparta, even though she was the wife of the brother of the most powerful king in all the mainland. This conflict was about achieving glory for the warlords, and about ransacking the royal treasury of the richest king in all the world. It was also about freeing the route up the Hellespont so no more bounty could be extracted!

Agamemnon was not disappointed by the old king's response. Priam had told the envoy that Helen wished to live in Troy now and that she was renouncing her marriage to Menelaus. She was married to Alexandros, prince of Troy, and the Trojan people had accepted her as one of their own. Priam bristled at the notion that his treasury should be expected to pay for her choice. He was hospitable to the envoy from Mycenae but had sent them away empty-handed after three days.

The day after the envoy left, Priam met with his war council to debate the reaction from the Achaeans and the council was evenly split on what would follow, or not follow. But they had received word some time later that Agamemnon had called all the warlords to Aulis and at that point the Trojan council knew what the reason was. Priam had immediately gone before the people, standing on his balcony overlooking the agora, and told the Trojans that war was likely.

When the council received a report on the size of the Achaean force, they were stunned. The city itself only housed about three thousand citizens, and the farmers and the countryside only about that much again. Priam sent out a desperate plea to all allies and to any king who had ever considered Troy a friend. There already was in place a loose confederation of Trojan alliances, forged with neighboring tribes and smaller towns, all eager to share in Troy's incredible wealth and benefit from its protection.

Most of the towns along the southern coast were closely allied to Troy and were obligated to offer troops and supplies. At least twenty such cities answered Priam's call and by the time the invaders arrived, Troy was packed with newcomers – war chiefs, soldiers and the stragglers who travel with the troops. There were thousands of tents just outside the huge walls, mixing in with the farming huts.

Part of the reason Agamemnon had commissioned an envoy to Troy was to have them scope out the landscape of the Troad and look for a suitable landing area. Two rivers, the Scamander and the Simeos, flowed across the Trojan plain. The Scamander was the larger of the two and provided the bulk of the water for the city. The late arrivals took a heavy toll on the water and food supplies, but behind the city was Mount Ida, a beautiful mountain area similar to Mount Pelion, home of the centaurs. Mount Ida contained numerous valleys and copses, with cold springs and pools, and an abundance of fig and olive trees. In addition, there were hundreds of scattered shepherds with herds of sheep and cattle. The Trojans and their allies knew they could leave the city and head north up the slopes with no danger of interference from the Achaeans, who were not known for surrounding a city and choking off the food and water supplies when they attacked.

When the ships reached the landing site, based on information Agamemnon had received, they sat idly in the water, waiting for the signal to disembark. A large Trojan force had rumbled out of the city well in advance of the landing and there were over three thousand warriors in full armor lined up for half a mile, three and four deep, waiting for the first warriors to come ashore. The war chariots were packed in deeply, two hundred in all, and above the warriors the Achaeans could see row after row of frightful-appearing helmets with dancing crests of various colors. Most of the Trojan soldiers wore bronze breastplates and kilts, with shin guards also made of bronze, with large figure eight shields. Many of the allies were dressed in fur skins and carried small, oval shields.

Agamemnon stood on his ship's brow, with Nestor, Menelaus and Odysseus at his side, assessing the Trojan forces. He tugged lightly on his pointed beard, taking in all aspects of the scene, from the topography to the chariots.

"The Trojans seem eager to fight," said Nestor, leaning on the thick railing. He had seen dozens of wars in his lifetime, but he was already beginning to think this one was going to be very different from any others; based on the size of Troy and its ability to mobilize its allies, this had the appearance of being a long and costly battle.

"We shall soon see," said Agamemnon. He turned and glanced back over the sea from which they had just come. He saw hundreds of ships spread out behind him, and the ships of Protesilaus next to his. The war chief from Thrace was preparing to leap ashore, standing at the bow of his ship in full armor and addressing his troops. The Trojans were watching Protesilaus as well and one war leader was already moving his chariot forward to intercept him.

"Where is Achilles?" grumbled Agamemnon, scanning the ships nearby. "I do not see the Myrmidon crest anywhere in the front lines."

"He stopped to fight at Tenedos," said Odysseus. "The delay has cost him the glory of being the first to land at Troy."

Agamemnon leaned back, still staring at the ship next to him.

"Let Protesilaus go first," he muttered. "I have not forgotten the prophecy that he who lands first on Trojan soil will also die first."

They heard a series of shouts and saw Protesilaus and his Thracians leaping from their ships. They began wading through the waist high water, shields held high, spears poised. The Trojan war leader that had sped toward the landing spot leaped out of his chariot and the others parted for him. He was tall and thick and carried himself with an ease that marked him as a magnificent athlete and warrior. He was attired in gray armor with a gray war helmet, and a bright red crest of horse hair. He gave the appearance of being a formidable opponent.

Protesilaus reached the beach first and was met by two Trojan soldiers. He cut them down with two swipes of his sword, obviously up against young soldiers with little sword training. He turned and screamed for his warriors to follow him, and then turned back... to find himself facing the Trojan warlord in gray.

There was a brief exchange of words between the two and then both charged. Agamemnon, Odysseus and Nestor watched with fascination as the Trojan neatly sidestepped two wild charges by Protesilaus and then drove his sword deep into his chest. Protesilaus spun away as the warlord jerked the sword free, and staggered back to the sea, clutching his chest, vomiting blood, his soldiers gaping at him. And then he fell face first in the surf.

The Trojan warlord did not utter a victory cry or even follow him. He simply moved after other invaders and began attacking with a vengeance. The Thracians broke and began running back to their ships.

"By Zeus, we go NOW!" screamed Odysseus. "Protesilaus has become the first Achaean to die and now it is time to spill Trojan blood."

Odysseus leaped out of the ship and splashed toward the Trojan ranks, waving for his Ithacans to follow. They had been watching his every move and poured out of their ships. Quickly, the god of war, Ares, took over and it became full-scale madness; the invaders poured from their ships by the thousands, shouting their individual war cries as they streamed onto the sandy ground. Warriors ran onto the Trojan plain while their attendants unloaded horses and chariots. The Trojans fought valiantly, bowmen filling the sky with arrows and others hurled large stones that could kill a man easily, crushing his head inside his war helmet. Slowly, the invaders began to push the Trojans back.

Agamemnon and Menelaus fought side by side, grunting heavily, swinging their swords, screaming advice to their men. Once Agamemnon caught sight of the Trojan warlord in gray and swerved in the other direction. He would find other Trojans to fight this day.

When Achilles came upon the sight, gaping from the deck of his ship, he was heartsick that he had missed the initial battle. He yelled to the oarsmen to row harder and then strapped on his war helmet, glancing at Patroclus.

"Zeus has granted us our dream, Patroclus!" he shouted, scanning the full-scale battle waging ferociously in front of him. "Think of our fathers."

As the ship struck bottom, he leaped into the water, followed by Patroclus and the Myrmidons. They ran onto the beach, sticking together, looking for warriors to engage. Several Trojans ran up to fight Achilles and Patroclus and were cut down with single swipes. Achilles stepped over one of the bodies, glancing down, and then ran ahead, looking for more enemies.

The sounds of bronze swords striking bronze swords filled the air, along with the grunts of surging soldiers and the screams of dying men. Blood spurted everywhere and horses reared on the Trojan side, neighing and trying to break away. It was pure bedlam, two armies of vastly different types engaging one another with no particular order or scheme. It was every soldier for himself.

Achilles swung his word with relish, sending four more Trojan soldiers to the ground and to Hades. Suddenly, he was against a warrior with a helmet made of boars' tusks, and who wore only animal skins. He was lean and muscular and covered with blood. Behind him were ten warriors, all at his command. He smirked when he saw Achilles and held up a fist.

"I am Cycnus, son of Poseidon," he shouted, a terrible scowl on his face. "I have fought in many wars and never been injured. I cannot be wounded." He threw back his head and a maniacal laughter rolled from his mouth. He then stared hard at Achilles. "It is your time to die, invader," he growled.

"We will see if you are truly invulnerable," spat Achilles. "Perhaps you have only been fighting little boys and women."

Cyncus growled in rage but he did not charge. Instead, he began to circle Achilles and the Myrmidons stopped looking for foes, watching the impending battle as it began to unfold. They sensed that Cyncus was a warrior who might severely test their young leader. He was far more seasoned than Achilles in the art of war and was overflowing with confidence that comes from much success. They glowered from the eye slots of their gray war helmets, watching with keen anticipation.

Cyncus feinted several times with his long spear and tried to lure Achilles in, where he could use the short dagger clutched tight in his left hand. Achilles feinted several times, but could not get Trojan to fall for his tricks, either. After several minutes, Achilles threw his spear so quickly that Cyncus narrowly escaped death. He smiled.

"Your spear is gone, warrior," he said, teeth gritted. "Now, you will taste my spear's fine point."

He bore in, jabbing with his spear as Achilles moved to his right, mindful of the dagger Cyncus held. Even Patroclus began to feel a gnawing in the pit of his stomach, wondering if his friend was in trouble. Then, suddenly, Achilles charged straight into the warrior, swinging his sword wildly. Cyncus was caught off guard and tried to defend himself by raising his dagger, his spear now worthless as Achilles was inside its danger zone. Achilles swung his sword relentlessly without tiring. Cyncus backed off, gasping for breath. A swipe of the sword cut his spear arm badly and he dropped the spear in the dust and jabbed with his dagger, striking Achilles' hand. Achilles dropped his sword, blood spurting from the wound, and Cyncus felt relief for a moment. But Achilles was in a fury now. He leaped at Cyncus and they fell to the ground, wrestling wildly. Achilles came up behind his foe and gripped his helmet strap in both his hands. He slid the strap across the warrior's throat and jerked hard.

Cyncus groaned, hands flopping wildly in front of him, eyes bulging. Achilles pulled back with all his might, snarling, twisting the strap tighter and tighter across the windpipe. Cyncus gurgled, desperate as he felt the life fleeing from him.

"Are you still invulnerable?' gasped Achilles, his arms throbbing with the pressure he was exerting. "Or can you die as well as any man, even if you are the son of a god."

Finally, Cyncus stopped struggling and blood poured from his mouth. Achilles stood, his eyes glazed over, and stared at his victim's warriors. They gaped at him in awe.

"Who are you?" one of them mumbled, filled with terror by what he had seen. He had truly felt Cyncus was invincible – until seeing this warrior choke him to death with the strap of his own helmet.

"I am Achilles, son of Peleus, king of Phthia," he spat out. "And I will be the death of Troy!"

He leaned down and picked up his sword and spear and charged into them, and they scattered like geese before a lion. Patroclus stared after his friend, stunned by his ferocity. The Myrmidons screamed their terrible war cry and ran in pursuit of the fleeing Trojans, filled with lust for battle after the stirring victory of their young leader.

All across the plain, the Trojans began to back away, dismayed at the size of the invading army and the prowess of the warriors. They fought hard while retreating, trying to carry their wounded and dead back with them. The plain became a sea of misery, on this the very first day of the siege of Troy.

On the ramparts of the wall, King Priam stood at the highest point, staring out over the sea of humanity in front of him, his senses reeling. He felt faint and sick to his stomach at the horrendous loss of life. He heard the screams even from this great distance and saw horses and men falling everywhere. He turned to his aide, Quintas, and leaned on him, looking again over the battlefield.

"Do you see my sons?" he muttered. "Where is Hector?"

Quintas pointed out across the plain.

"There, in the gray armor and red horsehair crest," said Quintas. "Remember, he told you he would be in gray, so that you could spot him from the wall at your ease. He is the only warrior I see, anywhere, with gray armor."

Priam glared out over the plain, nodding.

"He has killed many men, including the very first invader to come ashore," said Quintas. "You can be proud of Hector, sir. He will always be in the front and he will never give quarter, for any reason."

"Yes, yes," I know," muttered Priam. "But....we must open the Scaean Gates, Quintas. Our warriors are now retreating. They have never seen war like this. We have not been attacked for thirty years by a host of any size and this army is the largest that has ever been assembled, anywhere, I fear."

Even as Priam watched, the Trojans broke ranks and fled across the plain, with the Achaeans giving chase for half the distance to Troy. Then, the invaders stopped near the Scamander River, as if on command, and watched the Trojans disappearing behind the huge gates. Agamemnon's chariot moved to the front of the army. Drenched with sweat and blood, he stood tall and proud in his chariot, glancing over the host of soldiers he was facing, his back to Troy.

"We have landed on the Troad and we have given a magnificent account of ourselves," said Agamemnon, his voice booming out over the vast army. "The Trojans now know what lays before them, in the days ahead. This will be a short war. Still, let us return to our ships and unload our supplies and build a protective wall and our huts."

The warriors screamed loudly, shaking their spears and swords above their heads for a long time. Slowly, they began to break off, walking back across the field, looking for wounded comrades and for Trojan prisoners. It took until Helios had stabled his sun chariot down behind the far mountains for the Achaeans to desert the plain entirely.

Achilles and Patroclus were tireless. Achilles picked a spot at the far end of the invaders' camp away from the others, where he and Patroclus directed the unloading of their ships. Automedon enlisted a group of men to pitch the tents of Achilles, Patroclus and Phoenix. Food and drink were brought quickly, by serving girls from Phthia. They all stared at Achilles with admiration, as word of his fighting prowess had spread quickly through the camp.

Before they began to eat, Patroclus looked at Achilles's hand and drew back shocked.

"I thought you were injured," he said slowly, gaping at the hand. "I saw the dagger go in and blood pour out."

Achilles lifted the hand and turned it slowly. There was only a long scratch and no other marks on it.

"I thought the dagger stuck deep into my hand too," he said quietly. "But I see no signs now. It must have only pricked me, Patroclus; the blood must have been from one of those I killed."

Patroclus shook his head in amazement. He glanced at Phoenix, who was sitting in a large chair studying the two young warriors. He ran his hand down his long, white beard, remembering that Chiron had told him Achilles seemed to heal quicker than anyone he had ever known. Phoenix wondered just how much of the blood of the goddess flowed through the veins of Achilles... and if maybe there was the blood of Zeus Cloudgatherer in him, as well.

One of the first things that Achilles attended to was the placing of the chest which held the armor that Peleus had given him. He knew he was not yet big and strong enough to wear it in comfort, so he carried the huge chest to the back of his tent, near his sleeping cot. He placed it there and gazed on it for a long time, his mind racing back to Phthia.

"I will make you proud of me, father," he whispered. "And when I wear this armor, given to you by Heracles and forged by a god, it will be the most special day of my life."

For the next two weeks, there was very little fighting as the Achaeans built a long fortifying wall. They had to scour the countryside for wood for the wall and sent soldiers out for to cut down trees, and to search for food. Achilles was bored with it all, but recognized that such work had to be done. No one knew how long the war would last, but most of the warlords felt it could go on for perhaps as long as six months. That meant they would need a place to live, with some protection from marauding bands of Trojans...if they ever grew so bold. Based on the first day of action, few of the Achaean warlords were worried about that happening.

Meanwhile, the Trojans watched from their walls and guard towers, trying to make sense of all that was happening. The temples of the city were filled day and night with women, young and old, offering prayers for support and help to Athena, Ares, Apollo and Zeus. To Athena, the goddess of wisdom, they prayed for insight to make the right decisions; to Ares, the god of war, they prayed for victory in the field of combat; to Apollo, the god of beauty and all virtues, they prayed for courage; and to Zeus, king of all the gods and goddesses on Mount Olympus, they prayed for his help in enduring their tremendous ordeal. The other gods were important, but it was Zeus, the Trojans believed, who held the most power of all. Of course, the Achaeans were praying to the same gods for identical reasons, asking for the same blessings.

Achilles wanted desperately to get into the field and to fight Trojans. Already word of the exploits of the Trojan in the gray armor had been talked about in the camp, and when it was learned that his name was Hector, Calchas was consulted. He was brought to Agamemnon's tent during a war council. Calchas knew the royal family well during the several years he had lived on Mount Ida.

"Priam has many sons and they are, for the most part, a valorous crew," said Calchas, the warlords staring intently at him as he spoke. "Alexandros, you know about. He was abandoned as a youth on Mount Ida and brought up there by swineherds."

Menelaus interrupted to ask why Alexandros had been abandoned by the royals.

"It was prophesized that he would cause the doom of Troy," said Calchas "Priam and Hecuba could not bring themselves to have the beautiful baby destroyed, so they sent him away to Mount Ida to live. He came to Troy for the great festival five years ago and distinguished himself in boxing and archery. Then, it was revealed who he really was and he became a part of the royal family.

"Cassandra, his sister and a prophetress, strenuously objected but she was overruled by Priam. She left the meeting in anger, swearing that Alexandros would bring the city down."

There was a moment's silence.

"It appears this Cassandra is very wise indeed," said Odysseus. All the warlords laughed heartily, and Agamemnon bid Calchas to continue.

"There are many sons, as I said. By far the greatest, both in wisdom and in fighting, is Hector. He is the eldest son and Priam's favorite. He is a great warrior, skilled in all areas of fighting. He can run like the wind, fight with the spear and sword like no other Trojan. He is the city's champion, as well. The Trojan people love him and will look to him for leadership as the war progresses."

"He was the one in the gray armor we saw when we first arrived, who cut down Protesilaus after he leaped ashore?" asked Odysseus.

"Yes, that was Hector," said Calchas.

The warlords asked many other questions and drank lots of wine. They were in a good mood, for they felt the adventure had gotten off to a good start. As they were breaking up to return to their own tents, Agamemnon told them not to forget their duties of sacrifice.

"We need the support of the gods and goddesses in this great adventure," he said solemnly, on his feet, his eyes scanning the tent, staring into the eyes of the other chieftans. "Do not neglect to pay honor to the gods. The Trojans will be asking them for their support, as well, so we must be generous."

None of them were prepared for the way the war would go. After their protective wall and huts were built, the Achaeans gathered in front of

Troy day after day, issuing challenges and hurling insults up to the men watching from the high towers. Agamemnon rode back and forth in front of the walls in his chariot, shaking his long spear and deriding the Trojans for their cowardice; Menelaus and other warlords began doing the same. The Trojans merely stared down at them in silence, saying little in return. It was the plan that Priam had adopted in a long war council after heated debate. Some of the warriors were for opening the Scaean Gates and fighting to the death, while others were for holding back and waiting for reinforcements to arrive from the allies.

"We could not have dreamed that the Achaeans could bring together such a vast army," said Deiphobus, another son of Priam, when it was his turn to speak. "It would be pure folly to waste all our best men when we are so badly outnumbered. We must wait for our allies to send reinforcements. In the meantime, the invaders show no interest in surrounding the city and blocking us off from Mount Ida. We can have all the water and food we need from there."

And that was the truth of it. Agamemnon did not intend to blockade the city and cut off its supply route from Mount Ida. But when two months had expired, the invaders grew extremely restless. Unable to lure the Trojans out for a full-scale battle, they began to look at the cities down the coast from Troy with a growing lust. They needed supplies of their own; not only did the soldiers require food of all kinds, they needed to keep their fighting skills honed. They also were interested in looting all they could to pay for the expedition.

They were interested in more women, too. There were hundreds of women servants who had made the trip from the mainland, but the Achaeans heard stories of the beautiful women who lived in the towns south of Troy. Frustrated by the massive walls that seemed impenetrable and the Trojans' reluctance to come out and fight on a regular basis, the invaders began making raids down the coast.

The Myrmidons were in the forefront of the expeditions. With Achilles leading the way, the Myrmidons rolled out of their camp time after time to venture south. Achilles and Patroclus were in the front chariots, with four hundred troops marching behind them. After sacking the first two cities with ease, the natives were terrified of the very mention of the name Achilles and ran as soon as they saw the approaching army come into view. Often as they returned to their camp, Achilles was dejected. They had claimed considerable booty and many captives, but it was battle that Achilles longed for, and no one dared to stand before him or his Myrmidons.

Even Patroclus, who had always respected Achilles to the utmost, began to look upon him with a sense of awe, seeing him vanquish foe after foe with ease. No matter how strong or how skilled the enemy was, it made no difference to Achilles. He cut them down as a man playing with children. Physically, he was far above all others; but it was his confidence that was his biggest edge. He fought with a confidence that knew no boundaries. He never doubted that he was superior and that he would emerge victorious in every single combat he engaged in.

"The men are saying you cannot be injured," said Patroclus one night when they were sitting in the tent after a long battle in a town far to the south of Troy. "Even the Myrmidons are in awe of you, Achilles. Word has spread throughout the encampment. Everyone knows you are by far the best of the Achaeans. And, the Trojans already have a special name for you, according to our captives.

"They call you The Deathdealer."

Achilles leaned back in his chair, smiling faintly at the words. They made him feel good, of course; but he was also pleased that the glory would rub off on Peleus, as well. The more time he was removed from his father in Phthia, the more highly he regarded him. Peleus was a constant presence in his mind. Some times, he even felt like the king was at his side as he walked through the camp of the Myrmidons.

The Great Quarrel

The years began to pass with no real advances made in the invaders' primary objective – sacking Troy. The two sides had fallen into a steady routine. There would be bursts of war and then a long respite and the months began to blur together in a confusing haze, both in Troy and in the camp of the Achaeans. Fighting came to a dead halt during the long months of winter as the cold winds blew down out of the eastern mountains, forcing the invaders to seek warmth in their tents and huts. The Trojans huddled in their tiny homes, thanking the gods that they were fortunate enough to still be alive while many friends and comrades had died in the fighting. Priam and the royal family spent more time than ever in the temple of Apollo, praying for relief from the miseries of war. In the first two years of the war, Achilles was invited to a regular meal with the other warlords in the banquet hall of Agamemnon, which the high king had ordered constructed in the second year of the war. He wanted the hall so that he could host his captains and talk strategy….and get drunk. But as the years slipped by, Achilles stopped attending; eventually, the invitations stopped coming as well, and he seldom left the camp of the Myrmidons except to lead raids down the coast.

From time to time, his thoughts wandered to Iphigenia on Aulis and he continued to feel a great admiration for her. There was a rumor in the highest ranks of the camp that she had not really been sacrificed – that Agamemnon had ordered the priests to save her at the last minute and take her to some island in the sea, where she could spend her life in leisurely pursuits as the anonymous guest of a king who would never reveal her secret. But Achilles had no way of knowing if the rumor was true and he always dismissed the story from his mind as quickly as it came.

He had not thought of Deidamia much since leaving Skyros. He had found her attractive enough during his time there and was not opposed to marrying her, as Thetis had insisted. Deidamia used all her womanly charms and skills to keep him with her, but it the end even she knew it was hopeless. And when Odysseus came to Skyros and broke through the spell Thetis had put on him, Achilles had nearly banished Deidamia from his thoughts altogether. However, he was pleased when a newcomer arrived in the Achaean camp and sought him out, saying he had stopped at Skyros on the way and Deidamia had given Achilles a son.

While the other warlords and their soldiers were constantly chasing after the women of their defeated enemies in the various cities, Achilles and Patroclus cared little for such rewards. But, all of that changed in the ninth year. When the spoils of a small city he had raided were being divided, he spotted a woman looking at him in such a way that intrigued him. She was a handsome woman, trim and athletic appearing. She had long, brown hair that splashed off her shoulders, and a bewitching way of smiling. Achilles had felt his heart flutter when their eyes met and he had decided he wanted her to share his tent.

As was the custom, the high king was given first pick of all the captives and Achilles watched anxiously while Agamemnon walked through the line of captives, carefully eyeing all the women. Finally, the high king reached out and grabbed the wrist of a pretty woman and pulled her toward his waiting chariot.

An old man protested feebly.

"No, you must not take her," cried the old man, falling to his knees in front of Agamemnon, his long, white beard shaking. " I am chief priest to Apollo and she is my only daughter, given to Apollo at birth. No man can touch her, for she belongs to the god alone."

Agamemnon merely chuckled and pushed the old man aside, taking the woman, named Chryseis, to his waiting chariot. Having second choice, Achilles stepped out and selected the woman he had been watching. Her name was Briseis and Achilles took her back to the Myrmidon camp, along with twenty other women. He told Patroclus and Phoenix to each select a woman. After all three women were allowed to wash and apply perfume, they were then brought to his tent for supper.

The women where showed in by Automedon and they stood shyly by the entrance, half hidden in the shadows left by the dim glow of the lanterns in each of the tent's corners. Achilles, Patroclus and Phoenix were at the large table with their wine cups and had been drinking for some time prior to the women's arrival. Achilles stood up and walked over to them, his gaze locked on Briseis.

"Do you speak the Trojan tongue, or another dialect?" he asked. He was surprised and pleased to hear her words.

SHIP TO:

Name

Address

City

State/Zip

Phone

E-Mail

☐ Check if you do not wish to receive email offers

Call 1-800-451-4463 · www.iccoin.com/n5582

Or enclose completed card with payment in an envelope and mail to:

International Coins & Currency
62 Ridge Street, Dept. N5582, Montpelier, Vermont 05602

YES, I want to take advantage of your "Great American Favorites" set. (#46687)

☐ One Set: $5.95
☐ 5 Sets: $27.50 ($5.50 each)

☐ Check/Money Order enclosed. *(We can take payment from your checking account over the phone. Call 1-800-451-4463 M-F 9am-5pm EST.)*

☐ Charge my credit card (one only):
☐ MasterCard ☐ VISA ☐ AmEx ☐ Discover

Card No.

Exp

Signature

iccoin

FREE Shipping with code N5582

We'll include a big coin catalog with every order!

"We lived on the mainland for some time, before coming here to settle," she said in a tongue he could understand, though it was heavy with a Trojan accent. "I can speak several tongues. I hope you will hear my words and know their meaning."

He nodded.

"We have many dialects here in the Achaean camp," he said. "And after so many years of war, we have all learned to understand a little of the Trojan speak, as well."

"Don't be afraid of us," he said, smiling faintly down at her. "We may look like Ares, the god of war, during the battle time, but at the evening meal you will find that we are tame and hospitable enough."

He took Briseis gently by the elbow and led her to the table, the other two women trailing along behind. Patroclus and Phoenix both stood and bowed slightly as the three women stopped in front of them.

"This is Patroclus, my closest companion," said Achilles, placing a hand on the shoulder of Patroclus. "Some think we are brothers because we look and think so much alike, but we are only cousins." He paused and looked over at Phoenix. "And this is Phoenix, who is my mentor. He is the wisest man here in the camp, and still is as handsome as any man here."

Phoenix coughed at the flattery and took the arm of the woman he had selected, who was much closer to his own age than the other two women. Patroclus took his woman, Melisa, by the elbow and escorted her to a chair. The men sat first and then the women sat in the chairs that had been provided for them. Food was brought in and Achilles held his cup, motioning for the women to feel free to drink.

Food was served and they all ate heartily. There was plenty of fresh lamb, roasted on the spit outside the tent, as well as boiled vegetables and loaves of thick, tasty bread, with spices to dip the bread in. There were plates filled with olives and figs and two kinds of wine… the heavy wine with spices, and the other kind considerably thinned by adding water. The men drank the first and the women the second. After the meal, Achilles motioned to a servant by the tent opening and soon a bard appeared, carrying a lyre. He bowed to them and then took a seat at the far edge of the huge tent and began to sing softly.

As the song wore on, Achilles led Briseis to a large reclining cot, while both Patroclus and Phoenix left for their own tents with their women. Briseis stared at Achilles in the dim light and lifted a hand to glide slowly over his bare face.

"Most warriors wear beards," she said. "But you do not. Why?"

"There are two reasons," he said, lying back on one arm and staring at her, taken with her beauty. He liked the fact she talked so openly to him.

"First, in battle, a warrior might grab another's warrior's beard and thus control him for a moment," he said. "I could not allow that to happen. And secondly, it is the Myrmidon way, to be clean shaven. We are....different from the others here."

"Yes, I know," she said softly. She stared into his eyes.

"Everyone is terrified of the Myrmidons, when they know they are coming." She paused, tilting her face, still peering into his eyes.

"And they are afraid of you, most of all. They have a name for you."

He sat up, interested.

"What name?" he asked.

"They call you.... Deathdealer," she said.

He laid back on an elbow, nodding.

"They also say....you are a god," she said softly.

He stared at her, and she at him.

"I am not a god," he said finally. "I am a warrior. And a prince. That is all."

She shook her head.

"I think you are much more than a warrior and a prince." She leaned close to him and he breathed in her fragrance. He saw her firm breasts rising and falling beneath the thin chiton and he liked what he saw.

"I think... you are indeed a god," she whispered. "You are so handsome....and so brave....and so....invincible."

She moved her small hand to his forearm, touching it gently. She ran her hands over his bare chest and then pulled back, staring down at it.

"What is wrong?" he asked, concerned. He liked the way her hand on his flesh made him feel.

"The scar," she said softly, gaping at the four long marks running down his chest. She touched them with her fingertips; he watched her closely as she studied them, then turned her eyes back to his.

"What could have made these?" she asked. "They are not from a sword or from a spear. They are much different."

"A mountain lion, back on Mount Pelion, when I was just a pup," he said, leaning back and enjoying the memory. "I was with Chiron, my first mentor. A lion had begun killing women and children for food and we went after it. I found him first."

"What happened?" she asked, her eyes wide with suspense.

Achilles smiled faintly at her.

"He left me with these scars....and with that skin over there," he said, pointing at the lion skin draped over the chest Peleus had given him years ago. He walked over to the chest and picked up the skin, turning it over in his hands, studying it.

"It seems like a very long time ago," he said quietly. "And yet, it is one of my proudest moments. He attacked me and I killed him. Chiron was proud."

She asked to touch the skin and she gazed at it in wonder, then turned back to him, running both hands over his chest again. She loved the feeling of the rippling muscles and now that she knew the secret of the scars, she felt even closer to him than before. She snuggled up close as he embraced her. They lay silent for some time and then she gasped and looked up into his eyes.

"What is it this time?" he said, sitting up again. He was very close to her and could almost taste her. She was so small and vulnerable. She regarded him with wide eyes.

"I feel the power in you," she whispered. "I feel a power like no other man has ever possessed. Truly, you are Ares, the god of war, come to life in a real person."

She recoiled slightly: "I am afraid to be with you….but I am also afraid to get up and run away."

He reached out and took her in his arms. She looked up at him, trembling. He stared down into her eyes and then his gaze dropped to her lips, which had been reddened with the juice of berries. He slid a hand into her thick hair and gripped it easily.

"I am not Ares," he said softly. "I am Achilles. I want you to know me."

He motioned for the singer to leave and then laid Briseis down on the skins at the foot of his recliner, placing his lion skin from Mount Pelion on top of the soft pile. He moved next to her and slid his face to hers. He kissed her hair, then her cheeks, then her moist lips, hovering over her. She lay on her back, trembling from both fear and excitement. Slowly, her hands moved to his arms and she kissed him back. Achilles eased over her, on top of her as her arms slid around his shoulders. They made love for hours, until Diana was riding high in the night sky.

As the months slipped by, he grew very fond of Briseis. He brought her into his tent and she had complete use of it and began to regard it as her new home, sleeping there every night, even when he did not want to make love. When he began to play the lyre one night, strumming it skillfully, she gasped in disbelief.

"If I could tell my people that Deathdealer also plays the lyre, they would not believe me," she said. "And, Patroclus told Melisa that you have healed his wounds and that of other warriors, as well. How did you learn all of these things? Surely, you are a god."

He smiled at her questions and assertions. He told her of his youth on Mount Pelion and how Chiron had insisted he learn these virtues, as well as the art of fighting. She covered her mouth with her hands when he told her that he had lived with centaurs; she had never met anyone who actually knew one of the man-horse race and she could hardly make herself come near him after hearing that. But he only laughed at her and explained that centaurs were really two separate beings, and only gave the appearance of being one beast together.

In a short amount of time, Achilles began to regard her as he would a wife.

"She is good," he said to Patroclus as they were sitting alone by the seashore one day. "She makes love in the most pleasing way, much better than Deidamia. She is very strong, so that I don't need to worry if she is being hurt when she cries out. She is crying out because Aphrodite has opened up her heart to me."

Patroclus smiled at his friend and slapped him on the shoulder.

"I feel the same way about Melisa," he said. "Perhaps you and I are getting old and weak. Maybe the Trojans will be able to defeat us, because we are so preoccupied with women now."

Achilles glanced out at the wine-dark sea and reached down to scoop up the sand from the beach. He let the grains ease through his fingers and then turned his hand so all the sand fell back to the beach. He repeated it several times.

"It has been nine years since we came," said Patroclus. "Who would have thought it would take so long."

"It is the way that Agamemnon makes war," said Achilles, angrily. "Many times, Odysseus has told him to send a large force behind Troy and block off the supply routes that come down from Mount Ida. But he refuses. He says the Trojans will surrender soon enough. I think he is afraid to go home, back to Mycenae, because of what he fears might be waiting for him."

They eyed one another.

"You mean Clytaemnestra? Do you think she is she still plotting revenge for Iphigenia?" asked Patroclus.

"Odysseus told me, the last time we talked, that there was word from the mainland that she has taken a lover and they are plotting for the day Agamemnon returns," said Achilles. "That they have a terrible homecoming planned for him. But he is supposed to be the high king. He is acting like a coward; he should sail home immediately and march on Mycenae and restore his kingdom."

"What about Troy?" said Patroclus. "Does he just abandon this city?"

Achilles shrugged his shoulders.

"We can take care of Troy," he said. "It will still be here when he gets back."

There was a long silence as the two warriors reflected on all they had gone though. Together, they had sacked dozens of cities, killed hundreds of soldiers and brought back hundreds of captives, which they eventually sold. Their tents were filled with precious stones and ornaments they had earned through their victories. And yet neither of them was satisfied with the rewards. They seemed to have less meaning than ever before.

"We have enough of these things," Achilles had said one day earlier, looking around his tent, hardly able to find a place to sit. "What do I need with one more golden tripod, or one more chest of gems? Three times I have sent ships back to Phthia full of booty and Peleus sends word that the treasury is as full as it has ever been. I would much rather see my father and Chiron again than gain one more bauble."

Patroclus reached out and embraced Achilles and then held him at arm's length, staring at him.

"When I was a boy, I dreamed of having a friend like you some day," said Patroclus.

Achilles smiled and nodded.

"I never dreamed of having a friend, only of glory," said Achilles. "But, now that I have a friend like you, I'm glad that I do."

They walked back along the beach.

"Do you know that the Trojans think you are a god, Achilles?" said Patroclus. "The warriors say you can not be injured, in any way. And the women, watching from the walls, say you are as handsome as Apollo, and they too feel you are a god."

Achilles nodded.

"I have heard the stories from Briseis and from other captives," he said. He stopped and faced Patroclus, a grim look on his face.

"Chiron told me long ago there are two ways to win in combat," said Achilles. "One is by the power of your limbs; the other is through the might of your reputation. If they think I am a god and if they think I can not be wounded, then I have already defeated them."

Several days later, Patroclus confided to Phoenix that he was sensing a major change in the nature of Achilles.

"I think Briseis is very good for Achilles," said Patroclus, talking to Phoenix as they watched Achilles and Briseis walking down the seashore. "For nine years, he has done little other than train and fight. He has had women, of course, but Briseis is different. He enjoys spending time with her and talking about Phthia. He has even confided to me that he hopes she will bear him a son."

Phoenix raised his eyebrows in surprise.

"Achilles said that?" he asked. "Well, praise Zeus. He has finally learned to think about something other than killing. This is a big moment."

The very next day, a terrible plague struck the camp of the Achaeans with a fury. First, the animals began getting sick and dying. Horses, mules and hounds bellowed out in agony, and within days of showing the symptoms fell to the ground foaming at the mouth, legs twitching, and gave up their lives. Shortly after, servants and soldiers alike began dying the same way. The healers ran from tent to tent, attending to the sick, but to no avail; they had no medicines that could help fight this new plague. Even the great Machon, the finest healer in all the camp, had no answers. The funeral pyres burned all day and all night and a heavy stench hung constantly in the air for well over a week.

"What is wrong?" asked Achilles of Phoenix at the evening meal on the eleventh day of the plague. "This misery has been with us for ten days. I am told were have lost hundreds of soldiers to the hideous death. What is to be done?"

Phoenix advised Achilles to consult Calchas one again. After leaving Aulis, the old seer had returned to his home on Mount Ida and sought seclusion, trying to remain out of the war. Achilles sent heralds to find the old seer and bring him to camp. He was reluctant to come but at last showed up at the tent of Achilles, where Achilles and Phoenix were waiting for him. Calchas entered slowly and trembling. He leaned unsteadily on his staff, barley able to look at Achilles.

"What is wrong, old man?" asked Achilles. "You look as though you have been to Hades and seen the dark side."

"I might as well have, lord Achilles," he said in a trembling voice. "I fear that the news I must tell you will not be well received in some tents, just as it was not in Aulis those nine long years ago"

"You must speak, Calchas," said Phoenix. "The entire adventure is in jeopardy. If we have angered the gods, surely you can tell us that so we can make sacrifice and make amends."

"It is true, Apollo is very angry," said Calchas. "When the Achaeans took the city of Thebes they captured the daughter of Apollo's high priest, whose name is Chryses. The daughter is known as Chryseis; the priest begged Agamemnon to spare her, to leave her with him. But Agamemnon merely laughed at the priest and carted her away. The priest prayed to Apollo for revenge – and the plague is Apollo's answer. He is shooting his silver shafts of death into the Achaean camp without mercy, and will continue to do so until Agamemnon returns Chryseis to her father."

The words came like a bolt from Zeus himself. Phoenix and Achilles glanced at one another and knew immediately the full impact. They conferred quietly, Achilles nodding at the words of his wise mentor. At last, he leaned back in his great chair, frowning.

"It's time to face Agamemnon and to demand that he act like a high king," said Achilles. "I will force him to call a meeting of the warlords, saying that if he will not, then I will do so. Then, I will have Calchas tell them all what he has told us here. Agamemnon must make amends or Apollo with continue to visit us with the arrows of death and the plague will ruin our mission."

At the insistence of Achilles, Agamemnon finally called an emergency meeting, with all the warlords gathered around his great table. The long years of war had taken a toll on him in many ways; he was shorter and much heavier and more restricted in the way he moved due to several leg injuries. His face was etched with deep lines and his long, black hair had turned mostly gray. Menelaus had not fared much better. The two richest kings had suffered the most from the long ordeal; Odysseus was a spry as ever, both on his feet and in his mind, and Idomeneus of Crete, Diomedes, and the two Ajaxes and Achilles all seemed much the same.

When all the forty warlords had assembled, Agamemnon stood wearily and placed his hand on the great table, looking down. He still favored the long purple robe that he had worn when they first came ashore at Troy.

"The gods have surely turned against us," he mumbled. "Nine long years of war, and now this terrible plague. The air stinks with the smell of burning bodies, men and animals. There is no escape, it seems."

He sank into his throne chair and gestured for Achilles to take over.

Achilles stood and faced the warlords. Other than Ajax and Odysseus, he did not know any of them well. He had broken bread with them at meetings such as this, but generally he and his Myrmidons stayed apart from the others and did not know much about them. He recognized Diomedes as being an excellent fighter, having seen him in action and heard stories of his exploits. He also respected Idomeneus of Crete and Antilochus, the son of Nestor, of Pylos. Antilochus had befriended Patroclus and Patroclus respected him as a fine warrior. Of course, Achilles held Nestor in the highest regard, as well. But the thirty other warlords he knew very little about.

"The plague must come to a halt," he said, looking around the high king's tent. "In my concern for the fate of our adventure, I found Calchas and bid him come to my tent. He told me what has happened and I have asked him to come here and repeat his words." He paused, frowning. "He is afraid that his words may injure some, but I have sworn to protect him, with my sword if need be."

The warlords stared up at Achilles and knew how serious he was. They all remembered his effort to protect Iphigenia. No one could stand before Achilles, of that much they were all certain.

Calchas stood and walked slowly over to Achilles, a stooped and tired man. His weary eyes looked over the group and he shivered. Achilles placed a comforting hand on his thin shoulder.

"You may speak with truth," said Achilles. "No one here will harm you, I vow."

"Apollo is outraged and has taken up his bow to send silver arrows of death to the camp of the Achaeans," Calchas began. "He will not stop firing his arrows until he has been totally appeased."

Agamemnon frowned and waved a hand impatiently.

"So, what does Apollo want from us, seer?" he mumbled. "How many sheep must be killed to dull his anger? Or is it Trojan captives that he wants bloodied? We still have twenty or so and some of them are young and full of life. Will that do it?"

Calchas shook his head slowly, the long, white beard gently swaying.

"That is some of what the great god Apollo wants and demands," he said, "but there is more."

Agamemnon threw his arms up in frustration.

"Then tell us, seer; do not waste our time. What must we do to show Apollo we respect him and will do his bidding?"

There was a long pause and Calchas turned to Achilles for support. Achilles nodded at him to continue, a grim expression on his face.

"When the Achaeans looted the city of Lyrnessos, they also took the daughter of Apollo's high priest," he began. "The priest prayed to Apollo for revenge... and the plague is Apollo's answer. He is shooting his silver shafts of death into the Achaean camp without mercy and will continue to do so until the woman is returned to her father."

Agamemnon stiffened, leaning forward, his dark eyes staring hard at Calchas.

"And just who is this woman?" he asked, his voice thick with a growing anger.

"It is the woman known as is Chryseis, the daughter of Chryses."

The tent was filled with a long, ominous silence. Agamemnon's face turned red as he stared at the seer, then at Achilles. He rose slowly, hands on the top of the thick table, fighting to control his anger.

"Old man, you always have something bad to say, it seems. I have not forgotten Aulis ten years ago." He paused to let the words sink in to one and all, reminding them of his great personal sacrifice.

"If that is what it will take to placate Apollo, then so be it," he said, the words low and measured. "But, the high king will not go without his reward. When I was selected by the warlords to lead this expedition, it was also voted that the high king would receive the first pick of prisoners of any city we took. Such is his right, as leader."

He paused, staring around the congregation. Odysseus and the others nodded their agreement, not knowing what he would say next.

He turned his angry eyes on Achilles.

"If I must give up Chryseis….then I choose Briseis as mine."

Gasps were heard throughout the tent as all eyes immediately turned to Achilles. Everyone knew that he had taken Briseis into his tent and now considered her like a wife.

Achilles stood rigid, his eyes locked on Agamemnon. He felt a knot in his stomach and an immense anger swelling up inside him. The tension was thick as a cloud on high about to burst into a violent storm.

Ajax's voice cut through the silence like a sword ripping through a piece of cloth.

"Briseis belongs to Achilles," he said flatly, staring at Agamemnon. "We all know that. You will have far more than you can carry from Troy, once the city is taken. I will vote to give you twice – no, three times – your allotment, if you will now leave Briseis with Achilles."

Agamemnon was greatly relieved that Ajax had spoken so that he could look away from Achilles' terrible stare. He had not wanted to show his weakness and turn away first, but he was suddenly in fear for his life by the way Achilles was eyeing him.

"That she belongs to Achilles is no longer the case," said Agamemnon. "His rights are overruled by the rights of the high king. She is now forfeit."

Achilles placed his hand on the hilt of his dagger and several saw him do so. Odysseus, fearful that Achilles would attack Agamemnon and slay him then and there, and knowing it would take many men to subdue Achilles, came to his feet quickly.

"Lord Achilles, I beg you not to surrender your emotions to rage," he said softly, "but think calmly, as Chiron and Peleus taught you many years ago, back in Phthia. You are the greatest among us with sword and spear, we all know that and we all acknowledge that. But by our own code of conduct, Agamemnon has such a right. If he was determined to take my woman, I would not object. What is a woman as compared to the quest we are all on?"

Achilles glanced at the Ithacan and felt his rage subsiding. Odysseus was very wise to have invoked the names of the two men Achilles respected most in all the world to bring him to his senses. Then, he turned to Agamemnon, and the high king felt a chill go down his back when Achilles fixed his eyes on him.

"You are a man without shame, if you do this thing," said Achilles. "If you tried to take her from me with your sword, I would cut you down like a dog and everyone knows that. We are not at all equal in our abilities, but you sit on a higher throne due to the fact that you rule more men and rule a city that is larger and richer.

"I did not come to Troy with my Myrmidons because the Trojans had done us any harm, in faraway Phthia. I came in response to a plea from you and your brother and to earn glory as a warrior at Troy. But you care nothing for the sacrifices that I and the other warlords have made on your behalf. Now, you would take my greatest prize, even though I never get the first pick of anything. It is through my efforts that we took Lyrnessos, not through your efforts. You sat back and watched my Myrmidons do the work."

Achilles paused, his eyes boring into Agamemnon.

"Come and take Briseis; I will not stop you even though I could. But know this, high king: The Myrmidons and I will fight no more at Troy. We will wait for the winds to come, and then we will leave this place and sail home to Phthia."

Everyone sat stunned at his words. Even Odysseus did not have the heart, or the courage, to get up and speak after seeing how deep was the pain Achilles was feeling. Somehow, Agamemnon found the nerve to respond.

"Go then, if you will, Achilles," he said meekly, controlling his emotions for fear of arousing Achilles to immediate action. "Your power as a warrior may be unmatched, but we have other great warriors ready to fight on until Troy is taken." He wanted to say more but Athena, the goddess of wisdom, must have whispered in his ear that he had said enough. He sat back down, staring across the table at the prince of Phthia.

Achilles was not finished speaking, feeling the rage building again.

"You empty wineskin….you have the face of a dog and courage of a fawn," he spit out at Agamemnon. "But you know there will come a time when all the Achaeans will desperately long to hear the way cry of the Myrmidons; every time the Trojans and their allies get to close to your ships, you will look south to see if the Myrmidons are charging to the rescue. Instead of Achilles to save them, they will have to look to you, high king Agamemnon. And then we shall see what the Achaeans value the most – your empty words or my sword and spear."

Achilles stalked toward the tent opening with Calchas by his side, shaking like a leaf that had just fallen from the tree. At the opening, Achilles turned and faced the others.

"Mark the day that your high king cheated me this way," he said to them. "When Hector and the Trojans are at your ships, burning them one by one, you can remember that it was the work of Agamemnon that brought you this ruin."

He stepped out into the cool night and walked down the beach, Calchas struggling to keep up. Achilles felt a knot in his stomach as he left one campfire after another, heading for the Myrmidon area at the outer most edge on the southern point. He strode past the sentry, who stood at rigid attention as he moved past him, saluting Achilles with his spear. He walked into the tent, where Phoenix and Patroclus, wine cups in front of them, sat anxiously waiting for him.

"By the look on your face, it did not go well," said Phoenix.

Achilles paced back and forth, staring at the ground. His long, golden hair swirled as he walked, his gray tunic accentuating his trim physique. He finally stopped and faced them.

"I must surrender Briseis," he muttered.

"What?" gasped Patroclus, rising from his chair.

"What madness is this?" said Phoenix, his aged face wrinkled in deep concern.

"Agamemnon, the high thief, has agreed to give up Chryseis....but lays claim to anyone he wants as a replacement. He has chosen Briseis."

They were stunned.

"And you agreed?" asked Patroclus not believing what he had just heard.

Achilles turned on him, throwing his arms out wide.

"What choice have I? He is the high king and his word is law. Should I go charging back there and kill him? Is that what I should do, Patroclus?"

Patroclus sank back into his chair and muttered an oath. Achilles watched his closest friend begin sulking and knew he had no solutions, either.

"There are no choices," Achilles said finally. Suddenly, he felt very weary. He sought his chair and dropped into it, sagging against the back. They all sat in silence, until at last Achilles sighed and looked up.

"I must ask you to leave," he said. "And summon Briseis for me. She was going to be at the seashore with the other women until I called for her."

Patroclus nodded as he and Phoenix left the tent. Achilles sat by himself, lost in thought, then stood and walked to the low recliner that he loved so much. He laid down on the wooden cot, heavily covered with thick animal skins. He stared at the lion skin hanging on the armor chest, recalling the great thrill of facing the beast and overcoming it. Life seemed much more simple then, back with the centaurs and Chiron. He felt a strong and powerful longing to be home in Phthia. He placed his hands behind his head, locking his fingers, and let his head droop back to the cot, his eyes fixed on the top of the tent. He was still dreaming when he heard the footsteps and he glanced over to see Briseis moving slowly toward him. He sat up and smiled faintly at her.

"Patroclus says....you are worried," she said softly, coming to his side. "Is that so? How can anything worry lord Achilles?"

He reached for her hands and eased her down beside him. She smiled coyly and he felt a surge of passion moving within his breast. He had only loved two women in his twenty-six years of life, and he knew that he loved her far more than he had ever loved Deidamia. Part of that was due to the fact that he was older and appreciated a woman much more now than he had while living on Skyros, he reasoned; but part of it was Briseis herself. Deidamia was a princess and had been raised as such, without the same zest for life that Briseis had. Though well born, Briseis was not royalty and had an unreserved sexuality about her that Deidamia did not. She also appreciated all that Achilles had brought to her simple life, including the prestige of being mated with the most handsome and most respected of all the Achaean warriors.

"We can talk later," he said, taking her into his arms and pulling her in close. He gazed down at her perfect breasts, admiring them once again. He placed his powerful hands on them and gently squeezed; she gasped, her eyelids fluttering. She loved his hands on her body, anywhere. She slid her fingers along his powerful arms, relishing the feel of the hard muscles.

"Maybe I can make you forget your worries, at least for awhile, lord Achilles," she whispered, moving over him as he laid back on the recliner. Her fingers slid into his golden locks and she smiled down into his eyes. "You may be Deathdealer out there on the plain of Troy," she whispered, "but in this tent, you are my lovemaker."

He smiled widely at her words and pulled her onto him, her tiny body snuggling in closer. They made love for a long time. At last, she fell asleep on top of him and he held her tight. Tears formed in his eyes, thinking how he would tell her that she must leave him to go live with the high king. He had disliked Agamemnon almost from the moment they first met; he had lost all his respect for him at Aulis over the deceit with Iphigenia. And now, he hated Agamemnon more than ever. He swore silently that he would get his revenge on the high king, no matter how long it took.

He told her in the morning. Briseis collapsed against his chest, sobbing, her hands clinging to his arms.

"No, tell me it is not true," she whimpered. "I love you, Achilles. I will not go to live with anyone else. My place is here, with you."

"Our fate is out of our hands, Briseis," he said, stroking her long brown hair. He pushed her away from him, staring into her brown eyes, now wet. Her lower lip quivered as he smiled at her.

"I promise I will come for you when the time is ripe," he said. "You must be strong and face this with courage."

Already, he had heard the trumpets blaring throughout the encampment, in recognition of the sacrifices that would be made in the name of Apollo. Heralds moved through the various camps, advising everyone to burn any garments that might have been worn at the time a friend or family member took ill. Achilles walked to the tent's opening and pulled back the flap, gazing out into the new day. He saw funnels of smoke spiraling heavenward everywhere he looked, the mark of funeral pyres and of sacrifices. And then he saw two heralds carrying small signs bearing the insignia of Mycenae walking slowly toward his tent. They saw him and halted abruptly, very nervous, but he motioned them to continue toward him.

He turned and faced Briseis.

"He has not wasted any time, it seems," Achilles said softly. "The heralds from the Mycenaen camp are here already. You....must prepare to leave."

She backed away from him, hands over her mouth, and then turned to her small little trunk of clothes that he had allowed her to bring into his tent. She fell across it, wailing. Achilles watched for several long moments then, grim faced, stepped out of his tent to face the heralds.

They were men in their thirties, thin and unsuited for battle. They stared down meekly, one of them trembling visibly. He motioned them to come closer.

"I have no ill feelings toward you," he said. "You are not the ones to have made the decision, you are only carrying out your orders. The lady is in the tent," he added, motioning for them to go in. They slipped inside and he heard Briseis weeping. He was relieved to see Patroclus walking up to the tent, with Melisa at his side.

"I thought that Melisa might be able to help Briseis," said Patroclus, nodding toward the woman at his side. "She is her best friend. She will walk with her to the camp of the Mycenaens."

Achilles nodded and she slipped inside the tent.

"The sacrifices are under way," said Patroclus, wanting to change the subject. "Perhaps Calchas knows what he is talking about and Apollo will end the plague."

"Perhaps," said Achilles. He stood straight, saying nothing else. At last, Briseis emerged from the tent, standing tall and straight, her face dried of tears. Melisa was at her side and the two heralds were carrying her small chest of clothes. She stood in front of Achilles, looking up at him.

"I will not give myself to anyone else, lord Achilles," she said softly. "If any man wants me, he will have to take me and be satisfied with that. My love is for you alone."

He nodded solemnly at her and watched the small party walk away down the beach. She looked back at him once and then they were lost from view as they moved into the camp of the next group, the Cretans of Idomeneus.

"What will we do now?" asked Patroclus. "You have sworn not to fight any longer and the men know that. Are we sailing back to Phthia? Will we give up before Troy has fallen?"

Achilles stared at his friend and shrugged.

"I don't have the answers any longer," he said. "I will pray to my mother. Perhaps she will come and give me the advice I need."

A princess of Troy

When word reached Troy that Achilles and the Myrmidons had retired from the war, a huge shout erupted from the assembled troops. Soldiers lifted their spears high, shaking them, and Priam leaned back in his throne, smiling for the first time in years about news from the war.

"At last, we have something good to talk about, something that excites the troops," said the old king. Hector, Alexandros, Sarpedon and Aeneas stood before him, obviously well pleased as well. Sarpedon commanded the Lycian troops that had been with Troy since the outset of the war, while Aeneas led the brave Dardanians. Both Sarpedon and Aeneas were highly respected warriors and both of them knew what it meant that Achilles would no longer be in the field. All the warlords, except Hector himself, harbored a fear of meeting Achilles in single combat and were always nervous that he might call out a challenge to them; they would be forced to accept or be deemed a coward by their men.

"It is good news, to be sure," said Hector, measuring his words carefully. "But, no one man is the difference in such a war as this. Achilles may be the best of the Achaeans, though Ajax the Greater and Diomedes are great warriors, too. But Achilles is, after all, just one man."

"But he is the son of a god and seems invincible," said Sarpedon. "I have heard tales of men who went against him and who felt they should have wounded him, but that he is far too quick for them. No one can come close to harming him, it seems; he is indeed protected by a god."

"Helen says there is a legend among the Achaeans that he can not be injured," said Alexandros. "She had never seen him before the battle began here, but she had heard stories of him when he was a youth in Phthia. They say his mother, a sea nymph, dipped him in the River Styx to make him immortal and that the water of the Styx protects him from all weapons."

Hector chuckled at the story. He was a powerful man, with wide shoulders and a lean waist, taller than the average Trojan. He wore a closely cropped beard which was dark brown in color and he kept his brown hair closely cropped, unlike most of the Trojans who liked long, flowing hair.

"A woman's tale, no doubt," said Hector. "I don't believe it."

Priam rubbed his face hard and looked at the four captains in front of him. They were all good men and fine warriors, men he was well proud of. They had endured much over the nine years of war and the fact that they were still alive proved that they knew their business well.

"I have known many warriors in my day. I even saw the great Heracles when he attacked our walls, nearly thirty years ago," said Priam. "And I saw Jason and Theseus when they passed by. Standing on the walls and watching the battles these last ten years, I don't believe I have ever seen a warrior with the speed and skills of Achilles....except for you, Hector. You have the same abilities as Achilles."

"And you don't have the excuse of a goddess for a mother," laughed Alexandros, slapping his brother on the shoulder.

They all laughed heartily and then Aeneas grew serious.

"One captain told me that Achilles has killed well over one hundred of our soldiers in single combat," he said. "That does not include the hundreds he has cut down in wild melees. There is no doubt that he is the heart of the Achaean army, just like Hector is the heart of ours. I, for one, will be glad to know he is sitting idly by the side of his black ships, strumming his lyre.

"In the fifth year of the war, I was on Mount Ida with my sheep when he happened to come by," continued Aeneas. "He was making a pilgrimage to the Temple of Zeus in the deep woods. Neither of us wore armor and had just our swords. We met face to face; I had ten men with me and he had ten Myrmidons. He was a very formidable looking fellow. He had an angry look in his eyes that I have never seen before."

He paused.

"I think Achilles has a love for war that is unnatural, and makes him different than all other warriors."

They discussed other events in the long war and when it was time to depart they all agreed that the Myrmidons leaving the war was a huge factor in their favor. They offered a prayer to Apollo for making it happen, but Hector said it was up to the Trojans to make sure that the retirement of Achilles was taken full advantage of.

Hector walked down the cobbled street away from the palace, on his way to the agora to try and find his wife, Andromache. The citizens waved at him when they saw who it was and many a woman pointed him out to her children. He noticed that there were very few men under the age of fifty to be seen anywhere; either they had been killed or wounded by the long war, or they were now at the gates, planning to venture out onto the plain to see if the invaders were on the field this day.

Hector had promised Andromache that he would try and take some time off from the fighting. As the leader of the entire Trojan army and all its allies, he had been the heart and soul of Troy for nine long years. Not only was he first in war and first in valor, he was the leader in all the planning and was the one Priam counted on for all reports and assessments. So, it was not easy for him to excuse himself even though he had seen more battle action than any other Trojan; in fact, no other solider was even close to him in the amount of time spent fighting on the plain.

As the first born of Priam and Hecuba, he was also the one the other twenty-some brothers and half-brothers looked up to the most. He held a fondness for most of his brothers, but it had taken considerable effort for him to warm up to Alexandros. He had disliked Alexandros from the first time they met, twelve years earlier when Alexandros had come to Troy for a huge Dionisius festival, a week-long carnival of athletic games, wenching and drinking. He emerged from the archery contest as the victor and was declared the finest archer in all of Troy. He also won the boxing contest and incited envy among the sons of Priam. As Hector was about to challenge him to a wrestling match, Hecuba recognized the man and woman Alexandros was with as the shepherds she had given the baby to many years prior and ran down to his side, telling Priam who he really was. He was accepted into the royal family, grudgingly by some.

When Alexandros sailed off to the mainland on a peace mission, even his detractors felt he was becoming a man of reason and stature. But when he returned with the queen of Sparta, Helen, at his side, he was almost run out of Troy. Cassandra, his sister who had what is known as The Madness, ran wildly from the royal palace, pulling her hair and screaming that he would cause the ruination of the entire city. She claimed she had seen a vision of Troy burning and Alexandros and Helen starting the inferno.

When most others were for forcing the lovers out of Troy, Hector rallied to their side. He said he had information that the brother kings of Mycenae and Sparta would have started a war no matter what the cause and that Helen was not the reason the war was initiated. Hector said that it was the desire for control of the trade route to the Black Sea and the rumors of Troy's immense wealth that had brought the thousand Achaean ships to Troy, not revenge for the abduction of Helen.

In the years since the start of the war, Hector had come to like both

Helen and Alexandros. At times, he even felt sorry for them as they seemed to feel the weight of the world descending on their shoulders, due to their role in the start of the war. Nearly everyone who lost a brother, a son or a husband on the battlefield had, at one time or another, blamed the two lovers for their family's misfortune.

This particular day, Hector was anxious to be with Andromache. They had been married for twelve years and she was not only his wife but his confidant and best friend. Had the war not come, they would have been the heir apparent to Priam and Hecuba and would have some day been known far and wide as the benevolent rulers of the most prosperous city in the entire world. Since the invasion, they had all they could do to just keep their sanity amid the turmoil and destruction.

He found Andromache with their young son, Astyanax, busily chatting with two other women and their children while inspecting the fruits that had been brought in by merchants from the north. Andromache saw her husband approaching and quickly ended the conversation. She grabbed Astyanax by the hand and hurried to meet Hector, a wide smile on her lips. She was a tall, sensual woman who moved with grace. She was wearing a white chiton trimmed with deep purple and long earrings that jingled when she moved. She embraced her husband with great affection. She was extremely proud of Hector and knew the entire city loved him almost as much as she did.

"What news today, Hector?" she asked as they walked hand in hand up the cobbled street, back toward the palace. They lived in the very finest room in the entire palace, save for the room in which lived the ling and queen.

"Achilles has withdrawn from the war," he said matter of factly. "And his Myrmidons will fight no more, apparently."

"That is wonderful news, is it not?" she asked.

They passed under the palace's main archway and into the garden area. Servants were pruning the fig trees and bushes and smiled at them as they strolled by. Hector and Andromache treated the servants as equals and were the favorites of all the men and women who attended on the royal family.

"Yes, it is good news," he said, frowning. "But we must take advantage of it. The invaders will be despondent, now that their greatest hero sits by the seashore and sets his spear and sword aside. It is not that Achilles is so great a warrior as much as it is that his absence will make others less eager to fight."

He paused, facing her.

"I feel I must issue a challenge to the best of the invaders. I will lay the terms thus: if their champion wins, we will give back Helen and let them depart in peace. If I win, they will agree to pack up their tents and leave immediately."

She gasped, bringing her hands to her mouth.

"Oh, Hector....why must you take such a risk?" she asked softly.

He studied her face, a slight smile on his lips. Then he reached out for her and pulled her into his arms. She kept her hands to her mouth and shut her eyes, feeling his great strength all around her. And still she was afraid.

"Do you think there is a warrior anywhere who can defeat me?" he asked, softly. He knew how she must answer, being his wife; still, he wanted to hear her words.

"No, of course not," she said. "But...."

"But what?" he asked, moving her away so he could study her expression.

"The gods, we never know what tricks they might play," she croaked. "If you intend to do this, then I must go to the temple of Apollo and Athena tonight and pray. I must pray long and hard that they be with you."

He nodded.

"Of course," he said.

The next day, Hector challenged the best of the invaders to individual battle and three answered his call – Ajax the Greater, Diomedes and Odysseus. Both Menelaus and Agamemnon cited fresh injuries as the reason they did not accept Hector's challenge, but the warlords knew better. Not many Achaeans were willing to put their life on the line in a fight to the death with the redoubtable Hector, certainly not the two brother kings; each had far too much to lose besides his life.

But Ajax, always eager to escape the tremendous shadow of his cousin, was very pleased when his name was drawn from the helmet. Though certainly not afraid of the giant, Hector faced Ajax with a grim realization that he was in for the battle of his life... and indeed it was. Ajax nearly killed him with a spear thrust that drove through Hector's oxhide shield, and knocked him to the ground. He rolled frantically to escape Ajax's wild sword swings at him, and regained his feet only to find the giant in his face, hammering ferocious blows on top of his battered shield.

Hector had fought for his very life, his mouth dry and his breath coming in huge gasps. But eventually Ajax tired and paused to catch his breath and Hector used the brief respite to marshal his own strength. He began to drive Ajax backwards with his own blows. The warriors were flanked by a multitude of soldiers who had come to see the two great warriors fight and cheers rolled over them as they battled furiously. They fought for nearly an hour until at last two heralds, one from each side, moved forward to break them up and call a truce.

"Zeus loves you both and is pleased with your tremendous efforts," said the first herald, his voice quaking with excitement as he stood between the two warriors. "It is his will that we call this match a draw and end it now."

Ajax declared it was Hector's decision to make since he had issued the challenge, and so it was Hector who decided to call it off. The two champions exchanged gifts, Hector giving Ajax a silver-studded sword with a beautiful scabbard, while Ajax offered a huge buckle inlaid with precious jewels to Hector. They parted with a brief salute and the two armies drifted back to their respective camps. Though the armies of both warriors declared victory, most of the leaders on both sides knew that Ajax had done the most damage and had held the edge.

Patroclus related every detail of the battle to Achilles, who listened with great interest. He asked Patroclus questions about Hector's stamina and techniques, nodding sagely. Incredibly, in nine years of war, Achilles and Hector had never come close to pairing off on the plain. They had seen each other on many occasions but always they were both too far away and otherwise engaged for them to seek each other out. But Achilles knew that some day he and the great Trojan hero were destined to meet, and one of them to die. He knew it and he was anxious for that day to arrive. All heroes need a great foe, Chiron had told him years ago, and Achilles knew in his heart that Hector was his great foe. He was glad, therefore, that Ajax had not killed him.

As his anger subsided, Achilles grew bored with his self-imposed exile. He found his thoughts drifting constantly to Briseis. Through her, he had discovered a side of himself that he did not know existed; he was tender with her and enjoyed the way she made him feel with her soft hands and warm lips. He felt a warm rush from the way she looked at him and the way he felt when he saw her naked, bent over to wash or lying on the recliner, sleeping softly, waiting for him to come to her. A week after her departure, he had summoned another girl to his tent, a comely slave girl from Lesbos, but had found her unfulfilling and sent her away without making love. He had tried two other women, being able to satisfy himself physically with one, but not the other.

"Briseis has awakened something in me that I did not know was there," he told Patroclus and Phoenix late one night, after putting up his lyre. "I am furious at the indignity, of course, and I would slay Agamemnon for that alone; but, I must admit, taking Briseis from my tent has wounded me almost as deeply."

Patroclus and Phoenix were surprised that he talked so freely about his loss. Phoenix remembered that years ago Chiron had told him Achilles was far more sensitive and complex than anyone would ever know and now Phoenix was seeing that for himself.

The following day, Patroclus had even gone so far to approach Achilles and suggest that he go to Melisa and try to find relief from the pain of not having Briseis. It was a gesture of pure friendship, as Patroclus cared a great deal about Melisa. Achilles shook his head and slapped Patroclus on the shoulder, but declined the invitation.

"She is your woman, Patroclus; I can not take her," he had said simply.

Achilles began going to the seashore regularly and walking along it, alone and unarmed. He would slip past the single sentry on the southern tip of the camp and disappear into the dark of night, sometimes not returning until Helios was ready to start his long trek across the sky. Often, he would sit on the shore, pulling his knees up to his chin, and talk to his mother; he found comfort in asking Thetis why he had been so cheated by the fates.

"A short life with glorious deeds," he shouted once, to the dark and tumbling sea in front of him. "It seems that Achilles will be quickly forgotten, thanks to Agamemnon. No bards will sing of my deeds and my father back home in Phthia will have nothing to boast about. We Achaeans came to Troy and accomplished little other than sacking a few weak towns down the coast. Agamemnon is the supreme villain; first he dishonors his own daughter and tries to ruin my name, as well. And now he has taken Briseis from me. I could have killed him but the gods insisted I let him live. Still, I will have my revenge when Hector comes to the ships and burns them, as surely he will."

Several times he sprawled out on the sand and fell asleep, dreaming of victories before the Scaean Gates. He did not awaken until the waters of Ocean had crept up on him in the morning tide and soaked him from his feet to his waist.

Finally, he decided to take a trip behind Troy, up to Mount Ida. He had not been there for several years, not since running into the Dardanian prince named Aeneas. He had taken delight in the way Aeneas at first blustered, and then drew back, silent and trembling when he saw who it was that he was facing.

"Deathdealer!" someone behind Aeneas muttered and Achilles had seen the face of Aeneas, who he had heard was a brave man and good fighter, turn ashen with fear. Aeneas had made small talk in a dialect Achilles had trouble understanding and Achilles had merely stared at him, until Aeneas bowed slightly and turned and walked swiftly away. Achilles had not been in a temper to fight and, besides, he respected the fact that

Mount Ida was supposed to be a scared area – home to the temple of Almighty Zeus and considered a neutral ground by both armies.

Achilles had gone to the small, marble temple with the majestic statute of Zeus, and had sat there for a long time, talking to the great god. He had seen the women darting back and forth, those who served the god's temple and the two who were actual priestesses. They had been too frightened to approach him and he had finally stood, stretched hard and left.

Now, he wanted to go back to the temple high on the back side of Mount Ida and commune with Zeus once again. He told Patroclus and Phoenix of his plans and asked Automedon and eight other Myrmidons to travel with him. They set off in the early morning in two carts, each pulled by a team of two horses, making a wide circle around Troy, far to the south. There were few soldiers on the plain that day and those who did venture out would not attack when they saw the black pennant of the Myrmidons flying from the top of the carts.

It was a long trip, taking the better part of the day, and Achilles found his thoughts drifting back to his youth on Mount Pelion. The two mountains were very similar in their shape and with vegetation. The carts drove through areas of high grass and then dense trees – poplars, beech trees, and even elm and apple trees. They passed little huts where farmers lived and saw faces staring out at them as they moved by. Achilles wondered if Chiron was still able to ride his stout horse as easily as when he had left him; after all, he figured the man-horse was now in his sixth decade of life and was surely slowing down.

The sun was well past the halfway mark when at last he saw the temple in the distance. He hadn't planned what he would say to Zeus, but he knew it would come easily to him. Automedon halted the lead cart and the other one stopped behind it. Achilles stepped out of the cart and glanced about. It was quiet, with birds singing softly in the distance. He had seen no signs of life the last mile or so, either human or animal. As he walked to the temple he wondered if it was deserted, if the years of war had caused the servants of the great god to leave in despair. He glanced about and spotted the well where the drinking water came from and saw small huts a good distance away, where the temple caretakers once lived.

The Myrmidons relaxed in the long grass, sprawling out to nap or play dice. Achilles moved into the spacious temple, the cool of the marble floor feeling good against his bare feet. There were small wooden doors in four different spots and beautiful tapestries hung from the walls, giving evidence that the temple was still being used; if not, someone would have stolen the tapestries, he reasoned. He stepped to the large statue and peered up at the god he most admired. Zeus was the most powerful of all the gods; he gathered the clouds, scattered the winds, made the lightning, ruled supreme over the Olympians and controlled the destiny of men.

He knelt down before the statue and began praying softly. He heard a noise behind him; he swiveled like a cat and leaped to his feet in one motion, his hand flying to the short dagger that was in his belt. He saw nothing but knew he was not alone. He glanced about and then knelt again. He resumed praying to the god but this time all his senses were keenly alert. After several moments, he heard the sound again and recognized it as a woman's voice, singing softly. He titled his head, listening and trying to see from the corner of his eyes. He detected movement at the open back of the temple near the small bushes.

Slowly, he arose and walked past Zeus, who stared down at him with unblinking eyes. He glanced back over his shoulder and could see his warriors far away, several of them now sound asleep. He moved out of the temple, by the bushes, and saw a small path in the trees ahead. He walked onto the narrow, seldom-used trail and followed the sound. He could not make out the words or the tune; it was stranger than any sounds he had ever heard coming from a human throat, and it was intoxicating. It must be a wood nymph, he told himself. Only Thetis or one of her followers could make such a sweet sound. He moved like a wolf, his senses keenly alert, feeling the thrill of the hunt he had often experienced as a lad back on Mount Pelion.

He passed through a spot of dense foliage and then stopped abruptly, half hidden by thick bushes. There were three young women sitting in a clearing, by a stream. They were singing and washing linen, side by side. He watched in astonishment as one stood and walked slowly toward him. She was young and sweet and fresh looking, and he thought she was the most beautiful woman he had ever seen. She was wearing a white short chiton, belted at the waist, and red painted sandals; her long, dark hair splashed off her shoulders. She had a wild look to her but she also seemed vulnerable. He doubted Aphrodite herself could be as beautiful.

She walked to the edge of the clearing and stared at him without smiling. He looked into her dark eyes and felt a stirring in his breast.

"Come out," she said, holding her hand out slowly. Her voice was like music, as though she was singing when she spoke. Then she smiled: "You have nothing to fear; we won't hurt you."

The other two girls giggled and stood, turning toward him too. When Achilles stepped out of the thicket she gasped and took a step back.

"What is wrong?" he asked quickly. "Have I offended you in some way?"

She gaped at him and then turned and ran to the others. They chatted excitedly, in words he could not understand. He walked to them, arms stretched out, perplexed.

"I am glad you will not harm me," he said. "Nor will I harm you."

The one who had walked to him stood tall and faced him again.

"We thought you were from Troy, either a Trojan or perhaps a Dardanian. Or one of the allies. But you are not, we fear." She paused. "Who are you? Are you….a god come to visit us at last? Are you Apollo in mortal form?"

He smiled.

"I'm not a god," he said. Suddenly, he had misgivings and he glanced around to make sure there were no soldiers waiting to pounce on him. His hand moved to his dagger instinctively. She noticed his caution.

"No, you are not a god," she said. "Gods don't need their daggers for protection against three women."

He smiled again.

"But I am dangerous, if not a god," he said, suddenly feeling the desire to impress her. "I am a warrior, from the Achaean camp."

She turned and whispered to the others in a dialect he did not recognize. She turned back to face him.

"Who are you?" she asked. "How do men call you?"

"I am known as Achilles," he said.

She gasped, throwing her hands to her mouth and backed up. The others came to her side, ogling him.

"Deathdealer!" she mumbled.

"Widowmaker," said another.

They turned and ran to the stream's edge and retrieved their linens, tossing them in the small baskets they had brought them in. They ran off into the woods and Achilles decided to follow them. They moved quickly and he ran easily behind them, ducking under low-hanging branches and pushing aside thistles and bushes. When they saw they could not lose him, they stopped and the beautiful one approached him again. Her breasts were heaving from the exertion and she appeared tired.

"What do you want?" she asked nervously.

"You asked if I was Apollo," he said. "Now, I ask… are you a goddess yourself? I have never seen anyone as beautiful as you."

She blushed and looked over her shoulder at the others, then turned back to face him.

"No, I am a priestess of the Temple of Zeus," she said softly, her dark eyes staring into his. "We were passing by the temple on our way to the stream, to clean our clothes."

"I heard your singing," he said. "But I did not recognize the words or the language."

"It is our special language, known only to the gods and those who serve them," she said. She frowned up at him. "But, why are you here....the mightiest of the invaders? Why would the king of the Myrmidons come here?"

He was surprised that she knew the name of his warriors.

"I have taken time off from war," he said.

"You are feuding with the king of Mycenae," she said, surprising him again.

"How is it that you, a priestess on Mount Ida, know so much of the war?" he asked.

She stared at him for a long time and he felt a hunger growing in him that he had not known since he first slept with Briseis. But this was a different kind of hunger, he knew. Something about her stirred him in a way no woman had ever done before.

"I am not only a priestess," she said softly. "I go to Troy from time to time to visit my parents and my brothers and sisters. And I have stood on the wall over the Scaean Gate and watched the fighting." She paused. "I have seen you in the field, and have seen men flee from your spear." She paused again and he knew she was struggling for her next words.

"You are the city's greatest enemy," she said. "Everyone fears you. All but my brother."

He studied her face, drawn in by her beauty. He longed to know her better.

"And who is this brother, the one who does not fear Achilles?" he asked.

"Hector, tamer of horses," she said proudly, tilting her chin upwards.

Achilles frowned slightly and placed his hands on his hips.

"You are the sister of Hector?" he asked finally. "I know he has many brothers and sisters but I did not know he had one so beautiful as you."

She stiffened slightly. And then a slight smile broke across her lips. She studied his features, then frowned slightly.

"Up close, you do not look like a Deathdealer," she said. "I thought you would be far older and with a beard. Most of the Achaeans have beards. Do they not?"

He nodded.

"Most do, but very few of the Myrmidons have beards," he said. "In a fight to the death, anything can be a factor. I have heard of a foe clutching a man's beard and holding him by it while he drove his dagger home, into his heart. That will never happen to a Myrmidon."

She reached out a hand and touched his cheek faintly, then quickly withdrew her hand. He smiled at her, the feel of her touch lingering.

"I must go now," she said. "I have talked too long already."

She turned to leave but he called out to her.

"Wait!" he said. "I do not know your name."

She looked up at him with eyes that seemed to captivate his soul.

"My name does not matter," she whispered. "I am a priestess of Zeus and we will never meet again."

With that, she and the other two ran quickly away, darting into the forest. He watched them disappear and then shook his head and trudged back to the temple. He stopped to pay his respects to Zeus.

"Please, great Zeus Cloudgatherer, let me see this priestess again, some time soon," he said.

He returned to wake his Myrmidons and they drove back to the encampment, arriving when the moon chariot was riding high in the cloudless sky. Achilles was tired but he did not fall asleep quickly. He placed his hands behind his head, locking his fingers, and stared up at the top of the tent, visions of the beautiful priestess filling his mind.

Without Achilles and his Myrmidons in the field, the Trojans gained confidence. Day after day, they scored minor victories, pushing the Achaeans back. Among the invaders, only Diomedes seemed to relish the fighting. He raged across the plain for days, scoring tremendous victories in single combat. His greatest moment came when he killed Pandarus, one of the Trojans' finest warriors, in single combat and wounded a dozen other war chiefs of the Trojans, including Aeneas.

Hector also fought like a demon, scattering the Achaeans before him. He raced across the Troad in his chariot, his gray armor marking him as he went. He slew many with his long spear and many more with his sword. When Teucer, the cousin of Great Ajax and the finest bowman among the invaders, wounded eight Trojans, Hector sought him out. He saw Teucer send an arrow into the breast of another victim and then issued a challenge. Teucer tried to string his bow but Hector was upon him too quickly and struck him with his sword. Teucer fell badly wounded, but a loud cry went up from his soldiers and they surrounded him, fighting off Hector and the Trojans until Ajax came bellowing, racing to the aide of his cousin. Ajax threw the ailing Teucer over his right shoulder and trudged from the field, the Trojans making a wide path for the angry giant.

On another day, Odysseus slew eight Trojans and then was almost cut down himself; he was saved by both Ajaxes and had to leave the battle with his worst wound of the entire nine years. Even Agamemnon fought valiantly that day, until wounded by an arrow and driven from the field.

Each night, Patroclus brought news of the fighting to Achilles. During supper, the three men – Achilles, Patroclus and Phoenix – would talk about the war, and then Achilles would lay on his recliner and play his lyre. A week after his last trip to Mount Ida, he decided to go back, this time alone.

"Even the great Achilles can not travel all the way around Troy alone," protested Patroclus when Achilles told him he was leaving. "There are roving bands of soldiers about the city all the time, looking for bodies to loot, or worse mischief. Twenty of them would surround you and cut you down like a dog."

Achilles shook his head, unworried.

"I will be vigilant," he said, strapping a short sword to his side and placing his dagger in its sheath and sticking the sheath in his belt. He wore a brown tunic, belted at the waist, but no armor. "I have an urgent matter that I must attend to."

Patroclus walked outside the tent with him and to the pen where the horses were kept. Achilles' war chariot was pulled for the past five years by two magnificent black horses, Balius and Xanthus, but he would not use them this trip. They were well known by the Trojans and their appearance would be a certain giveaway as to who was in the chariot. He selected two brown horses and a sturdy chariot that was not his own. He bid Patroclus farewell and set off for his long trip around Troy.

He encountered no marauding bands along the way. Once, a chariot pulled along side of him, with two Trojans it, and they brandished their spears. He stared at them and they suddenly swerved to the left and disappeared. Though he could not be sure, he reasoned they must have recognized him and decided they wanted no part of trying to bring him down.

The chariot moved along the back of the city and onto the common trail that was used by many of the allies coming into Troy from the rear. Within three hours of leaving the Achaean camp he had pulled up near the Temple of Zeus. He secured the horses to a tree, near a pile of lush grass, and walked to the temple.

There were over a dozen men and women in the front of the temple when he arrived, praying near the statue of Zeus. He walked into the temple and lingered in the back until they left. Several of them gaped at him and began whispering as they hurried past, eyes wide. If they did not know him for who he was, they at least recognized him as a tremendously handsome warrior.

He stayed for nearly an hour and was disappointed that he did not see her. There were three other priestesses there and he thought he recognized one as having been with the one he sought. She seemed to recognize him too and after several minutes of soft chanting she departed out the back. He left the temple, standing in front, in the gathering darkness. He was about to return to his chariot when he heard the voice.

"You are here again," it said. He turned to see her; she was more radiant than ever. He smiled and nodded.

"Deathdealer has returned," she said.

"My name is Achilles," he said, walking up to her. "What is your name, daughter of Priam?"

She paused and they faced each other in silence. Then he reached out and took her hands in his. She gasped and stared to withdraw them, but he held them fast, staring at her. Her gaze fell on his hands.

"These hands have killed so many," she said. She rubbed the back of one hand gently with her hand. "The hands of death."

She smiled up at him and he was struck by her beauty once again. Her eyes had a sparkle that he had never seen in any other eyes.

"I need your name," he said softly.

"What is in a name?" she responded.

"I want to have something by which to know you. When I return to the camp of the Myrmidons, I want to be able to think of you. To do that, I need your name."

"You will think of me?" she asked.

"Yes, I will think of you," said Achilles. "Perhaps often."

She eased her hands away and turned quickly. She glanced back over her shoulder. He came to her and gripped her waist and turned her around gently. Her hands flew to his arms and she felt the coiled strength of his muscles. She had never felt power like that before.

"I....I must know if I can trust you," she said, her voice soft and low. "Trust must come...before all else," she whispered.

"Yes, of course," he said and dropped his grip on her waist. "I will not hold you against your wishes."

She looked at him surprised.

"Achilles does not just take whatever he wants?" she said, arching her eyebrows.

He shook his head. "You are free to leave," he said, a pained expression on his face.

She walked several steps away, then swiveled and faced him. It was dark and he could scarcely see her features.

"Will you come again?" she asked.

"Yes, I will come again," he said. "When?"

"In four nights, when Diana is at the very top of her ride across the sky," she said, glancing up at the moon goddess just starting her long trek through the night. "If you come then, to the temple, you will see me."

"And who shall I ask for, if you are not here?" he said.

"I am Polyxena," she said finally.

He nodded. And then she was gone.

On the fourth night he repeated his journey, on guard for any treachery. He wondered if she had taken word to Hector that Achilles would be coming this way, alone and almost unarmed. He only wondered as if to amuse himself, for he did not care who would try to stand in his way. He had grown weary of not fighting and he would take on anyone who dared confront him. Anyone, or any number.

It seemed the trip took far longer than the first two times. He passed a few elderly men and women and children on the path but the last mile it was totally deserted. Diana was high in the sky when he tied the horses up and walked quickly toward the temple. He had never seen it at this point of time; bathed in the light of the moon, with deep shadows all about it, he realized it was the perfect place for a trap. There was an opening in the temple roof above the statue of Zeus and the moonlight shone directly on the statue. As he walked into the large temple, he stopped to stare up at the king of the gods. He could have sworn he saw the statue move....

Polyxena had come to the temple much earlier, her mind spinning with thoughts that were quite alien to her. She had sworn to remain a virgin, giving herself only to a god. In recent years she had despaired of ever meeting a god, but then her eyes had fallen on Achilles that day by the stream. She had never seen anyone so gloriously handsome or with such a wonderful physique. Every muscle seemed to stand at rigid attention; he was, she thought, beautiful to gaze upon.

Still, she had not allowed herself to think much about him, until her fellow priestess had come running breathless to her and told her he was back in the temple. She had come to see for herself and had been overwhelmed by him once again. When he took her hands in his and she placed her hands on his arms and felt the power, she was sure that he was a god. She had heard the stories, told throughout Troy, that he was invincible because his mother was a sea goddess. Even Hector, one night long after dinner, had told the members of the royal family that Achilles seemed more than mortal.

"I would fight him, of course; that is my duty, and I shrink from no man," Hector had said, feeling the wine. "But they say even mighty Ajax is afraid of Achilles."

"And you had your hands full with Ajax, brother," teased Deiphobus.

Hector grimaced and threw his wine cup at his brother and they all laughed heartily. And then Hector had grown very serious.

"If the gods and goddesses take to the battlefield, no man has a chance," he said, his voice low and thick. "So it seems with Achilles...."

His final words had sent a chill down her back and Polyxena had wanted to hate Achilles. She had never imagined meeting him and when she did, she had been taken by surprise at his gentle nature, at his clean-shaven face, and by his magnificent body. He was more handsome than any man she had ever known, including her brother Alexandros, who most women fell in love with at first sight. And when her hands touched the arms of Achilles she felt a strength that was of another world.

Yes, she had wanted to see him again, in deepest night, when no one else would know. She had heard stories of her half-sister Cassandra, whom many claimed was mad, being visited by a god, and of other women being visited by gods, seduced, and having great children. Maybe, she thought, Achilles would be her god!

She stood behind the statue of Zeus, trembling slightly, even though the night was warm. She had heard his approach and leaned against the statue, suddenly weak and frightened. She had peered around it and had seen him standing in the moon's light, his long hair touching his shoulders, his muscles glistening....and she knew at that moment that he was indeed a god, come to rescue her from this simple life she lived.

She eased out from behind the statue and he saw her. Slowly, they walked to each other and stood face to face in the moonlight, Zeus watching from on high.

"Come with me," she said at last, slipping her hand into his. They left the temple and walked down the path he had first followed to find her. A short way in, she detoured to the right and they ducked under some tree limbs and hurried along. Twice he tried to speak to her but she lifted a finger to his lips to silence him. He felt her trim body move next to his when she did so and he felt an excitement growing in his loins that he had never known before in his entire life.

Shortly, they came to a small clearing where sat ten small huts. She led him to the third one and they slipped into it. There was an opening at the top, where the moonlight streamed in. She glanced up and he stared at her neck and shoulders, a fire in his body that he could not contain.

"When Diana is taking the chariot by overhead, the light is wonderful," she whispered, her voice intoxicating. "When it rains, I have to cover it. But tonight, it is wonderful."

She turned her eyes on him and he took her in his arms. She gasped slightly but did not resist; he kissed her lips once, twice and then he lost count. He pulled her in, smothering her face and cheeks with hungry kisses. His hands slipped her thin garment from her shoulders and it fell to the earth. She swooned, groaning, her arms flying around his neck and they sagged onto the thick mound of animal skins that made up her bed.

"Achilles," she whispered, her fingers moving through his long, golden locks. "My god has finally come....."

He was up at dawn and saw Polyxena sitting in the corner, wrapped in furs, smiling at him. He yawned and stretched and crawled over to her on all fours, like an animal, growling. She giggled and then slid her hands in his tousled hair. He smiled at her and sat up, hugging her. He kissed her gently and then held her for a long time as she nestled against him.

She ran her hands over his chest, across the scars. She stared at them and then placed her lips on the scar.

"Your body is like no other I have ever seen," she whispered. "Even this scar. Tell me, what is it from?"

She sat mesmerized as he told her about the lion. When he was finished, she eased her fingers over the thick scars. She cuddled up next to him again, her head resting on his chest.

"There has never been a man like you, Achilles. A man who fights lions as a youth and yet who would die to protect the young daughter of his greatest enemy. And who withdraws from a war he loves to protest the actions of a king who steals a slave girl from his tent."

He pushed her gently from him, peering down into her eyes.

"How do you know so much?" he asked. "Who told you about Iphigenia and about my quarrel with Agamemnon?"

She shrugged.

"Troy is full of spies and storytellers, men who travel back and forth between the camp of the invaders and the city," she said. "Many nights, the house of Priam is treated to after-dinner stories of all the invaders and what they went through to come here. I have known about Iphigenia for some time but didn't believe it because I didn't think Deathdealer was capable of such acts.

"But now, after knowing you, I understand," she said. "You are much different than I had ever dreamed. And, I am falling in love with you, my Achilles."

They were overtaken by passion again. Polyxena was casting a spell over him that no other woman had ever come close to. After another session of lovemaking, he admitted to himself that he was in love with a priestess of Troy!

"I must go," he said finally, standing, and pulling her up with him.

"Will you come back?" she asked shyly. "Or, was this just for the moment?"

"I will come back," he said, looking into her eyes. "I promise you that, Polyxena. I will come back."

The death of Patroclus

Patroclus paced in front of Achilles on his recliner. "The war goes poorly. Our comrades are cut down," he said. "The Trojans and their many allies grow bolder and bolder. Hector stands in front of the Achaean army and challenges anyone to come meet him in single battle, knowing that you rest by your ships and will not hear his challenge. Even Great Ajax, because of his numerous wounds, does not answer the challenge even though he fought Hector to a standstill only a short time ago.

"It seems the gods have turned against us. Odysseus is also suffering from many wounds. Agamemnon and Menelaus seem to have lost heart, and Nestor never leaves his tent any more. Idomeneus talks of taking his men back to Crete. Only Diomedes and Antilochus seem to fight on as always, never wavering.

"The common soldier is weary and wondering when he will see his homeland again…or if he will ever see it."

He halted to see if his words were affecting Achilles.

"Do you not care at all?" Patroclus asked in frustration, arms outstretched. "Does the fact that the Achaeans are being humiliated bother you in any way? Or has the injury which Agamemnon did to you outstripped all other feelings that you once had for your friends and comrades?"

Achilles put down his lyre and stared hard at Patroclus.

"Ever since you came to Mount Pelion, eleven long years ago, you have been my brother, Patroclus," he said finally. "The brother I never had. But even you can not know everything that is within my heart.

"I came here to Troy not because the Trojans wounded me or my father, but because I saw a noble mission and a chance to test myself against other warriors. I was just sixteen when we sailed for Troy, and now I am over the twenty-six year mark. I have fought hundreds of individual battles, always with victory, and we have sacked a total of twenty cities. The Myrmidons are the most feared warriors in the field and no one dares to stand before them unless they are vastly superior in numbers.

"Our tents outside, where we keep our spoils, are bulging to the tops. We have taken enough golden tripods, golden ingots, enough jewels and necklaces, gems and trophies to make Phthia wealthy until the end of time."

He paused, staring up at Patroclus.

"And what has it gained any of us? Everyone knows I am a far better man than Agamemnon in the field, but still he can take my most prized possession from me, a woman I once cared for a great deal. So what have I gained, Patroclus? Tell me, my brother, what have I gained from all of this foolishness?"

Patroclus stared at him and then shrugged. He walked to the tent opening and peered out into the night for a long time. Then he came back to stand before Achilles.

"Agamemnon knows he has done wrong and is sending a peace emissary to you, tonight. They are waiting to hear from me to see if you will allow them to come meet with you. It is Ajax and Odysseus and Nestor. And Phoenix. They are outside now. Can they come in and talk to you?"

Achilles leaned back, his mind going in many directions at once. His pride had been severely wounded and so was the name of his father, Peleus. He had not grown weary of the fighting; in fact, he loved it as much as ever. But he could not even think of Agamemnon without the anger welling up inside of him. He wanted to embarrass the high king and to show him for the kind of man he really was – so swallowed up by greed that he was no longer capable of acting with any regard to honor. He wanted to see his fellow warlords, but he did not want to talk about the issue of Agamemnon's insult. He nodded to Patroclus.

"Show them in," he said at last.

They filed into the tent one after the other, following the two heralds that came with them from the tent of Agamemnon. The heralds bowed low to Achilles as they entered, and then Achilles stood and greeted the others warmly.

Ajax came first, huge as ever; he had a noticeable limp and his arms were scarred with recently-healed wounds. He nodded at Achilles, his features glum and almost hidden by the long, thick growth of reddish-brown hair that covered much of his face.

Behind him came Odysseus, also limping, and wearing the sly grin that Achilles had seen from the first day they met. His dark eyes darted around the tent, taking in everything. He was much smaller than Ajax, but almost as wide. His craftiness had made him every bit as terrible a foe as Great Ajax in the thoughts of the Trojans.

Last came Nestor and Phoenix, comrades in age and wisdom. Both had lived seven decades and were greatly admired for their vast knowledge. They liked to sit together with a full wineskin nearby, and spin tales of mighty heroes and wonderful deeds. Achilles knew he would get an earful from both before the night was over.

"It is good to see you all," said Achilles, his eyes moving over them one by one as they stood behind chairs set for them by his servants. "I know the evening is late enough that you have all eaten, but let us enjoy fine wine that came to this tent through one of the many adventures of the Myrmidons… all some time ago, as there have not been many adventures of late."

The servants scurried around the table, filling everyone's wine cup and placing thick loaves of bread in the middle of the table, with knives to slice them and small cups of honey for the men to dunk the bread in. And then they departed quickly. The heralds from the tent of Agamemnon stood near the opening, tall and straight, and would remain there unless ordered by Achilles to leave. But he wanted them to stay, so that their lord, the high king of Mycenae, would get a full report of all that was said. They made small talk, drinking their wine and eating the bread dipped in honey. Ajax ate the most, saying little. A man of his size needed lots of nourishment.

At last, Odysseus cleared his throat and stood, looking down the table at Achilles.

"We have come a long way together, you and I, Achilles," he began, the impish smile now gone from his face. "Remember the words of Peleus and Chiron, how proud they were to be sending you off to war, for they knew the mighty deeds that you were capable of. And so do all of us, and the entire Achaean host. No one doubts that you are the finest warrior in all the world, that Zeus has bestowed upon you physical gifts that surpass those of all others.

"It is certain that Lord Agamemnon was not thinking clearly when he demanded that you surrender Briseis to him. I, for one, counseled him against such a brash move, and so did Nestor. Ajax made his feelings against the move well known. But the high king was not willing to listen, so angered by having to surrender his own sweet girl.

"Now, he realizes the grave error he has made. Not only do we miss your great skills and the war-like nature of the Myrmidons, but your very absence from the field has given new courage to the Trojans. Hector has run amuk, knowing you sit idle by your ships. Even now, his campfires dot the plain just beyond our wall. They are poised, ready to strike hard tomorrow. They believe they can breach the wall and burn our ships, and that we will all perish here by the seashore.

"Agamemnon called Ajax, Nestor and me to his tent hours ago and begged us to ask you to rejoin the battle. Not only will he return Briseis to you, but much, much more. He has instructed his servants to heap treasures upon you – including seven tripods and ten talents of gold; twenty bright cauldrons and twelve strong horses. Also, seven women, all young and attractive. He will swear by Zeus that he had never touched Briseis, knowing she pines for you and that she has no interest in him at all."

Odysseus paused to let his words take affect, then continued.

"Not only all of this will he give to you, but when Troy is sacked you can have your choice of all the beautiful women, taking any ten you want. And all the gold and bronze that your ships can carry back to Phthia. And then," he said, pausing again for impact, "he will give you seven small cities to rule over, in the kingdom he is lord of.

"All this, the high king has sworn to us, and will do so again to you. All that he asks is that you swallow your anger and return to the war.

"But if that won't bring you to your senses, think of the rest of us. Hector knows no fear and only you can stop him now. He thinks there is no man equal to him…. not even you, lord Achilles."

Odysseus nodded at Achilles and then sat back down. After several moments, Achilles stood and faced him.

"You speak well, king of Ithaca," he said quietly. "No man is better suited to either the sword or the word. But as powerful as were your words, they have not turned me from the feeling in my heart. I know now that the king of men is a cheat and a liar. How can I still serve him? Are there enough riches anywhere on earth to buy my services when I despise the man who wants to buy them?"

Achilles looked at each of them deliberately, one after the other. Nestor studied Achilles intently, surprised and impressed at how the warlord from Phthia had matured in his years at Troy. Nestor realized at that moment that Achilles was not only the master of the battlefield, but that he was now on a journey to be master of himself.

"I no longer care anything for the riches of this world," Achilles continued. "I would much rather see my father in Phthia and race through the meadows on Mount Pelion with the man-horse than to remain here trying to win more spoils of war. Agamemnon sits by his tent and waits for the spoils to come to him, goods that other men have earned, and then when things don't go his way he reaches out and takes hard-earned rewards from others. Is that fair, is that just?

"My mind is set, Odysseus. He has made this what he has. It is Agamemnon who will have to take to the field and hold off mighty Hector, if he can. As for me, I will pack my ships tomorrow and set sail for Phthia on the next day. In just three days of sailing and two more days of travel, I will be back home to serve a real king – Peleus."

He sat down, knowing that the others would still have something to say. It was Phoenix who stood next, hands on the table, looking solemn-ly at Achilles.

"You are like a son to me, Achilles," he said, his voice low and weak with age. "If you go, I must go also, as Peleus instructed me to stay by your side at all times. But, I beg you to take control of your pride….to rule it and not let it rule you. Even the gods know how to be won over by prayer and reason, and change their attitudes. As great as you are, Achilles, you are not a god.

"Until now, all men were with you in this matter. But now that Agamemnon has told us all that he was wrong, the mood may shift against you if you do not manage to change your thinking and rescue the Achaeans."

Achilles faced his old mentor with a kind expression.

"All you say may be true, Phoenix," he said slowly. "But you ask for something that I can not give. I can not let Agamemnon have his way in this matter until he realizes who he is, and what he has done to me, who came to serve him. Justice is my king, not Agamemnon."

There was a long silence around the table and Phoenix nodded slowly, recalling the conversations he had with Chiron, long ago in the palace of Peleus.

"Beware when Achilles thinks he has been wronged, or someone he cares about has been injured," said Chiron. "When that happens, nothing can turn his thoughts from seeking revenge. He will die fighting for what he believes in, right or wrong. His passion for fairness in all matters is a strength, but it can also be a weakness, for he can carry it to an extreme and alienate even the gods with his stubbornness."

Phoenix remembered how Achilles reacted when he felt Patroclus had cheated him in the foot race the first day they met, and how he felt when his name had been used to deceive Iphigenia. He was willing to break Patroclus's arm over a race and he was willing to die in defense of Iphigenia, if need be. No, Phoenix knew there was no sense in talking to Achilles any longer. He had made up his mind on Agamemnon. He had weighed the value of more fame and wealth on one scale against the injustice he felt had been dealt to him by Agamemnon's acts on the other scale, and had made his choice: justice would be served before man, even if that man was the high king of the Achaeans.

Then Ajax stood and faced his cousin.

"Achilles, I surely know how magnificent you are in all things. I tested you years ago and found that my size and strength were little compared to your strength and skills. I have deferred to you ever since, in all matters, and look the other way when men say how much greater you are than I am.

"But, you are wrong to let your anger continue to blindly guide you." He glanced around the table, then walked to the tent's opening, turning back to look again at Achilles.

"I am leaving, for I know now that nothing will placate you."

Achilles nodded at him, with a certain sadness in his eyes.

"You always speak your heart, Ajax, and I admire you for that. But you do not choose to recognize how Agamemnon has used me and used all of us. I will serve him no longer, that much is certain."

Phoenix, Odysseus and Nestor rose and thanked Achilles for his hospitality, then walked out into the night with Ajax, the heralds trailing behind them. Now they had the task of reporting the unhappy news to Agamemnon, and preparing for the next day's onslaught knowing that Achilles would not be with them.

Achilles sat silently at the table for a long time after they departed, his mind full of conflicting thoughts. He wanted to see Polyxena again before sailing for home; perhaps he would ask her to go with him, or even take her by force if she said she could not leave. He left the tent and walked down to the sea. It brought him great comfort to visit the seashore and listen to the tide as it came in each night. The steady rumbling of the waves soothed him and he felt he could talk to his mother there, or to Zeus Cloudgatherer. He moved slowly down the beach, the campfires of the Achaeans in the far background, and the fires of his own Myrmidons close behind him. At last, he returned to this tent, seeking a few hours of sleep before the advent of day.

As the pink fingers of dawn played on the horizon, the Trojans and their allies were up and making ready. They had slept on the plain the two previous nights, pitching tents and setting huge fires to roast their meat on. They were in high spirits for the first time in many months as Hector walked through the encampment, offering words of encouragement to the warlords, and even to the common soldiers. At morning's light, they were assembling, pulling on their armor and war helmets and buckling on their scabbards and short swords. The warlords grabbed their long spears and headed toward the chariots, the common fighting man preparing to march out behind the leaders.

The Achaeans wore grim expressions as they filed out of the huge gate to face the Trojans. Agamemnon tried to rally them with a bitter speech about their mission, telling them they could not return home to their families and friends with defeat hanging around their necks. At the end, he raised his long war spear, shaking it at them, and rode out the gate in his huge chariot, his terrible war crest wavering in the crisp air, his long, purple robe flying behind him as the horses raced ahead.

In his wake came the other warlords in their chariots – Diomedes, hungry for battle, and Menelaus, Odysseus, Great Ajax and Little Ajax, Idomeneus, and the other lesser-known warriors. Thousands of foot soldiers trudged out behind the chariots and the Trojans and their allies raised a tremendous shout, anxious to confront them. The two armies surged toward one another, with the great heroes searching out familiar chariots and war crests from the other side, to issue challenges to.

The armies came together shortly after dawn, and it quickly turned into one of the most terrible days of the entire ten years. Both sides were anxious to rout the other and the fighting was as fierce as any man had ever seen. Ajax led the way, striking out with a fury, his horses running down foot soldiers, his chariot wheels rolling over screaming men. He thrust his spear everywhere, his mouth foaming with anger, his eyes staring out from each side of the long nose guard on his helmet. He quickly used all six spears that he carried, shouting to his driver to hand them to him one at a time and then casting them with all his might at Trojans. Three times he leaped from his chariot and attacked soldiers with his sword, cutting them down; he had never felt so powerful, so overwhelming. He wanted the world to see that he could fight even with Achilles in his tent.

Diomedes fought in such a fury that he slew ten Trojans within a short span of time and then had trouble finding anyone to stand against him. His chariot raced across the plain, his driver looking for pockets of fighters so his chieftan could issue challenges, and climb down and engage. But when the Trojans saw the chariot of Diomedes advancing, they turned and fled, no one wanting to stand before him.

Odysseus also fought exceedingly well, sending a dozen Trojans to the land of the dead. Idomeneus, highly skilled with the war lance, ran through several Trojans with his great spear. Menelaus engaged in a brutal fight with a skilled Trojan soldier named Peisander and was severely tested before running the Trojan through the abdomen with his sword. Even Agamemnon gave a good account of himself that day.

But at midday, the fortunes of the battle swung in the other direction. Hector had taken a break, exhausted, and pulled off his war helmet, staring up at the heavens. He pleaded with Zeus and Apollo to turn the tide, to give strength to the Trojans. And then, his spirit renewed, he roared back into the fray.

Suddenly, the Achaeans were retreating. A warrior named Socus wounded Odysseus with a spear and Diomedes was struck in the foot by an arrow shot from in the midst of the Trojan army. The two great warriors moved closer together, panting from exertion, and found themselves shut off from the main body of Achaeans. They were surrounded by a host of Trojans who rushed at them, eager to bring down two of their most feared enemies.

"Diomedes, we are in trouble!" Odysseus shouted out. "I have been sorely wounded and my Ithacans are cut off from me. I need your help!"

The warlord from Argos limped over to him, blood pouring from his foot, perspiration streaming down his face. He had ten Argives with him and he turned his eyes on the Ithacan.

"We may go down fighting right here, Odysseus!" he shouted. "Zeus has turned against us."

Flanked by the ten warriors of Diomedes, the two warlords gripped their swords as the Trojans surrounded them, a blood lust racing through their veins. There were at least ten times as many Trojans, and Odysseus felt a hot tremor down his back. Then he saw the huge figure of Ajax in the distance, marching to another part of the battle with his Salamians.

"Ajax! Ajax!" shouted Odysseus, waving his sword high above his head. "This way! Diomedes and I are trapped!"

Ajax stopped in his tracks, peering over the heads of the others and, seeing what was happening, screamed his war cry and raced toward them. The Trojans turned in his direction and braced to meet the new threat. The battle turned into a bloodletting of staggering dimensions. Ajax and his men attacked the Trojans from one flank, while Diomedes and his ten warriors and Odysseus came at them from the other end. Terrible screams of agony ripped the air as the two sides fought frantically, swords hacking in every direction. A Trojan screamed wildly as a sword took his right arm clean off; another's head went rolling in the dust, helmet firmly on top. Two of Diomedes's men were driven to the ground with spears firmly planted in their abdomens. The hundred Trojans and the Achaeans of Diomedes and Ajax fought wildly, screaming their war cries and shouting to one another for help.

Hearing the clamors and the clashing of weapons from all across the vast plain, Achilles hurried out of his tent and climbed onto the bow of his ship. The gates to the encampment were wide open and he stared out them onto the Troad. Huge clouds of dust rose up in dozens of spots where the chariots were moving and he heard the screams of men and horses mingled together. He saw the Achaeans giving ground and felt a knot in his stomach. He searched for the gray armor of Hector, and finally saw him leading a tremendous charge on the western flank. He looked unstoppable and the Achaeans began to break and flee from Hector and his soldiers.

The rout was on and the Achaeans fled for the safety of their great wall and trenches. The Trojans and their allies poured behind them, shouting and running as fast as they could. The Achaeans tumbled over the trenches and the long spikes they had driven into the earth, pouring through the gates. One gate swung shut and Hector leaped out of his chariot. He lifted a huge rock and ran at the gate, slamming the stone into the wood. With his soldiers watching, he slammed the stone into the wood three more times, and the last time the wood splintered and caved in. The Trojans poured through the battered gate and for the first time ever were inside the camp of the invaders.

Pandemonium ruled as Achaeans fought desperately, some even climbing onto their ships and spearing down at the advancing Trojans.

Patroclus climbed onto the bow of the ship besides Achilles, panting with the exertion of running from the gates.

"I have been up by the gates watching," he shouted, staring at Achilles with wide eyes. "Odysseus and Diomedes are wounded and are just now limping toward the ships. Ajax came to their rescue, but he was wounded and is now retreating, as well."

"What of our high king?" asked Achilles, still intent on the battle scene in front of him. "I heard he was doing well, for once."

"Early on that was so, I am told," said Patroclus. "But he has been wounded by an arrow to the arm and has left the field. Among the chief warlords, only Idomeneus and Antilochus are still in the field. I fear a rout is under way and the enemy will soon be at our gates... and at our ships." Achilles grimaced, torn for the first time by conflicting emotions. While he was pleased to see Agamemnon's rejection of him forcing horrible consequences, he was also moved by the plight of his comrades. He saw a chariot race past with a wounded man in the arms of Nestor, who was struggling valiantly to hold onto him as the driver guided the chariot toward Nestor's tent.

"Go see who that wounded warrior is," said Achilles.

Patroclus nodded and leaped from the ship's bow and raced for the tent of Nestor. When he arrived, he saw Nestor and several others bending over a soldier. It was Machon, the finest medicine man among the Achaeans. His death would be a huge blow to the Achaeans.

"How bad is it?" said Patroclus to Nestor. The old man looked up at him, his white beard shaking. "Achilles wants to know."

"What does he care?" asked Nestor. "He will soon have his wish. The gods are against us now, it is obvious. Hector is fighting like a man who knows Zeus will protect him. Our finest warlords are wounded and out of action. The army is retreating. And Lord Achilles sits in his tent, without a care in the world."

Patroclus gaped at Machon writhing on the ground as other doctors tried to assist him. There was a broken shaft of an arrow protruding from his right thigh and he grimaced as the others began cutting the arrow out. Patroclus was preparing to depart when Nestor gripped his arm with his aged fingers. He wore an expression of heavy concern.

"Listen, Patroclus, you are his closest friend. He will listen to you. If Achilles will not take to the field, ask him if you can wear his armor…. and lead the Myrmidons. If the Trojans see you in his armor, they will think Achilles has rejoined the battle and they will lose heart. They may even turn and flee."

He paused, staring hard into the eyes of Patroclus.

"It is our only hope, Patroclus. Without the Myrmidons, we are lost. All the Trojans will be inside our gates and burn our ships and none of us will ever return to our homes."

The two warriors gaped at each other, separated only by forty summers of living. At last, Patroclus nodded.

"I will do my best, Nestor," he croaked. He turned and raced away.

Achilles was still on the bow of the ship when Patroclus returned. He saw his friend's great anxiety and when Patroclus motioned to him, Achilles climbed down to him.

"The entire army is on the verge of destruction," Patroclus spit out. "I have just come from the tent of Nestor. Machon has been severely wounded. Nestor says we are about to lose our camp, and our ships.

"I know that you have wanted the gods to favor the Trojans so that Agamemnon will be derided for what he has done, but we have many companions who will perish. Will you not swallow your anger and lead the Myrmidons onto the field, for the sake of all those who have befriended us the last ten years?"

Achilles frowned heavily and turned aside. He stalked alongside the ship, gazing first at the sea and then at the gates, then at his friend. He motioned for Patroclus to follow him and they ran to his tent. Inside, Achilles picked up his sword and swung it wildly in the air. Then he turned to Patroclus, a wounded expression on his face.

"Patroclus….how can I fight now? I care deeply for my comrades, but where were they when Agamemnon was doing this great wrong? Except Ajax, no one raised a voice against him, not even Nestor. They all knew what the high king was doing was unfair, yet they were silent, letting me carry the indignity and the shame by myself.

"Yes, finally they came to their senses. But it was too late. I tell you,

Patroclus, there is a higher duty in life than stealing another man's riches. That's what I've learned here at Troy. Together, you and I sacked many cities. We took whatever we wanted, and I felt good about it. But no more. Not since Agamemnon took what was rightfully mine and I had to sit still and bear it, only because he rules more people.

"I love combat, as it pits one man against another on terms they both accept. No man has to fight me if he chooses not to; he can just stay within the confines of the city's walls and be safe. Combat is done on equal terms, between men of equal persuasion, and that is the beauty of it.

"But I have had my fill of taking what is not mine. I no longer desire to carry a single gold tripod or ingot from Troy back to Phthia. Not a single one, or any slave that is not willing to go. That is the grave lesson I have learned from Agamemnon.

"No, I will not rise to save him."

He rammed the sword deep into the wood of the banquet table, where it stood quivering from the impact. Patroclus knew it was useless to debate the issue any longer. He turned to his only other hope.

"Then….will you allow me to wear your armor onto the field and take the Myrmidons with me?" His voice had an urgency to it that Achilles had never heard before from his friend of many years.

There was a long silence as the two warriors regarded each other, each hoping the other would see his reasoning and accept it.

"Whose idea is this?" Achilles said finally.

"It….is mine," said Patroclus. He did not want to lie to his best friend but there was too much at stake for him to tell the truth. If he admitted that Nestor had hatched the idea, he was afraid Achilles would not accept it. But Patroclus knew if it came from him, the chances were far better that Achilles could not turn away from it.

"Do you know what you are saying?" asked Achilles sternly. "To wear my armor will mean that all eyes will be upon you. Hector himself may decide to challenge you, if he thinks it is not me, or senses that it is really me and I am not myself."

The two men continued staring at each other for long moments, realizing that this was a decision of profound consequences and that there was little time to waste.

"I do," said Patroclus. He came to Achilles and gripped his forearms. "You are the best friend I have ever known, dearer to me than any brother could be. We have been through many things together and if the gods will it, many more. But Achilles, I want this chance to fight for our comrades, and to give them breathing space."

The thick shoulders of Achilles began to sag, and Patroclus knew the decision was made. Achilles walked to the cot where his armor rested. He lifted the bronze breastplate, holding it at arm's length, the first armor that Peleus had given him ten years earlier back in Phthia. It had a huge emblem of an eagle carved on it, in bright red. He walked to Patroclus and handed it to him. Then he turned and grabbed his greaves.

Patroclus placed the breastplate over his chest and Achilles moved behind him, snapping it in place. Patroclus picked up the greaves and placed them over his lower legs, and fastened his sandals good and tight. Achilles retrieved the war helmet with the dancing crest, made of red, stiff horsehair. He handed that to Patroclus and then went for his sword. Patroclus stood in front of him, peering out through the eye slits on each side of the long nose guard. His physique was so similar to that of Achilles that Achilles felt he could pull it off, at least from a distance. Up close, one might notice that Patroclus was a bit shorter and his arms not as big and muscular. But that was the only difference.

"I will keep my own spear," said Patroclus, laughing faintly. "I never could quite handle the Pelion ash. It is too heavy."

Achilles nodded. He dropped a thick hand on his friend's shoulder and stared hard at him.

"Promise me this, Patroclus," he said. "Win breathing space and push the Trojans back past the Scamander River, halfway to Troy. But go no further. Do not try to take the city by yourself, my great friend. It is not yours to take alone. When that day comes, I must be in the field, as well.

"Promise me that, Patroclus," he said, "or I will take back my armor."

Patroclus nodded.

"As Zeus is my witness, I promise," he said.

They nodded solemnly at one another and then Patroclus departed. He ran into the camp of the Myrmidons, shouting the war cry. Instantly, soldiers poured out of their tents and huts, carrying their armor and weapons, to see what was happening. They had waited patiently for this sound, and they were ready. Achilles stood by his tent, heart pounding, as he watched the horse handlers running to the pens to bring out the horses. He saw Xanthus and Balius pawing the ground, glancing about them and then at Patroclus as he neared them. Automedon raced over to where Achilles stood, fastening his belt about his waist, his short sword at his side.

"Is it true that Patroclus will lead us….in your own chariot? Wearing your armor?" Automedon shouted, excited and confused all at once.

"Yes, it is so," said Achilles. "It is his plan!"

Automedon turned to leave, but Achilles gripped his arm and spun him around.

"Automedon....let him go no further than halfway, to the Scamander. No further. Do you hear me?"

Automedon nodded.

"And keep him away from Hector," Achilles growled, his voice edged with tension. "Do not let the chariot go in the area where Hector is fighting."

Automedon nodded again.

"I hear you, lord Achilles," he said.

He ran off to the horse pen. Soon, the Myrmidon war cry cut the air again and Achilles stood stiffly as the war chariots moved past, Patroclus in the lead. He nodded stiffly down at Achilles, the horses snorting and prancing. Xanthus seemed to look at Achilles and tried to stop, but Automedon's whip cracked above his head, and he began prancing again. Ten more chariots of the subleaders filed by and then the Myrmidon foot soldiers, at a trot, moved past, all saluting Achilles with their spears as they went.

They ran into the beleaguered part of the camp, shouting their war cry and the Achaeans turned to gape at them, unable to believe the Myrmidons were finally coming to their rescue. Weary from their great drive forward and now disheartened at the prospect of Achilles back in the war, the Trojans began to retreat. Soon the Myrmidons had forced the lead Trojan group back to the battered gate and they passed out into the melee beyond.

Achilles ran to the ship and climbed up on the bow, hands above his eyes to shade the sun, staring for as long as he could. The Myrmidons sent up another dust cloud and he could see where they were headed. Then he heard the shouting....overwhelming cheers of joy on the behalf of the Achaeans and groans of dismay from the Trojan side.

Unable to see any more through the huge dust clouds, he climbed down and walked to his tent, a knot growing in his stomach. He grabbed his favorite drinking cup and poured wine into it, and drank it in one greedy gulp. He sat the cup down and looked up through the opening at the top of the tent into the blue skies above.

"I drink to you, Zeus, monarch of the gods. My beloved friend has gone into the battle with my blessings, and my armor and reputation to protect him. I pray that you give him the strength to score a great victory, but that you also give him the wisdom to draw back when the time has come to retire. Let him save our ships, Zeus, I pray, but let him also return safely to the camp of the Myrmidons."

And then Achilles dropped into his large chair. He felt a sense of doom gnawing at him. Minutes later, he jumped up again, arms outstretched to the sky.

"Zeus!" he shouted. "Protect Patroclus! He is a good warrior, but not a great one. But he is indeed a great friend, to me and all who know him. Do not let him meet Hector today!"

The blood surged through Patroclus' veins and his temples pounded like never before. He held his head high, feeling like a god in the armor of Achilles. He saw the reaction from the Achaeans as he raced toward them and they heard the war cry of the Myrmidons. Warriors fell back, spellbound, shouting the name over and over, ramming their spears into the air above their heads.

"Achilles!"

"Achilles comes!"

"It is Achilles…we are saved!"

Automedon cracked the whip again and again as the horses raced across the plain, the other war chariots trying to keep pace. They flew past the ranks of the Achaeans, out into the midst of the fighting. The Trojans and their allies screamed in panic and began fleeing.

"Alilia…alilia….alilia…..alilia….alilia….."

The Myrmidon war cry was everywhere. The warriors had been pent up too long, and were in a fighting frenzy. They sliced through the heart of the Trojan army, hacking at the soldiers with a fury the Trojans could not defend against. Soldiers fell to the ground by the score, writhing and kicking in their death throes, and still the Myrmidons came on in their black armor, chanting their chilling war cry.

"Alilia…alilia….alilia…..alilia….alilia….."

Patroclus was flush with success. He drove his spear into body after body, jerking it free each time and shaking it above his head. Automedon handled the chariot like a master driver, swerving in and out of the ranks of foot soldiers, searching for soldiers to run at. Patroclus leaped from the chariot on one occasion and chased down two Trojans, who finally turned to face him, great fear streaking across their features.

"You….are not Achilles!" gasped one.

"An imposter," said the other, gripping his spear with a renewed hope. He charged at Patroclus, who neatly sidestepped the thrust and rammed his sword deep into the man's abdomen. The soldier screamed, gripping the sword blade with his hands, and staggered off before falling face down in the grass. The other soldier, seeing Patroclus without his sword, charged. Patroclus met him head on, swinging his short shield with such force that the soldier staggered back. Before he could regain his footing, Patroclus leaped at him and drove his short dagger into the man's thigh.

The warrior screamed and tried to hobble away. Automedon leaped from the chariot and handed Patroclus a spear and Patroclus hurled it at the injured soldier. It struck him between his shoulder blades, just above the armor, and he tumbled into the grass, dead before he hit the ground. Patroclus ran up to him and retrieved the spear and then took his sword from the other body. He turned toward Automedon, a blood lust raging through him.

"More!" he shouted to Automedon. "The entire Trojan army is fleeing before us. We can take Troy today!"

They ran to the chariot and Automedon grabbed the reins and they sped off, the Myrmidons falling further behind them. They raced toward the retreating line of soldiers, heedless of where the rest of the Achaean army was, and heedless of the words of Achilles.

Sarpedon, king of the Lycians, was wiping blood and sweat from his brow when he saw Patroclus heading in his direction. He squinted, holding up a blood-stained hand, trying to get a better look.

"That looks like Achilles, but something is different," he said to his driver, who was also watching the chariot. Sarpedon had earned a reputation among the Trojans for his expert sword play and had sent many an invader to Hades over the years. He was a strong fighter and a smart fighter, willing to wait for the right moment to strike. He was a handsome man with a short, dark beard, and was very close to Hector; they had become fast friends during the ten years of war. Hector valued his leadership as much as his fighting prowess.

"Let's take a closer look," he said to his driver, leaping onto the platform of the chariot. The driver turned the horses toward the oncoming chariot of Patroclus.

Patroclus saw it was Sarpedon who now confronted him, and was pleased. He gripped his spear tighter, turning toward Automedon.

"That is Sarpedon, the Lycian, who comes now," he said. "He will be a good test, Automedon. He is a worthy foe. Slow the horses, so I can get a good cast at him."

The two chariots neared one another, the drivers tense, holding the reins, the warriors pulling out long spears and jostling them in their grip, preparing for a cast. As the horses sped by the other chariot, each threw with all his strength. Sarpedon's spear missed the mark and he jerked his shield up as he saw Patroclus's spear heading right for his chest. The spear crashed into his shield and knocked Sarpedon from the chariot. He fell heavily on his back and rolled in the dust, gasping for breath. He struggled to his feet, dazed. Automedon wheeled the chariot around and Patroclus leaped from the platform, pulling out his short sword. With armor clattering about him, his horsehair crest nodding, he ran at Sarpedon and began raining blows down on him. Still dazed from the fall, Sarpedon staggered backwards, warding off the blows.

"You are…not….Achilles," he groaned.

"What does that matter now?" screamed Patroclus. "I am a better man than you, Sarpedon, and you are about to enter Hades."

With a mighty thrust, he knocked Sarpedon's boar's tusk helmet from him and sent the Lycian leader sprawling to the ground again. Sarpedon struggled to his feet, blood pouring from his mouth and nearly helpless. He held his sword up but his strength was now gone. Patroclus ran him through with his sword. Sarpedon fell into the dirt, moaning the death rattle.

Patroclus pulled his sword free, staring down at Sarpedon. This was the twentieth warrior he had killed already today, and his limbs were growing weary. He stared at the handsome Lycian for a moment and felt a stab of sadness at what he had wrought. But he shook his head quickly, muttering, "This is war. A warrior can not afford pity or sympathy, or he too will soon be on his way to Hades."

He picked up Sarpedon's helmet as a war trophy and threw it at Automedon, who caught it and placed it on the railing of the chariot.

Several Lycians had seen Sarpedon's death and still thought it was Achilles who was raging. They ran to where Glaucus, Sarpedon's captain, was resting between battles and told him that Achilles had just killed Sarpedon. Glaucus leaped to his chariot.

"We must rescue the body; someone go and tell Hector what has happened," he shouted as his horses started toward Sarpedon. A hundred other Lycian soldiers ran toward the spot where the battle had taken place, shouting and moaning.

Ares, the god of war, was basking in his glory as bedlam took over. The Myrmidons caught up to Patroclus, proud that their war chief had scored such a great victory. They were determined to capture the body to take back to the camp and were hoisting it onto the rear of a chariot when the Lycians charged, enraged. The two groups met head on, neither giving or asking any quarter. Many soldiers were sent to Hades in a short period of time. Patroclus staggered back from the melee, nearly overcome by exhaustion. He hung on the chariot, gasping for breath as the Myrmidons forced the Lycians backwards.

"You need to rest, Patroclus," shouted Automedon, leaning over the railing. "It has been hours now since you took the field. Even Achilles rested."

Patroclus nodded, wiping the perspiration from his face. And then he saw the gates opening in the distance.

"The Scaean Gates are open!" he shouted to Automedon, pointing at Troy. "Look, they have opened the gates because the Trojans are fleeing. We can take the city if we hurry!"

He leaped into the chariot as both he and Automedon, in their great excitement, forgot what Achilles had made them promise. Patroclus turned toward the Myrmidons and saw that the other troops were now heading toward them, as well.

"Look! All the Achaeans are coming. Everyone sees what is happening.... the Trojans are in total flight! They think Achilles is among them and they are terrified."

He turned back to stare at the open gates in the far distance, and he felt drunk with power. He forgot how tired he was from hours of fighting. He licked his dry lips and tried to spit, but there was no moisture. He was on fire with an ambition that he had never known before while living in the immense shadow of Achilles.

"Go!" he shouted toward Automedon, pointing at the thousands of soldiers fleeing in front of him. "To Troy!"

He turned and swung his arm high in an arc for the Myrmidons to follow him. The war cry split the air, over and over and over.

"Alilia...alilia....alilia.....alilia....alilia....."

Glaucus staggered back, bloody and spent, devastated that he could not retrieve the body of his leader. He fell into the chariot, leaning over the rail in total exhaustion as the Lycians retreated from the Myrmidons.

"Go and find Hector," he groaned. "He has to come save us."

The chariot tore away toward Troy.

Near the gates, Hector was trying to rally the troops and stop the flight. He stood in the gate way, shouting at the soldiers, trying to remind them of their duty to protect the city. Above him, the wall was lined with old men, women and children, all screaming down at the soldiers, trying to find loved ones. Hector glanced up at the faces racked with pain, and feared all might be lost. Then the first of the Lycians reached him, crying and shaking.

"Sarpedon has fallen, to the sword of Achilles," he shouted. "The Myrmidons have taken his body back to the invaders camp. Glaucus pleads for you to come."

Hector felt a hot shiver run through his body. So it was time for him to meet Achilles at last, he thought. He screamed his war cry and ran toward his chariot, which was standing idle at the side of the gate, his driver, Cebriones, waiting for instructions.

"To the plain by the Scamander," he shouted. "I will meet Achilles and settle this once and for all. If I kill him, the tide will turn."

The chariot took off against the flood of humanity coming toward

Troy, and several of the war chieftans saw Hector going toward the battle. They paused and began to stop their fleeing troops, pointing toward Hector's chariot. The soldiers began to take heart and pulled up. Slowly, the army began to turn and head back to the plain, all following the courage of Hector.

Thoughts of the impeding battle gripped Hector's mind. He knew Achilles was the greatest warrior he would ever face; he had seen him from afar, and marveled how he never seemed to tire. Hector was proud of his own stamina, but deep in his soul he wondered if he could match Achilles blow for blow without tiring. He shook his head, tossing such thoughts aside. "I must not waver," he told himself. "If I do, Troy falls today."

The Myrmidons saw the chariot of Hector speeding toward them, as did Patroclus. He felt a knot in his stomach when he realized whom he would soon be facing in a fight to the death. He smiled grimly, his hand reaching for a long spear. And then, suddenly, he remembered the words of Achilles.

But it was too late. Hector's chariot was closing in; Hector was even shouting at him. And then, suddenly, Hector stopped shouting, a stunned expression on his face as the chariots sped by each other without a spear being cast.

"That is not Achilles!" gasped Hector to Cebriones. "By Zeus, it is not Achilles! How can that be?"

Their chariots swung wide, bouncing on the rocky plain, but Automedon was a master driver and he cut short the swing and suddenly Patroclus had a clear shot at the back of Hector's chariot. He threw his spear and it hit Cebriones square in the back. The driver threw up his arms with a horrid scream and tumbled out of the chariot, rolling in the dirt. Hector had to leap for the reins, gasping, and pull the horses in. He had no time to mourn for his driver, a lifelong friend who had helped him tame horses on this same plain long before the invaders arrived. He pulled the horses up and leaped from the chariot as Patroclus sped down on him again, another spear in his hand.

"I see who you are now," Hector shouted, even though Patroclus could not hear him. "You will pay dearly for killing Cebriones."

Patroclus fired another spear, but Hector easily evaded it as Automedon wheeled the chariot around again. Patroclus shouted at him to halt, and when he did so Patroclus leaped from the chariot, sword in hand. He wanted to meet Hector in an equal contest of fighting and slay him. He felt invincible.

A terrible pain in his right shoulder almost dropped Patroclus and his helmet flew from his head. He wheeled, gasping, and saw the Trojan warrior Euphorbus in front of him, shaking his fist at him, smiling hideously. He had cast his spear at Patroclus from behind, striking him in the upper shoulder and knocking his helmet loose. Patroclus staggered, blood in his mouth, reaching for the helmet of Achilles that was laying in the dust. He scooped it up and stood back up just in time to see Euphorbus retreating. Patroclus spat at him and sneered in disgust; here was a man who struck from behind and then ran when confronted.

Patroclus turned and his eyes grew wide with shock. Hector was in front of him and before Patroclus could move, the prince of Troy drove his sword deep into his abdomen. Patroclus spit blood in a fountain, lurching forward, hands on the blade, staring at Hector, who smiled grimly at him and then twisted the sword.

Patroclus groaned loudly, knowing he was dead. He fell to his knees, vomiting blood, gaping at the ground. Hector's foot struck his side and pushed him to his back. Patroclus stared up as Hector leaned over him and jerked the sword free.

"You thought you could take Troy by pretending to be Achilles," growled Hector. "But I have killed you. You will not enter Troy, Patroclus; instead, vultures will feast on your body before the walls of the city you thought to sack. That is your reward for killing Cebriones, my lifelong friend."

Patroclus felt his life slipping away, yet still he responded.

"You boast now, Hector....but Achilles will avenge me," he said feebly.

"Not so!" shouted Hector, exultant in his moment of triumph. "I will slay Achilles just like I have slain you."

"It is Apollo who struck me down," Patroclus groaned. "He robbed me of....of...."

He tried to say more but he was too weak. He heard the tumult around him and the shouts from both sides. He knew that a terrible battle would now begin for his body, and he hoped the Myrmidons could save it and take it back to Achilles for an honorable burial. He lifted his head one last time, staring at the legs of the soldiers racing around him. And then Patroclus died.

Hector bent down and stripped him of his armor, taking the breastplate and helmet to his chariot. Already another driver had taken the place of Cebriones, and Hector motioned for him to take the armor into the city. He had won the greatest trophy anyone had gained in ten long years – the fabled armor of Achilles.

The Myrmidons were stunned and furious at what they saw. Hector was stripping the armor of Achilles from the body of Patroclus. They screamed hideously, dozens of them trying to get at the body of Patroclus.

But the Trojans, flush with new life, surged into the fray; many of them still thought it was Achilles lying dead just outside the gates, and they were in a frenzy, as well. They thought their champion had killed the greatest of the invaders and they were determined to take the body of Achilles into Troy so that everyone could mock it, and scorn it.

The battle was the most furious in the ten long years of war. No one backed off a single step, no one gave any quarter. Helmets flew with heads still inside them and arms were hacked off. Arrows flew into the melee from warriors who were too timid to enter the battle with swords as terrible screams, of both rage and pain, filled the air. Horses leaped and kicked, trying to escape the madness, and chariots overturned.

Hector was crazed, foaming at the mouth, eyes wide with a reborn fury. He mounted his chariot and sped off for another section of the battle, leaving the body of Patroclus for others to fight over. He was in search of men who lived, not the dead.

Menelaus confronted Eurphorus, who had been boasting that he had dealt the most telling blow on Patroclus, and nearly cut him in half with one vicious swing, sending his soul straight to Hades. Great Ajax stood over the body of Patroclus like a lion protecting its cubs, swinging his sword at whoever dared to venture close. Two Myrmidons grabbed the arms of Patroclus and began pulling the lifeless body from the fighting, but two Trojans grabbed his ankles and began pulling the opposite way. The body was jerked back and forth, and struck by countless sword thrusts aimed at living men.

"We cannot return to the camp without the body of Patroclus!" one Myrmidon shouted. "It would be better if the earth opened up and swallowed us all whole than to face Achilles with the body in Troy."

Finally, Menelaus fell back and found Antilochus, the son of Nestor and Patroclus's best friend outside of Achilles. Menelaus gripped him by the arms, his face and hands covered with the blood of other men.

"Go tell Achilles what has happened," he shouted. "He must come and frighten the Trojans away, or we risk losing the body!"

Achilles had been pacing the tent, unable to sit. He thought that Patroclus had been gone far longer than was necessary to force the Trojans back, and he knew the Trojan threat was now long gone from the Achaean encampment.

"Why doesn't he come back?" he mumbled, striking his fist on the banquet table where they had sat together so many nights.

He finally stormed out of his tent and stalked through the deserted camp. Only a few injured men and cooking women were there, and they glanced up at him in awe as he strode past them. He glanced up at the sun chariot and shook his head, muttering to Zeus. Soon, he was at the large gate, now battered and broken in spots from the tremendous fighting that had taken place around it. He gazed out over the plain and saw that the action was far beyond the Scamander, near the city of Troy. And a huge fluttering grew in his stomach as he saw a lone chariot racing toward him. As it drew nearer, he recognized it as belonging to Antilochus.

"Achilles!" shouted Antilochus, leaping from the chariot as the horses came to a halt, panting heavily and foaming at their mouths. "I bring terrible news.

"Patroclus has been killed by Hector and the battle for his body rages still. We need you to come to save the body from being taken into Troy!"

Achilles gaped at the young man that both he and Patroclus had come to like and admire. He stumbled forward, gripping Antilochus by the shoulders.

"What do you say?" he shouted. "Tell me again!"

Antilochus had to look away, unable to bear the pain in Achilles's face.

"Patroclus is dead, lord Achilles," he moaned. "Hector cut him down and has sent your armor into Troy. Now, the Trojans want to steal the body, too."

Achilles threw his arms upward, fingers reaching for the sun. A long, terrible scream issued from him and he stood as if frozen, his body shaking. He sank to his knees, still stretching for the heavens with his hands.

Antilochus fell back in fear; always he had felt awe whenever he was in the presence of Achilles and now he trembled, not knowing what to expect from him. He gaped at Achilles as he dropped his face to the ground and began pouring dirt over his golden locks. He moaned loudly, beating his head against the earth.

"It is my fault.....my fault!" screamed Achilles. "I should never have let him go. His heart is always concerned with others….never with himself."

Achilles moaned, pulling at his hair. And then, suddenly, he stood back up and stared at Antilochus. His face was streaked with tears and dirt, and he looked like a ghost from Hades, his face ashen white. He was wearing a gray tunic, belted at the waist, and he held out a hand to Antilochus.

"Give me your dagger," he groaned, his voice shrill. Antilochus gasped, afraid he meant to plunge it into his own heart and join Patroclus in the afterlife.

"Nooo…no," mumbled Antilochus, staggering back. "We need you,

Achilles. Do not go to Patroclus in Hades. We need you desperately in the world of the living."

Achilles' lips were drawn tight, and his eyes were on fire with hate.

"Give me your dagger, Antilochus, or I will take it from you," he said.

His hand shaking, Antilochus reached for his dagger and handed it to him. Achilles lifted it to his tunic and cut the fabric from his shoulder. The tunic fell to the ground, and Achilles stood naked except for his loin cloth, muscles rippling. He grabbed Antilochus' arm and moved to his chariot.

"Take me to Patroclus," he commanded, his voice hard and measured.

Antilochus nodded and the driver stepped out of the chariot, frightened by the appearance of Achilles. Antilochus grabbed the reins as Achilles stood next to him in the chariot. Together, they raced across the plain. They sped past hundreds of mutilated bodies, past the Scamander, nearly red with blood. They moved past overturned chariots and moaning men, many dying and others merely wounded. Achilles paid no attention to any of it, his eyes riveted on the Scaean Gates.

They could not get close to the body for the multitude of warriors fighting. Antilochus pulled the horses up and waited, his heart pounding, not knowing what Achilles would do.

Achilles jumped down from the chariot and walked in a daze toward the fighting. When men saw who came, they stood up and fell back, awestruck. The fighting ceased in the outer areas as both Trojan and Achaean stared at Achilles. Quickly, the fighting ceased all the way to where Patroclus lay in the dust.

Achilles stopped when he could go no further. He glanced all around and it seemed the sun was shining on him alone. He lifted his arms above his head.

"Patroclus!" he screamed. "I am here. Achilles is here!"

His voice sent a wave of shock through the Trojans. They stopped to gape numbly at him.

"Achilles is here!" he shouted again.

The Trojans began to back up, glancing about them. Those who had been trying to pull the body of Patroclus dropped his ankles and backed away, trembling in fear that Achilles may see them and charge.

"Achilles is here!" he shouted a third time.

Then he dropped his arms and stared out over the huge body of warriors. An eerie calm settled over the host. Ajax nodded grimly and stooped to pick up the body of Patroclus, battered almost beyond recognition. He slung the corpse over his right shoulder and began trudging away. The

Trojans offered no more resistance, still watching Achilles, and the Achaean army parted to let Ajax pass.

He moved to where Achilles stood, and their eyes met.

"Take him home, Ajax," said Achilles.

The giant nodded and lifted the body onto the back of the chariot of Antilochus. Achilles faced the Trojans again. Those in the front rank were in awe, wondering if they were indeed seeing a god or a godson.

"I am coming, Trojans," he said, his arm raised, pointing at them, his voice loud yet strangely calm. "Tell your women and children, tell your wise old men, and tell your warriors that Achilles will sit by his tent no more. We will mourn for Patroclus for nine days....and on the tenth day Achilles comes."

He paused.

"And first of all, I come for Hector."

With that, he turned and walked back to the chariot of Antilochus.

The Trojans broke ranks and filtered slowly back into their city, their spirits now broken and dashed. The longest and most bitter fighting of the entire war had been seen that day, and yet they knew the toughest days lay ahead – for Achilles was back, and he was coming as he had never come before.

The calm before the storm

Once again, as they had been doing on a regular basis for nearly ten years, the Trojans and Achaeans sent their women and old men out onto the battlefield to retrieve the bodies of the fallen soldiers, and to bring the wounded into their respective camps. The two groups scurried about the field, some picking up weapons that could be used again. A pall hung over the plain as never before; the smell of death was everywhere.

Achilles and Phoenix waited patiently in Achilles' tent for the body of Patroclus to be cleaned and brought to them, but at the last moment the old mentor departed, saying he was unable to face Patroclus in death.

Achilles had seen the battered corpse for only a few moments as it was lifted from the chariot and taken to the tent where bodies were prepared for burial. He stood rigid as the stretcher was carried past him, his eyes lingering for a moment on the once handsome face of his finest friend. He was surprised by the depth of his own emotions; he had always known he loved Patroclus like a brother, but seeing him in death had a stunning effect on Achilles.

After the body was brought to his tent, Achilles nodded to the men who had borne it and dismissed them. He moved haltingly inside the tent and, with the oil boat lamps flickering, stared down at Patroclus. He had been cleaned and wrapped in white linen. His face was badly bruised, his eyes shut, but the features were clearly those of Patroclus. Achilles threw his head back, tears streaming down his face, and moaned loudly.

"Why did you go? Why did you not remember my words of warning?" he mumbled. "Did you think the gods would let you take Troy alone, Patroclus?"

He sank into his chair and stared at the body for a long, long time. Then he left the tent and walked down the seashore, wanting to be alone.

It was dark and it had been one of the most exhausting days in the long war, for everyone on both sides. He saw the funeral pyres burning near the city of Troy, where most of the common soldiers were disposed of. Only the warlords and chiefs from noble families were given a prolonged mourning period, inside the gates. For the common soldier, the grieving came and went quickly, as the war would not wait for anyone but a prince or a king.

He sensed a deep gloom descending on the camp of the entire Achaean host, for the losses had been many. In addition, Patroclus was well loved by all who knew him. Nestor had said on several occasions that he was the most popular warrior in the entire camp, as he always had a smile and a good word for everyone. Living in the shadow of Achilles was not easy, Nestor had said, and yet Patroclus had managed to do so with grace.

As he reflected back on all the good days on Mount Pelion and in Phthia, of the cities they had sacked together, of the many adventures and battles where they had been side by side, Achilles sat in the grass, far down the beach, and began to weep softly.

"Patroclus, you were a friend like no other," he said, lifting his face and staring up at the heavens, dark and gloomy. "I promise I will not forget you, and that others will know your name for ages to come. Whenever men speak of Troy and of Achilles, they will also speak of Patroclus."

He lowered his head to his knees, which he had drawn up close, and sat huddled for a long time. He prayed to Zeus and to his mother, asking for guidance.

Finally, he stood and turned around to face the path he had come over some hours before. The fires of the Myrmidon camp were far off in the distance. He had walked further than he realized. He turned again and saw Troy dimly in the flickering light of dozens of funeral fires in front of the walls.

"Damned city," he thought. "What misery you have caused to so many people. But your day is coming quickly, just as mine is. I know our destinies are intertwined. You shall perish, I know; but the same fate awaits me, of that I am equally certain."

He had a fitful night of sleep, broken by repeated nightmares of savage combat. Twice the ghost of Patroclus appeared to him, reaching out and pleading with him to avenge his death. "Hector must pay," said Patroclus in a sorrowful voice. "You owe me that, Achilles."

The second time, the image of Patroclus was so clear that Achilles jerked awake, perspiration pouring down his face. Patroclus had accused him, pointing a finger at him, for not caring enough about him to deny him his request: "Why did you let me go onto the plain leading the Myrmidons, Achilles? Why did you not stop me, thereby saving me from this horrible end? Achilles....my death was caused by you!"

Achilles sat in the semi dark, the oil boat lamp casting strange images on the walls of the tent. He thought he saw a ghost moving in a far corner, and he called out for Patroclus and then to his mother, Thetis. But there was no one there and he laid back down, his hand on his dagger, clutching the hilt.

Dawn finally came. He awoke to the sounds of sad singing and for the first time he thought of Melisa, the woman Patroclus had loved, as he had loved Briseis. He walked to the tent opening and peered out, his throat thick and his mouth dry. He felt like he might vomit and he turned away, bent over, gripping his stomach. Then he straightened.

"I will not be a woman," he said to himself. "I am a warrior; death is part of life, and the acceptance of death is the part of being a warrior that all must face."

He stomped out of the tent and made his way through the camp, the brown loin cloth his only piece of clothing. Men and women fell back as they saw who it was that marched through the camp. He stopped in front of Automedon's tent and called out to him. Automedon came running, buckling on his belt and dagger sheath.

"Yes, Achilles," he muttered, standing before his warlord. He was still a handsome man, though in his fourth ten-year span of life. Seeing him gave comfort to Achilles and he reached out for his forearm.

"Automedon, old friend," he said. "Assemble all the chieftans and Phoenix. Tell them to come to my tent immediately." He turned and walked back the way he had come, head held high, sniffing the cool air that came in off the ocean. He remembered how much Patroclus had loved the sea, its smell and its embrace when he went swimming in it after a hard day's battle.

He waited for the chieftans to come to pay their respects to Patroclus. First was Phoenix, seeming more bent and aged than Achilles had ever seen him. He greeted Achilles sadly and walked over to where the body of Patroclus lay. He stood in silence for a long time, then walked slowly to a chair and sagged into it. Then the others filed in silently, ten in all. Only three of them had been chieftans when the war had started, but had moved up the ranks through the death of others and by their own valor. They paid their respects to Patroclus then stood before Achilles, waiting for his words.

"Patroclus is gone; we will never see him striding through our camp again, laughing and talking, as was his style," Achilles said, his voice soft and low. "But now....we need to plan funeral games for Patroclus, to honor him as a great warlord."

He gave orders to the various chiefs, one to plan the boxing and wrestling, another to plan the racing and spear throwing, another to plan the chariot race and yet another to organize the mock battle. To Automedon he gave the task of arranging the huge feast, which would take place after the games, as well as the sacrifices.

But to Phoenix, he gave the hardest task of all.

"Go to the high king of Mycenae and tell him I am ready to fight again," said Achilles. "Tell him I want nothing. Nothing at all. No gifts, no gold, no captives. I do not want it said that Achilles profited from the death of Patroclus. First, we will send Patroclus to the Elysian Fields in the manner befitting a great hero and warrior; then we will spend nine days in contests and feasting, to honor him."

He gritted his teeth and leaned on the heavy banquet table, all his weight on his knuckles, the thick arms bulging with muscles, long veins running down the front of each arm. He glanced around the tent at the men he had fought so many battles with.

"We will mourn nine days for Patroclus – and then we will make war like no one has ever seen before."

The Myrmidon chieftans nodded their approval. Only Automedon dared ask the question that many were thinking.

"Lord Achilles," he stammered. "Your armor....is gone. Hector has taken it. What will you wear into battle?"

Achilles stared at Automedon.

"That," he said, "has already been taken care of. You will see when the tenth day arrives and we take to our chariots."

The next morning, work began on a huge funeral pyre. Myrmidons went to Mount Ida to bring back wood on mules. It was built down the coast, out of view of the Trojans, something Achilles insisted on. Six horses and twelve cattle were slaughtered, their blood serving as a means of purifying the event. Four Trojan captives, two men and two women, were taken to the pyre, tied to it, and their throats slit.

Then, Patroclus was carried in on a stretcher, his body blue and stiff, his long, golden hair tied behind his head in a knot. Achilles walked behind the stretcher, tears pouring down his face. Behind him came Phoenix and Automedon and Melisa, followed by a hundred Myrmidons, and behind them nearly a thousand warriors and camp people. Achilles wore his red tunic, tied tight at the waist with a thick leather belt trimmed with gold, and around his shoulders he wore a long, white cape. A purple ribbon was tied around his head in mourning.

Two priests chanted for a long time. Achilles sang a short song, strumming his lyre, paying tribute to the exploits of Patroclus, who he called "the finest of the Achaeans" and also "the best-liked of the Achaeans."

Each of the Myrmidon warlords cut a lock of hair from his own head and placed it near Patroclus. Achilles had Melisa hack off a length of his hair and he placed it gently over the dead man's body. Achilles was handed a torch and he set the funeral pyre on fire. He stood back, eyes fixed straight ahead as the flames grew and grew. Patroclus was at the top, nearly ten feet off the ground. It took some while for the flames to reach him, and Achilles had to look away as they began to consume him. Phoenix came to his side and touched his shoulder and they moved slowly away.

Achilles walked along side the sea, tears still streaming down his face. And then he stopped and looked at Troy in the distance.

"Somewhere in that city, Hector lives," he mumbled. "Tonight, Hector can hold his wife and drink his wine and laugh with his friends. But very soon, Hector dies!"

When the great fire had finally died away, the ashes and bones of Patroclus were gathered by servants and placed in a vase from his own tent. Nearby, a mound of earth was fashioned and the vase was carefully placed in the mound. Here his mortal remains would rest throughout eternity, while his soul wandered through the Elysian Fields.

What followed were the most lavish funeral games yet held in the ten years the Achaeans had been at Troy. They moved out of the encampment, beyond the walls onto the plain after receiving word from the Trojans that they would honor the long truce. In truth, the Trojans were glad of the respite from war and filtered up to Mount Ida, restoring their water chests with cool mountain water and picking basketfuls of figs and olives.

But there was also a sense of doom enveloping the city. Men met in taverns at night, whispering that Achilles would soon be back at war, in a new spirit of anger that had them all frightened. Women moved quietly through the streets to the seven temples, praying to their gods and their goddesses that somehow Achilles be placated.

Priam fretted in his palace, staring at Hector every time he saw his son walk by. Hector knew what was on the minds of everyone, that he would soon be sought out by Achilles for single combat. He talked lightly and smiled to all who greeted him, clasping their forearms and presenting an attitude of confidence.

"The war is going well," he told everyone. "We have had many good victories of late and the invaders have suffered great losses. I think Zeus favors us now."

But in his heart he knew what was coming. He spent much of the nine days with his wife, holding her tight late at night, staring into the small fire in their hearth, stroking her long, brown hair. He sensed how nervous she was; he saw it in her eyes and heard it in her voice. He also picked up his young son, just four years old, whenever he saw him. He loved to hold Astyanax high and dream of the grand future that would some day be his as the grandson of Priam, the son of Hector, tamer of horses.

But finally he too went to the walls, on the seventh day of the truce, to peer out across the Troad, watching the invaders maneuvering near the funeral pyres. Standing next to Aeneas, the two friends leaned on the ramparts high above the plain where so many of their comrades had died over ten years.

"What does it all mean, Hector?" asked Aeneas at one point. "We fight and kill and burn the bodies; they fight and kill and burn the bodies. Ten long years and nothing is gained, it seems. Is it all for the pleasure of the gods? Do they like to sit on their golden thrones on Mount Olympus and watch these foolish mortals destroy one another?"

Hector was about to answer when he saw four women approaching. It was Helen, with three handmaidens. He saw that she was coming to see him and he straightened, smiling as she approached. Her hair was a somewhat darker than when she first came to Troy, but she had the same beautiful figure, with ample breasts, a trim waist and long legs. She wore a blue chiton and white sandals. She had little bells hanging from her ear lobes that jingled softly as she moved and her lips were full and red. Her blue eyes had a way of looking deep into your eyes. Hector had to admit that she was the most beautiful woman he had ever seen, even though he loved his Andromache deeply and felt she was very beautiful, as well.

"Hector…. Aeneas," she said, bowing slightly to them both. "What a delight to find Troy's two greatest champions here at the same time."

Hector smiled at her, as he was accustomed to her flattery. It was a guileful style that Helen had learned early in life, to compliment her great beauty. Aeneas had not spent a great deal of time near the wife of Alexandros. Like the Myrmidons, Aeneas was clean shaven and his bare cheeks flushed a bit when her eyes caught his and held them.

"Helen, it's good to see you," said Hector. "Aeneas and I were just discussing the merits of war and warfare."

She arched an eyebrow, smiling at them. Her handmaidens stood behind her, also enjoying the opportunity to be with such famous men. Everyone in Troy knew of the exploits of Hector and Aeneas had earned a solid reputation as a warrior, as well. And both were handsome men, well proportioned with a graceful way of moving.

"Well, I think men need a means to express themselves," she said.

"They are always in pursuit of glory and fame, and the battlefield is the surest place to find it."

"Not all men," said Hector. "It seems that some prefer to sit with their women and dream of romance while their brothers are in the field, facing death."

She smiled faintly at his words.

"Yes, Alexandros is.... not so eager to fight as are you, Hector. Or Aeneas. I have chided him many a time, but you know how he can be."

Hector nodded at her and turned back to gaze at the Achaean camp again. Helen moved next to him, standing so close that her left breast touched his right arm. He noticed it, of course, but said nothing; nor did he remove his arm. He knew she was frightened by what she saw when she came to the wall, and that she needed to feel his strength.

"They are still mourning?" she asked.

"Yes," said Hector.

"How much longer will it go on?" she asked.

"Two more days," said Hector.

She turned to look up at him and he glanced down into her eyes. He felt a tightening in his throat; she surely was the daughter of Aphrodite, the love goddess, he thought. I see how Alexandros could not resist her.

"And then.... Achilles will fight again?" she asked, searching his face.

"Most likely he will," said Hector. "He has been severely wounded by the death of his great friend." He shrugged. "And he knows I have brought his armor into Troy."

There was a pause in the conversation and Aeneas stepped forward.

"We have several men who can stand up to Achilles," he said, nodding his head, in an effort to show both Helen and Hector that he was not afraid of Achilles' return. "They say he is the son of a sea goddess and is invulnerable, but I do not believe that."

"Yet, they say he has not suffered a single wound of any kind in ten years," said Helen.

"All that means is that he has not come face to face with Hector, or me," said Aeneas, chuckling. Helen laughed too; even Hector forced a wry smile. Then Helen placed her hand on Hector's arm.

"Be careful, Hector," she said. "You are Troy's heart. The city can not stand long without you to guard it."

He stared down at her, a lump in his throat. She ran her hand softly over his thick muscles and then she turned and left, her handmaidens following her. Hector and Aeneas watched her slip away, down the wall space, until she was lost from view.

"Some times, I think she is a goddess, come down to live with mortals....and to taunt us," said Aeneas.

Hector placed a hand on his friend's shoulder.

"I've thought that myself at times," he said.

The funeral games of Patroclus brought out the finest athletes of the invaders' camp. Five champions entered the chariot races and the horses pounded over the plain, with Diomedes coming in first, defeating Antilochus and Menelaus along the way. Achilles awarded to him a beautiful slave he had captured along with Briseis, and a three-footed cauldron fashioned of gold.

Epeius, second only to Ajax in size, won the boxing match and received a strong horse for his efforts, while Odysseus and a powerful warrior named Milos tied in the wrestling match, neither being able to throw the other down. Milos tried to overpower the smaller warrior, but Odysseus showed his great wrestling skills by outmaneuvering Milos and nearly tripping him to the earth twice. Achilles gave them each a golden tripod and a beautiful red tunic.

Odysseus also won the race when the lesser Ajax, in the lead, tripped and fell near the finish line. The last event, a mock battle, was the most daring and drew just two contestants. Diomedes and Ajax faced each other without armor, with the rules being that the first man to draw blood would be declared the winner. All of the soldiers were very interested in this spectacle and even the Trojans tried to watch from their walls far away. It was a very serious undertaking, as both men considered themselves to be the greatest fighter after Achilles. They feinted and parried with their spears, banging their shields together. Ajax towered over Diomedes, but the smaller man was scowling and chanting the entire time, not intimidated by the size of Ajax.

They fought a long time, but neither could gain a solid advantage and it appeared they would continue until one of them was maimed, or worse. Finally, Achilles intervened, halting the contest and praising them both. The prize was the beautiful armor of Sarpedon, whom Patroclus had killed just before his own death. Achilles had rammed the spear of Patroclus into the ground and hung the breast armor, sword sheath and shield from the spear, in view for all to see. He divided the spoils between the two heroes and they nodded their approval.

When the games were over, a huge feast was held and then it was time to prepare for battle once again. On the last day of the truce, Achilles walked to his tent, Phoenix and the Myrmidons steaming along behind him. He turned to face them at the entrance.

"Tomorrow, we fight," he said. "Be ready at dawn."

Then he disappeared into his tent. He walked to the chest by his cot, the one he had brought all the way from Phthia. He knealt and opened it. He stared at the armor that Peleus had given him those many years ago.

"You said I would wear this armor on the most special of days," he whispered. "That day has finally come, father."

He pulled on the armor, even putting on the helmet. He walked to the tent opening and heard a huge roar. His men had not left and were still standing there, waiting. He strode down the beach, toward the tent of the high king. Phoenix had arranged the meeting on the final day of the truce and Agamemnon knew he was coming to make his demands. He could do nothing but wait.

Achilles marched through the various camps – past the Argives and the Athenians, past the Locrians, the Salamites and the Ithacans, and through five other camps. Everyone fell back in awe as he moved swiftly by.

Agamemnon sat in his tent, drinking wine, staring nervously at his heralds standing watch outside the tent. Menelaus, Ajax, Odysseus, Nestor and Diomedes were all with him, for he was afraid to face Achilles alone, not knowing what kind of a temper he would be in. At last, the heralds came hurrying into the tent.

"Achilles comes," one of them said, wringing his hands. "He comes...."

Agamemnon sat down his wine cup and adjusted his long, purple robe around his shoulders. He fidgeted with the huge ring on his middle finger, his eyes glued to the opening of the tent. When the figure of Achilles filled the opening, he swallowed heavily and stood up.

"Welcome, prince Achilles," he said stiffly. "It has been a long time since this tent was honored by the presence of the best of the Achaeans."

Achilles stared hard at the high king from his eye openings in the great helmet. Agamemnon had never seen such grand armor and he was visibly shaken. He wanted to go to Achilles and grasp his forearms in a token of respect and friendship, but he was too intimidated by the warrior facing him. He thought quickly how the Trojans would feel the next day when they saw Achilles in the field, and he had to fight off a wry smile of satisfaction. He dared not show any expressions until he could discover what mood Achilles was in.

"I have prepared many gifts for you, Achilles," he said. "More prizes than any warrior has ever seen from our ten years at Troy. Come see for yourself; they are piled high in the waiting room at the back of the tents.

"And Briseis if waiting for you, of course. I have not touched her in any way and she still loves you. She is ready to go back to your tent, as well."

Achilles said nothing, his eyes never leaving the face of the high king. At last Agamemnon swallowed heavily, a look of anguish on his face.

"Are you....not satisfied by all that I have offered to you?" he croaked, lifting his hands weakly in frustration.

"Give your gifts, or keep them, Agamemnon," said Achilles, using the high king's name for the first time. "I have no interest in them; not even Briseis. I only have one interest in life now, and that is to avenge Patroclus. Only the death of Hector will satisfy me. I will lead the Myrmidons into battle tomorrow. As for you and your trinkets, do with them as you will."

He turned and strode out of the tent as Agamemnon collapsed into his chair, shaken and exhausted by the emotional ordeal.

Hector was up at dawn in his small sleeping room. The other side of the bed was empty and he went looking for Andromache. He found her in the small adjoining room, kneeling in front of a statute of Athena, eyes shut, fingers intertwined and locked tight, lips barely moving. He listened to her prayers and then came up behind her, gently touching her hair.

"Ooohhhhh!" she gasped, startled. When she twisted and looked up, he saw that she had been crying. He lifted her up to him and embraced her, his face deep in her hair.

"How long have you been awake?" he asked.

"All night," she whispered, her voice hoarse. "Hector...."

He held her away from him, gazing at her face.

"You are so beautiful," he said. He kissed her gently, and then hard. She swooned into him. Then he took her hand and led her into their son's room. Astyanax was still sleeping and Hector could hardly look away from him.

"The future king of Troy needs his sleep," said Hector, glancing down at Andromache. He moved away from her, back to his room, and began putting on his armor. He stopped suddenly, as though a god had grabbed him by the throat. He could scarcely breathe and had to swallow hard twice. He was shaken to his soul; was it fear that had suddenly, for the first time in his life, touched him?

He finished dressing, shaken by the feeling. He snapped on his greaves and walked to the main room. Andromache was sitting there, holding Astyanax, who still had sleep in his eyes. Hector held his gray helmet with the red horsehair, and Astyanax pulled back from it, whimpering. Hector set it aside and took the boy into his arms. Andromache stood too and leaned into Hector, needing to feel his strength this morning, of all mornings.

"Please, Hector….don't fight Achilles," she whispered, staring up at him. "Let his anger cool before you meet him. Let him fight others for two, three days before you face him. Please, Hector, do this for me and for Astyanax."

Hector frowned and set the boy down, looking at his wife of many years.

"Andromache, how can I ask others to do what I won't do? Achilles wants to fight me, and only me. It was I who killed Patroclus; I am proud of that."

He paused, glancing around the room.

"I am not afraid of Achilles," he said. "He is a good man, but so am I."

"They say he cannot be injured," she croaked, hands moving to her mouth, shaking. "They say he is the son of a goddess."

"He can be injured, and killed, for that matter," said Hector with finality. He picked up his helmet and moved toward the door. He looked back at her. She stood trembling uncontrollably, and he wished he could run to her and hold her one last time, but he couldn't. It might weaken him and he needed all the strength he could muster. He knew this would be by far the most trying day of his life.

"Fix my favorite supper," he said. "I will be a hungry man after today's fighting."

And then he was gone. Andromache ran to the window and peered out, watching her husband move down the street, toward the Scaean Gates. Other warriors were saluting him and falling in behind him. She staggered back to the bed she shared with Hector and fell onto it, sobbing softly.

The Moment of Truth

As he stepped out of his tent and faced the bright light of dawn, Achilles felt a raw power moving through his entire body. He had eaten sparingly before retiring, because he wanted to feel the hunger this morning….to feel lean and light, like a lion on Mount Pelion about to pounce on an unsuspecting lamb. He drank some heavily watered wine when he first arose, knowing his body needed liquid. And then he put on the splendid armor again. That which had years ago seemed so heavy to him was now so light he did not even notice how different it was.

He hefted the Pelion ash in one hand, his war helmet in the other. His blonde locks, cut short by Melisa ten days earlier, were corralled by a band of red cloth, tied tightly at the back and in the front. He wanted there to be no chance of flying hair hindering his vision today.

The Myrmidon camp was alive with activity and he moved to the smoldering ruins of a campfire. He stood straight as a mighty spear, searching for Automedon. He heard the horses behind him and swiveled to see his chariot moving toward him. Automedon was naked to the waist, with a rope over his shoulders, holding the reins tightly as the two black horses, Xanthus and Balius, pranced, rearing their heads. They had caught the excitement that was in the morning air and they were anxious to run.

"Lord Achilles!" shouted Automedon, breathless with anticipation, his arm muscles quivering. "We await your command."

Achilles glanced around the camp. Warriors were racing to him; soon he was surrounded by more than one hundred warriors in black armor. Only a few of them had been with him from the outset, all ten years. Others had come as reinforcements from Phthia through the years.

"Today, we avenge Patroclus!" he yelled, the veins standing out in his neck. He glanced around, his eyes falling on each man in front. He pulled on his war helmet and then he rammed the Pelion Ash aloft. Then war cry of the Myrmidons roared from his lips.

"Alilia…alilia….alilia…..alilia….alilia….."

Agamemnon was in the best spirits he had been in for a long time. He was also up early, dressing for war and marshaling his troops. When he saw the Myrmidons marching down the beach, heading for the gates and the plain beyond, he smiled over at his brother, who had joined him to break the fast. They had eaten well in anticipation of a great day on the field. The other warlords came to the tent and were standing behind Agamemnon as the Myrmidons went past.

"I don't like that man," Agamemnon muttered to Menelaus as he watched the chariot of Achilles speed by, "but what a sight this is. The Trojans will surely be brought down; maybe we will even ride into Troy before the day is over."

The entire Achaean host, including all of the soldiers who were not too hobbled by injury to fight, was ready to go. Soon, the entire army was moving across the plain.

Hector had mobilized his army as well, and the Trojans now advanced across the plain from the opposite direction, far from the confines of the city. The two vast armies neared the Scamander and the Trojans were filled with anxiety and fear when they saw the black armor of the Myrmidons and the chariot of Achilles in the lead.

Achilles was searching desperately for the gray armor of Hector and the white horses that marked his chariot. Automedon leaned forward, gasping from the sheer power of the moment, his temples pounding. Suddenly, within one hundred yards of the Trojan advance troops, he cracked the whips and the horses took off.

A scream of hysteria broke out among the Trojans who saw they had been picked as the first to feel the wrath of Achilles. They broke and fled, running over other Trojans who, in turn, turned and ran. The war cry of the Myrmidons ripped the air and suddenly the entire field was a surging mass of fighting men.

Automedon took the chariot directly into a pack of soldiers as Achilles leaned over the rail, swinging his sword in powerful strokes. Warriors, Trojans and allies, fell like stalks of wheat before a sickle. The Myrmidons were in a blood frenzy and Agamemnon was close behind, fighting wildly and filled with confidence. Diomedes, not wanting to be lost in the shadow of Achilles, veered off to the right, with Ajax going to the left. Idomeneus followed behind Achilles, his Cretan warriors marching to the sounds of a loud flute; Ajax the Lesser followed his namesake, his long snake curled up on the floor of his chariot. But Odysseus was content to hang back and watch, smiling slyly and picking his spots.

Achilles could not get enough. He cut down at least twenty soldiers in the first swing through the lines and then they were up to the banks of the Scamander. He leaped out of the chariot and his Myrmidons followed him; they caught hundreds of the enemy in the swift running stream. It became a massacre, Trojans dropping their weapons and fleeing, the Myrmidons and Achaeans chasing after them and cutting them down. Soon, the riverbank was strewn with armor and weapons and overturned chariots, while the water was choked with bodies and was turning red.

With no enemies left standing Achilles surged out of the swollen river and climbed back into the chariot. Automedon moved the horses toward Troy while Achilles scanned the plain, hoping to find someone foolish enough to face him in single battle. He threw back his head and gave the war cry again, and scoured the area in front of him. Suddenly, he stopped his search. He saw a stout warrior in splendid armor off to his right, just dispatching an Achaean solider. He recognized the chariot and jumped from his own chariot, yelling out to him.

"Aeneas, friend of Hector….come test yourself against Achilles," he shouted.

Aeneas turned, gasping, blood running down his arms, his spear still in the abdomen of his foe. He placed a foot on the man's chest and jerked the spear free, then faced Achilles. He had no time to experience fear; he was aware that his heart was pounding like nothing he had ever experienced before but he was far too proud a man to run away at this point.

"So, you are Achilles," he mumbled, in a dialect that Achilles recognized as Dardanian. "I hear you are the son of a god; well, so am I, Achilles. My mother is Aphrodite, or so they say."

"The goddess of love can not protect you here," growled Achilles, lifting his spear. "This is the playground of the god of war. Ares rules today. Prepare to enter the Underworld, Aeneas."

Aeneas lifted his shield but did not advance. He had heard many stories of the power of Achilles' arm and he was bracing himself for the throw. But it never came; instead, Achilles advanced right up to him, parrying with the spear as if taunting him. Aeneas moved back, using his shield to block the spear thrusts. He saw Achilles grinning and he fired his own spear. Achilles ducked beneath the cast and drew back his spear. He faked a throw, causing Aeneas to fall back – then Achilles threw the spear with all his might. It crashed against Aeneas' shield with such force that Aeneas fell backwards, tumbling to the ground. He rolled and stood up, dazed. Achilles was on him with drawn sword. They rammed into each other and Aeneas was knocked back again, but managed to keep his feet.

He was stunned by the power of the man he was facing. Never had he felt such terrible blows. Suddenly, a great fear gripped his throat, but still he would not lay down and die like a dog. He grimaced and mumbled a prayer to Aphrodite, knowing his end was at hand.

Achilles was unaware that the Dardanians had seen Aeneas was in dire trouble and were racing to his side. Suddenly, he glanced about and saw that there were twenty warriors flanking him. Aeneas sighed heavily as the warriors moved around him, shields raised high. One of the Dardanians spoke to Achilles.

"You can not slay us all, great Achilles," he said. "And we will not let Aeneas fight you alone. We are going to retreat; do not follow."

Achilles smiled faintly and lowered his sword arm. He admired the loyalty these men were showing to their warlord. They knew he could cut down many of them in the front if he was so inclined, but they were willing to die for Aeneas. But it was Hector he wanted, not Aeneas. He raised his sword in a salute.

"Go, Aeneas," he said. "You have good men. We will meet again another day."

He saw his chariot standing still some ways off, Automedon battling with several soldiers trying to control the horses. He sprinted toward the chariot. When the Trojans saw him coming they turned and ran off.

"What happened to you?" shouted Achilles, climbing into the chariot. "Why did you not follow me?"

"I was cut off," Automedon shouted. "Where to now?"

Achilles surveyed the field, then pointed toward Troy.

Let's find Hector....or take Troy, whichever happens first," he shouted.

The chariot jerked into motion. Achilles leaned over the railing again, swinging his sword, shouting the way cry. Everywhere he went, the soldiers turned to flee. He looked back over his shoulder at one point and saw the plain was full of Achaeans, chariots racing every direction, men jumping over bodies and shaking their swords and spears. It was a great day for the Achaeans!

Priam stood on the wall, shaking in fear for his warriors and his city. He had never been witness to a full rout like this in the long war. He could see Achilles and his Myrmidons headed toward the city and he sank against the wall, weak in the knees. His aides rushed to his side, gripping his elbows. He gaped at them.

"Order the gates opened," he said weakly. "Save the soldiers. They are all flying before Achilles. There is no hope!"

The large Scaean gates swung open and the soldiers poured in. They ran into each other and over each other in their haste; women waiting for them on the other side screamed and ran to each soldier they recognized. Troy was in a panic.

Hector raced across the plain from the west, where he had been fighting against the men of Diomedes and Odysseus. He was bloodied, but not from wounds of his own. He had killed or wounded at least ten men, and was arm weary and sore. He tried to rally the troops but now he knew it was useless. He stared ahead at the wide-open gates as his driver kept the horses racing full speed. He was in the last ranks of the flight.

Hector passed through the gates and heard them swinging shut behind him as men strained on the ropes that moved the massive wooden doors. He climbed down from his chariot and removed his war helmet, shaken at the sight of the defeated city. Nearly everyone was wailing and men were slumped against the inner wall, stripping off their war gear, bloodied and broken in spirit. Priam came to him, with twenty followers in long robes trailing behind him. His father looked older and more frail than he had ever seen him.

"Praise be to Apollo, and to Zeus!" Priam said, falling into him and embracing him. "I thought Achilles would find you." Hector stiffened at the words and pushed the old man gently from him.

"So even you think I am not his equal," he said. Priam saw that his words had wounded his son and shook his head sadly.

"You are the equal of any man who ever fought, even the mighty Heracles," said Priam. "But who knows who the gods will favor. Today, they favor the invaders."

A tremendous shout erupted from the wall above them, and they both threw back their heads and gaped up. Warriors were shouting down at them.

"What are you saying?" shouted Hector.

One of them ran down the stairs and came to Hector, breathless.

"Achilles has stopped before the walls. He is shouting for you to come meet him in single combat," said the warrior. "What….do we tell him?"

Priam swallowed hard, eyeing his son with horror.

Hector stared at the old man and the men behind him, all looking sorrowfully at the ground. Then he glanced around him. All the battered warriors and even the women were watching him. It seemed the entire world, even the gods on Mount Olympus, were anxious to see what Hector would do.

He looked the warrior in the eyes.

"Open the gates," he said to him.

Priam screamed and grabbed his arms, but Hector shook him off.

"Father, I have no choice. I must go, or all of Troy will think I am a coward and then the city will surely lose all hope."

Priam shrunk back, nearly faint. Hector pulled his war helmet back on and walked to the gates, which were slowly creaking open. The moment of truth had arrived.

Achilles was waiting in his chariot, Automedon breathless beside him. The Myrmidons were standing a long distance off, and some were even taking off their heavy helmets. The rest of the Achaean army was now arriving, thousands of them, stopping behind the Myrmidons. They knew that something incredible was transpiring before their very eyes.

When Achilles saw the warrior in gray armor moving out from the gates, he smiled grimly and stepped down from the chariot. He grabbed his Pelion ash, which he had saved for this moment alone, using other spears all day long. He began walking toward Hector.

Priam turned to the stunned warriors sitting all around him, spreading his arms out wide.

"Do not let him be out there alone!" he shouted. "Stand, you sons of Troy, and go with your champion!"

Many of them leaped up, pulled their helmets on and hurried out the gates behind Hector. They were shocked at the scene that greeted them. The entire Achaean army was spread out before them, but the warriors were no longer eager to fight. They stood motionless, whispering to one another, transfixed by what was about the take place in front of them.

Hector and Achilles moved toward each other, neither aware of anything else that was going on around them. Their eyes were riveted on one another; but while Hector saw what looked to be like a god approaching him, Achilles saw only the man who had killed his best friend. One came to the battle hoping to somehow survive, the other came with the utmost confidence that revenge was near.

They stopped ten yards from each other.

"When you slew Patroclus you boasted of your might and what you would do to me if ever we met," growled Achilles. "I was told that by men who were there. Now is the time to make good on your boast, Hector. But, I say to you....prepare to enter the Underworld, for that is where I will soon send you."

Hector stared at the warrior in the magnificent armor and he felt his legs weakening.

"Let the gods decide who they favor today, Achilles," he said, his voice low and firm. "But if they should favor me, I vow to return your armor and your body to the Achaeans, so you may have a decent funeral. And should they favor you, I ask that you do the same, that you allow Troy to honor me, as well."

Achilles glared at the man he had come to despise so deeply and he felt the anger rushing up inside him. The power was flowing into him. He welcomed the surge as though Patroclus had come to life in front of him. A hot tremor ran down his back and his muscles twitched several times. When he spoke again, his voice sounded like thunder to all who heard.

"Hector, don't speak to me of any terms or conditions. Between a lion and the lamb there is no agreement, nor is there between you and me!"

He lifted his spear and gave his war cry.

And then something unimaginable happened – something so shocking that not even the gods and goddesses, leaning forward in eager anticipation from their perches on high, could have ever thought it was possible.

Hector turned and ran. He did not stop to reason why. He simply began to run, carrying his spear at his side, his shield dangling off a shoulder. He raced along the high wall, his mind filled with terror. Dimly, he heard the roaring all around him, as if the sea had come up and engulfed him, the heavy waters pouring over him, the sea god roaring at him. His head throbbed and he could barely feel his feet hitting the earth as he ran. Those on the walls of Troy gaped down at the scene, their hands gripping the top of the thick stones, not willing to accept what their eyes were telling them. Priam had not come up, but heard the terrible screaming and fainted into the arms of the men who were at his side. They carried him to a stone bench and laid the king on it, hovering over him, fearful that his heart had given out.

The Achaeans stood transfixed at first, and then raised their spears with a mighty roar. It was the loudest roar ever heard on the plain of Troy in all the hundreds of years the city had stood, in one form or another.

Hector felt his heart pounding as though it might leap out of his chest and a thick dryness possessed his mouth. He wanted to quit running, but he could not. His legs would not obey him. He ran to the end of the wall and then cut to the right and raced along another section, glancing back over his shoulder. Achilles was close behind him, saying nothing, grimly pursuing, like the god of death.

Hector raced along the back side of the city, past the watch towers and the wide trail he had often taken up to Mount Ida, back in the peaceful days….how many years ago that now seemed. He ran to the third corner and then turned and raced along the final wall. He turned again and was back in front of the city. He saw his own troops staring at him in silence. He gaped beyond them, into some gray future… where he saw his wife, Andromache, alone in a courtyard, sobbing, with their small son at her side.

And then he stopped running. He came to an abrupt halt, and turned to face Achilles. His lungs were heaving from the exertion; he could have gone longer, but he was finished with running. Achilles stopped too, staring at him with no expression.

"It is time," said Hector, gasping. "Let us see who the gods truly favor today."

Achilles threw the Pelion ash spear with such force that it knocked the shield from Hector's grip and sent it flying into the dust. Hector bent to retrieve the shield and circled slowly as Achilles smiled at him, holding his sword high. Hector thew his spear, but Achilles knocked it away with his sword without a glance. As Achilles advanced on him, Hector drew his sword and stood his ground. For one brief moment, he remembered the stories he had heard from those who had seen Achilles in action and how they talked about the force of his blows.

Then Hector felt the force, over and over. Achilles was in front of him, slamming tremendous blows onto Hector's upraised shield. Hector had never felt such power, but he suddenly felt a surge of pride and he swung back with power. His sword banged into Achilles' sword and their bodies collided. They gaped into the other's eyes, the war's two greatest warriors, bent on destroying each other.

Achilles slid his right leg between Hector's legs and pushed with his hips. Hector flew back and tumbled to the ground, rolling to his side. He had been caught in an old wrestling trick. He leaped to his feet just in time as Achilles was on him again. He swung wildly at Achilles, sideways, trying to take his head off at the neck.

It was a fatal error. Achilles leaned to his right and with all the strength of his body rammed his sword into the open spot under Hector's left arm, where the armor stopped. The blade drove deep into the hard flesh, and Hector screamed in horror, jerking away, desperately trying to stop the blade from penetrating further. Achilles pushed into him, forcing the blade in deeper; Hector clutched at the blade with his hands, until the blood ran down his fingers.

With an incredible burst of strength, Achilles jerked the sword upward and lifted Hector off the ground and then slammed him to the earth. Achilles stood over him, gaping down, his mouth grimly shut. Hector writhed on his side, staring up at Achilles, his hands a bloody mess, still gripping the blade. He could feel the blade deep inside him, and his eyes rolled backwards. He fought for his breath and knew he was slipping fast.

"The spirit of Patroclus can rest now," gasped Achilles. He placed his foot on Hector's quaking body and ripped the sword free. The pain was excruciating; Hector tried to speak, but sank back to the ground. The pride of Troy, the tamer of horses, was dead.

An eerie silence had engulfed the field all during the battle. Now, a tremendous roar rose up from the Achaean ranks and the warlords all ran forward to congratulate Achilles and to leer at the body of the Trojan they all feared the most. Several stabbed at his body with swords, to see if he was dead or acting. Achilles motioned to Automedon, who ran to his side.

"Give me the rope you brought along," he mumbled. Automedon took it from his shoulder and handed it to Achilles, who bent low and wrapped the thick strand around the ankles of Hector, tying it tight. He pulled off Hector's helmet, looking at his full face for the first time. The others gathered around closer, staring down. Someone spit on the body and others shouted at Hector as if he could still hear them.

Without a word, Achilles walked to the chariot and tied the other end of the rope to the back edge. Then he climbed into the chariot. Automedon climbed up beside him, his eyes wide.

"Drag the body before the walls of this damned city!" commanded Achilles, his voice cold and hard. "This man killed my best friend, the finest man I ever knew, and boasted that he would also kill Achilles. Let's show the Trojans their champion now."

Automedon grinned and cracked the whip. The horses bolted, then took off.

The spectators on the wall reeled in horror as the chariot raced in front of them, the lifeless body of Hector, naked and battered, bouncing and flopping along behind. A large cloud of dust rose up as the chariot streaked by. Men hung their heads in sorrow, unable to continue watching and women wailed loudly, tearing their hair and beating their breasts. Hecuba and Andromache had received word in the palace that Hector and Achilles were in a duel to the death, and they had come racing to the wall together, holding hands, weeping. They stumbled down the stone walkway on the wall, gaping onto the field, hands over their mouths, not believing what they were seeing.

"Hector, my Hector!" screamed Andromache. "Nooo....Apollo.... you must .... stop this!" She fainted, sagging to the cold stones as women flocked around her. They lifted her up and carried her off the wall, taking her back to her house.

Hecuba's watery eyes stared down on the scene, and then she too fainted.

A deathly doom settled over all of Troy. With Hector dead, the fighting spirit was gone. No one wanted to venture out of the city.

For two days, Achilles showed up on the plain, dragging the body of Hector past the shocked citizens again. Then he retreated into his tent, leaving the body of Hector outside behind a stack of wood. Agamemnon and the other warlords met daily in the high king's tent to discuss the situation.

"How can we fight if the Trojans won't even come out of the city?" shouted Agamemnon. "Now they are so afraid of Achilles that we may have to wait another ten years to get them to fight again."

Ajax sat slumped in a chair, nursing a cup of wine.

"I think he should give Hector's body back to the Trojans for burial," he said at last. "Hector was a great warrior; I barely defeated him in our single combat. He deserves more respect than to lay unburied by a pile of wood."

"Who's going to tell that to Achilles?" asked Idomeneus. "Whoever it is had better be prepared to defend their life. I, for one, will not face him with such a request. I don't think Achilles is in his right mind now."

"I think it's time we considered cutting off the city from its supply route and from Mount Ida," said Odysseus. "We can starve them out, if we have to, without even throwing another spear."

None of the others were interested in that plan at all.

"What glory is there in defeating your foe by starvation?" sneered Diomedes. "I'd rather pack up my ship and sail home than do that."

The others agreed with him, and Odysseus merely shrugged. He knew how to end this war but he also knew the others would never agree to such a plan.

"Who can understand Achilles, anyway?" continued Agamemnon. "He quits fighting because I take one slave girl from him. Then, I offer him more treasures than any one man could possibly hope for….and he says he's not interested. I tried to have the heralds deliver the items I promised him and he turned them away."

He paused, taking another long drink of sweetened wine.

"What kind of a man is this I am forced to deal with?"

"You never did understand him," said Odysseus. "He is different than other kings and princes. Far different."

"I know that, Odysseus!" shouted Agamemnon. "I just don't know how to deal with him, is what I'm saying."

Odysseus smiled faintly, so that the high king would not see him. He knew that only he understood Achilles even a little bit, and he had to work hard at it. But, it was worth the effort, he told himself. Very well worth the effort.

They fell into another foul mood, drinking and muttering well into the night.

In Troy, Priam was also in counsel. He had fallen apart at the sight of his favorite son being so battered, but two days after Hector's death

Priam somehow found the strength that had made him an effective ruler for nearly forty years. He called twenty of his sons to his chambers, along with several of his most trusted counsel. They talked for hours about how to get Hector's body back, Priam listening attentively to all that was said. At last, he held up his hands for silence.

"I do have a plan," the aged king said. "It came to me last night. Zeus sent me a dream. And he sent me a messenger, as well. I wanted to see if any of you had a better plan. But since you don't, I will do what Zeus advised me to do in the dream, and what the messenger told me to do."

They all sat waiting for the words to follow.

"I will dress as a beggar and go to Achilles on bended knee. I will beg for my son's body," said Priam, trying to hold his head up despite the pain of his words.

The group erupted in shouts of protest. None spoke louder or more passionately than Alexandros against the idea. Priam let them rant, then silenced them again.

"Achilles has a father waiting for him back home in Phthia," he said. "I will appeal to him on that basis, as a father to a son. I have been told that he is very fond of his father."

"Told by whom?" shouted Deiphobus, another son. "This is madness, the king of Troy going alone to see Deathdealer."

"As I said....by Zeus, in a dream," said Priam calmly.

The protests continued but Priam was no longer listening. His mind was already made up. He glanced over at the statue of Zeus in the corner of the room and nodded. He felt sure that he saw the statue nod back.

Late the next afternoon, as the sun chariot was heading back to its stable beneath the sky, a wooden cart with two men left Troy. It was the type of cart not used for war but for carrying bodies back to the city. It rumbled over the plain, now void of any living men. It drove past rotting corpses that had not yet been taken in, and past the Scamander. It paused on the invaders' side of the river and the driver, a young man, turned to the rider, an old man.

"Are you sure, great king?" he asked softly. "Deathdealer is a terrible man. I fear he will slay us both and hang us on his spear, outside his tent, for the vultures and dogs to fight over."

Priam shrugged, his face lined and battered with years of pain. His long, white beard hung straight down, no longer nicely combed and cleaned by the servant women who fussed over him. He wore the oldest robe he could find and an old cap on his head to hide the bald spot.

"Go on, Demander. We have no choice. See?" he croaked, pointing a crooked finger at a chariot moving slowly toward them. "The sentries have already spotted us and are coming to check on us."

The Achaean chariot pulled up next to them, one soldier motioning for them to stop their cart. Two mid-aged soldiers glanced over at them, sizing them up carefully.

"Who are you, and what are you doing on the plain, this close to the camp of the Myrmidons?" one soldier demanded in a stern voice. Priam knew enough of the dialect that he could converse with him.

"I have come as a messenger from King Priam, to see Lord Achilles," he said. "Will you be so kind as to escort us to the great prince's tent?"

The soldier stepped out of the chariot and drew his sword. He walked up to the Trojan cart and stared at the two inside, then looked around.

"You seem harmless enough in this old cart," he said with a sneer. "Follow us."

He led the Trojan cart inside the wooden wall and to the gate that would allow them into the Myrmidon section. He saluted the sentry as he moved past and then halted his chariot and motioned for them to pull up.

Priam glanced around, his heart in his throat, fearful that he might find the body of Hector lying somewhere in the open. He saw the many tents and small huts, and knew the large tent they were now in front of belonged to Achilles. There were lights flickering inside the tent in several places and he could make out the silhouette of large banquet table. He thought he saw a shadow moving inside the tent.

"Stay here and I will see if lord Achilles will allow you to come in, old man," he said.

He disappeared in the tent and Priam could see two figures talking. The man emerged, shaking his head.

"Lord Achilles is in mourning, he does not care to see anyone," he said.

"Priam took a deep breath.

"Tell him," he said softly, "that the father of Polyxena wishes to see him."

The warrior went back inside and returned immediately, his eyes wide.

"Achilles will see you," he said, looking perplexed.

Priam trembled as he entered the tent. Achilles stood several feet from him, dressed in a red chiton, unbelted and hanging straight down. His eyes were sunken in and he did not look to be the world's most invincible warrior. He appeared to be, like Priam, a man in deep emotional distress.

"Leave us," said Achilles to the soldier, who quickly departed.

Priam gaped at Achilles, not knowing what to say or do. He had rehearsed his speech a dozen times and knew it well. But confronted at last with the emotions of all that had happened, he was at a loss. His shoulders sagged and his knees buckled.

Achilles leaped to his side, taking his elbow to steady him.

"Are you all right, sir?" he asked quietly. Priam stared at him, stunned by his voice, so soft and low, and by the touch of his hands. These were the hands that had slain his beloved son.

"I would like to sit, if I might," he said. "It's been a long ride from Troy. These old legs are not used to such a trip."

Achilles walked him to a cot and helped him to sit. He moved to the cot across from it and sat down, staring at Priam.

"Patroclus and I….used to sit on these cots and talk about Phthia," said Achilles.

Priam nodded, his eyes filling with tears.

"I used to sit on cots similar to these and bounce young Hector on my knees," he said. "Polyxena, too, long before he went off and got killed, and before she left to become a priestess on Mount Ida."

Achilles felt a stab of sorrow in his chest.

"Tell me about Polyxena," he said. "I have not seen her for some time."

"She came to me last night," he said. "I had a dream from Zeus and he told me to come to you, to plead for Hector's body. I awoke, shaking, and saw movement in my bed chamber. Hecuba, my queen, is staying in the house of Hector with Andromache. I was alone. I was afraid. I am not a young man any more. But it was Polyxena. She came to me, from Ida, to talk.

"She is the one who convinced me to visit you, lord Achilles. She told me she has met you and you are kind at heart. She said you would listen to the pleading of an old man, thinking of your father back in grassy Phthia."

Achilles arose and walked away, his back to Priam. He stood by the large table for a long time, Priam regarding him with a mixture of curiosity and frustration. He came back and sat down. Priam saw he had been crying.

"You need food and wine," mumbled Achilles. "How thoughtless of me." He went to the tent opening and barked some commands. Immediately, three servants came in to sit wine, bread, meat, vegetables and honey on the table. Achilles helped Priam to stand and led him to the table. They ate slowly and quietly.

"I have not eaten much for over a week," said Achilles, fingering the bread and the meat.

"Nor have I," said Priam.

They finished, then leaned back, eyes on the other.

"You remind me of my father, King Peleus," said Achilles.

"Do you miss him?" asked Priam, his eyes locked on the eyes of Achilles. He was trying to measure him to see if he was two different men – one who could drag the body of a foe wildly in the dust behind his chariot, and one who also could express the kind of compassion that Polyxena claimed to have seen in him.

"Yes, surely," said Achilles. "And Chiron, my mentor. I spent many years with him on Mount Pelion, learning to fight, and to sing, and to heal and many other things, as well."

"I see Chiron also taught you the art of compassion," said Priam.

Achilles nodded.

"It took great courage for you to come see me," he said. "I admire courage above all other qualities." He paused: "And I despise greed the most."

"I admire compassion in great warriors," said Priam. "For a weak man to have compassion means very little, for he has nothing to give in to. For a warrior to have compassion is a gift from the gods. Hector had it, too."

Achilles started to respond, saying Hector had shown no compassion to Patroclus, but he did not. He did not want to wound this old man any more. Achilles felt the anger he had harbored for so long beginning to drift away.

There was a long pause as the two men silently regarded each other.

"Do you want to take Hector's body back in the morning?" Achilles asked simply.

Priam was stunned. He looked at the young warrior, his lower lip trembling.

"You will permit me to, sir?" He asked, afraid his senses were leaving him.

"Yes," said Achilles. "Will you spend the night? You are too tired to go back to Troy tonight, I fear."

"Yes," said Priam, shaking. "I will sleep right here, on this cot, if Lord Achilles will allow it."

Achilles moved to the opening again. He called the servants back, talking in a low tone. They nodded and ran off. He came back, staring down at Priam. The old king peered up, struck by the majesty of the young warrior. He seemed to have transformed himself in the time since Priam had arrived. At that moment, even to Priam, he seemed almost like a god.

"Sleep well in my tent, king Priam," he said. "I have instructed my guards to stand alert at the entrance all night. They will also find a spot for your driver to spend the night. I will sleep in the tent of Patroclus. Hector's body will be cleaned and wrapped in precious linens. You will have an escort back to Troy at dawn."

He turned to leave. But Priam's voice stopped him.

"Lord Achilles," he said, his voice husky for the first time. "Peleus can be proud to have raised such a son."

Achilles walked slowly to the tent of Patroclus. Entering, he felt a ghostly vision and turned around quickly, searching for the image of his dear friend. The tent was dark as no oil lamp had been lit, and he saw nothing. He walked to the cot where Patroclus had slept night after night, for ten years, often with some woman but also often alone. Achilles sank onto the cot, heavy in thought for a long while. Then he stood and walked to the end furthest from the entrance. He grabbed some furs and spread them on the floor and lay down on them.

"Shade of Patroclus, forgive me for showing such hospitality to the father of the man who killed you," Achilles said quietly. "You would be justified in being angry. But, he made me think of Peleus in faraway Phthia, and I hope other men will show Peleus such kindness if ever he needs their help. With no young son there to assist him, Peleus could be at their mercy."

He had a difficult time surrendering to Sleep and was certain that when he did, he would have ugly dreams. But once he fell drifted away, he dreamed not at all; or at least none that he could remember come the morning.

They met briefly in the morning, at dawn. Hector's body was placed into the cart that had brought Priam and the old king quivered as he grasped the forearm of Achilles in gratitude. Before Priam left, Achilles promised him a nine-day truce so that the Trojans could honor Hector with funeral games like the Achaeans had done for Patroclus.

And then the cart rumbled off toward Troy, the king taking his greatest son back to the city he was raised in.

It was on the fourth day of the truce that Achilles decided to visit Mount Ida. Priam speaking of Polyxena had touched his heart and he wanted to see her again. He wondered if she would hate him for killing Hector; he was prepared to accept it if that was the case. As strong as were his feelings for her, they did not approach the need he felt to avenge the death of Patroclus.

He followed the same trail, going alone. He gave almost no thought whatsoever about running into Trojans or their allies. He drove the chariot by himself; as before, when people saw him, they fell back in fear. He heard the name "Deathdealer" on several occasions and knew he was recognized by everyone who saw him. His fame was great before the battle with Hector and now it had become legend.

Tying the horses to a tree, he walked to the temple of Zeus, noticing there was activity inside. He stepped into the temple and was greeted by gasps. There were several temple workers present and nearly a dozen others. They were all praying to the great god, probably for the end of the conflict that had raged for so long.

A priestess came up to him and bowed.

"Is lord Achilles looking for Polyxena?" she asked. He nodded and she pointed toward the trail that he had taken the last time. He nodded again and moved out of the temple and down the trail. He saw the hut where he had spent such a pleasurable night, and slipped through the small doorway but found it empty. There was a smoldering fire in the center of the area where the huts stood, but no men or women.

Two small children, a girl and a boy, saw him, and motioned to him. He moved to where they were and looked down at them.

"She is down by the stream," said the girl. Achilles smiled at her and walked to the stream. Polyxena saw him coming and stood up from her washing, her eyes locked on his. He stopped several feet from her, searching her face for signs of her feelings.

"Did you have to kill him?" she asked, her voice so low he could barely hear her.

He nodded.

"Yes," he said.

"Did you have to dishonor his memory and his family by dragging his body before the very walls he was sworn to protect?" she asked, tears streaming down her face, her hands clasped tightly together.

He sighed.

"Yes, I did," he said. "Hector knew the rules and accepted them. He stripped Patroclus of his armor....my armor. Hector knew I could not let that go unanswered and that he had to pay the full price for his insult. He laughed when Patroclus warned him to beware of my anger. Hector is laughing no more."

She stood trembling, torn by conflicting emotions of dedication to her brother and her affection for Achilles.

"Has ever a woman been in such a terrible situation as I am?" she moaned. "In love with the man who killed her favorite brother."

Achilles was touched by the depths of her suffering. He wanted to reach out to her but he did not know how to do so.

"The gods alone understand the ways of life," he said finally. "There are few easy answers. We mortals can just live as best we know how, hoping that the gods will impart enough wisdom that we can make life tolerable."

She wiped her eyes with the back of her hands.

"What do you know of a tolerable life?" she asked. "You are young and handsome, with a storehouse of treasures. You have a kingdom waiting for you and already you are a legend. People say you are the son of a goddess and can not be harmed, even that you are a god yourself.

"When the war is over, you will sail away with your warriors and return to a hero's welcome in faraway Phthia. You will marry a princess and have many children to climb over your lap in your old age. Bards will sing of your deeds and your name will live forever.

"That sounds like a tolerable life to me, lord Achilles."

He stepped to her, stopping directly in front of her.

"If I ever return to Phthia, I will ask you to go with me," he said. "You can be that princess you spoke of, if you so desire."

She gasped, staring up at him. She was already beautiful beyond compare, but her vulnerability made her even more special to him. She turned away and he saw her shoulders shaking. He placed his hands on her bare shoulders and pulled her back to him. He kissed her dark hair lightly and she sagged into him. Her hands came to his, covering them only halfway, so small were her hands against his.

"I need time....to pray to Zeus for understanding," she said. "And to think."

He nodded, backing away. She stood for a long time, then turned. He was gone, and her heart sank. She moved through the rest of the day in a daze, hoping he would show back up at any moment and take her to her hut. But he did not. She ate sparingly at night with the others, then retired to her hut. She lay silently on her thick bed of furs and was starting to drift away when she heard the welcome sound. She looked up and saw him standing in the doorway, unmoving.

Polyxena felt her heart pounding. She sat up slowly. The fur cloak covering her fell away, leaving her half naked, the soft glow of the oil boat offering scant light. She knew he would not move further until she asked him to.

"Come to me, Achilles," she whispered.

He laid down with her and she slid her hands up his powerful arms again. She swooned to her back, pulling him down on top of her. Polyxena and Achilles became one that night, forever.

The Queen of the Amazons

The line of warriors moved quickly toward the city in the distance. There were over four hundred of them, some on horseback, some in chariots but most in wooden carts pulled by mules. Shields hung from the sides of the carts and copper spear points pushed up into the bright light of day in huge numbers. They had come a long, long way, heeding the call of distress from Priam over two years earlier.

As the column passed the small farms, the residents regarded them with great curiosity; children ran to their mothers, shouting and pointing; the mothers came out and gasped in stunned surprise, as well.

The warriors smiled grimly, nodding at the farm people they passed. They were used to shocking people over the long route.

"Amazons!" muttered one man, scratching his head under his wool cap. "Women warriors. By Zeus, I never thought I'd see the day!"

Alexandros had left Troy in his silver chariot to greet them, with ten more warlords lined up behind him in their chariots. He had come out the Scaean Gates during the last day of the truce, as the body of Hector was about to be consumed by fire. He rode to where the Amazon column had halted, about one mile from the city. Alexandros pulled up his horses and jumped from the chariot. He strode up to the lead horses, his silver armor shining in the sunlight, his horsehair crest on his war helmet dyed blue. He was a strikingly handsome man, but Penthesileia, the leader of the Amazons, was not interested in his manliness, only in the fact that he was a Trojan prince.

"Greetings, Penthesileia," he said, hoping she could understand his language. She nodded solemnly, then titled her head, indicating she could not understand. He tried several other dialects and finally she spoke.

"I understand this tongue," she said, her voice husky and thick. She had sharp features, but was far from beautiful; her build was trim, but she had thick arms, developed from considerable use of the sword and spear. Rumor was that she was also a skilled boxer, able to hold her own with most men.

She dismounted and strode to Alexandros, embracing him stiffly, in a formal way. They were the same height, but her head crest was much taller than his, giving her the appearance of being taller. She wore a thin breastpiece, mostly leather but trimmed with bronze. She also had fore-arm covers of thick fur, as did all the Amazons, something that the Trojans had never seen before. She wore high greaves, protecting her legs from the top of the ankle to her knee. And she wore a kilt with a design similar to what the Assyrians wore. Her hair was braided and hung almost to her waist.

"It is good to see you," said Alexandros. "Thank you for answering our call."

She looked past him, to the city in the distance.

"So this is Troy," she said. "We have heard of your struggle."

"We have lost our greatest warrior, my brother Hector," he said sorrowfully. "He was killed by Achilles in single combat."

Her eyes brightened at the sound of the name she had come to know so much about.

"Achilles," she said with a forced smiled. "The son of the sea goddess." She paused, searching the face of Alexandros. She thought him soft and knew at a glance she would not want to have to depend upon him in battle. Nor would she want him in her bed, despite his good looks. "They say he can not be injured."

"Yes, that is what they say," said Alexandros.

"Well, we shall see about that," she said. She walked back to her horse and climbed astride. She leaned next to the rider next to her whispering, and she nodded. Then she looked back at Alexandros.

"We are ready to fight as soon as possible," she said. "We will camp outside the walls tonight, facing the Achaean camp."

Alexandros nodded his agreement.

"I must return to Troy immediately, to witness the funeral fire of Hector," he said. "We will talk again in the morning."

The huge fire lit up the dark night inside Troy as the entire city and many of the allies living in tents behind Troy came to pay their respects. Andromache and Astyanax stood bravely as the other members of the royal family prayed and cried. Then they retired into the house they had once shared with the prince of Troy, their lives to be never the same.

When dawn came, the Achaeans were surprised to see the new tents that had sprouted up outside the Trojan walls. Agamemnon and several other warlords sallied forth, eager to engage in battle again after the long truce for the funeral games of first Patroclus and then Hector. Agamemnon had not agreed with the long truce that Achilles had given the Trojans, but he knew better than to argue about it with Achilles. He had no heart for another long emotional battle, and so he sat in his tent and sulked.

"Now, Achilles has become the high king, making these decisions for us, decisions that only I have the right to make," he cried out. His angry outburst fell on deaf ears, though. The others were too pleased with the turn of events that brought Achilles back to the war and removed Hector from it to care about Agamemnon's feelings.

A small portion of the Achaean host moved toward Troy, curious about what troops they would see in the field of combat. When the advance scouts came back with the news, they were startled.

"Amazons!" spouted Agamemnon, straining his eyes to view the troops moving toward him. "We are to fight women now?"

Many behind him chuckled at the thought. But they weren't chuckling for long. Penthesileia was the veteran of many campaigns. She was a clever fighter, as well as an angry fighter. She did not like men in general, and these men in particular. She was cool and poised, riding into battle at the head of her four hundred troops, with the other Trojans and their allies at their side. The Amazons preferred cavalry charges, darting in and out on horseback between the chariots, a much more mobile force than the Achaeans were accustomed to.

The first pass was a soft one for both sides, but as the Achaeans were wheeling their chariots in a wide circle to come back and go again, the Amazons brought their horses about abruptly and charged after them from behind. Their swords swung wildly, catching many of the Achaeans off guard. Screams filled the air as the Amazons cut through the ranks of the enemy, much to the shock of both the Achaeans and the Trojans.

"By the grace of Apollo, look at them!" shouted Alexandros to Aeneas. "They are wicked, wicked women!"

Aeneas was shocked at the dexterity and the speed of the Amazons. They rode among the chariots, striking from all directions. Several of the finest soldiers were cut down, killed by women! Agamemnon shouted at his driver to pull the chariot off to the side, while he surveyed the field. Odysseus pulled up beside him, having just narrowly missed being cut down by one of the women, and finally killing her with a swift stab with his spear.

"These women can fight," exclaimed Odysseus, a wry smile on his lips. "I wonder what they would be like in the bed chambers."

Agamemnon grunted and watched as Penthesileia cut down another solider. She leaped off her horse, stripped the dead soldier of his armor and tossed it to the chariot that trailed along behind her for the purpose of gathering armor from her victims. It was now piled high and Agamemnon was stunned by the scene.

"She has more booty than anyone except Achilles!" he stammered. She leaped back on her horse and glanced around. She saw Agamemnon and Odysseus watching her and spurred her horse over to them.

"By Zeus, she's going to challenge us both!" gasped Agamemnon. "Will the pleasure of running her through be yours or mine, Odysseus?"

They both prepared for battle, pulling their war helmets down over their faces and grabbing their lances. But she stopped a good distance away, leaning forward on her horse to stare at them.

"I am looking for Achilles," she shouted. "You are warlords of high rank, that I can see plainly enough. I will spare you both if you go find Achilles and tell him I am here to take revenge for the way he treated the body of Hector!"

Agamemnon and Odysseus glanced at each other in astonishment.

"She wants Achilles!" laughed Agamemnon. "Let us go find him."

"Wait!" said Odysseus to Agamemnon. He then turned to the Amazon queen, a sparkle in his eyes.

"Do you know what you ask, woman?" he shouted. "He is by far the best of the Achaeans. He was too much for Hector, who I suspect was far better at war than you are. He is not interested in fighting women. I suggest you go pray to Artemis and Athena for some wisdom, then go back to wherever it is you come from."

She spurred her horse up closer, glowering at Odysseus. Her helmet wore no nose guard and her entire face was uncovered.

"I do not know who you are, soldier, nor do I care," she said angrily. "But if Achilles is not in the field soon, I will come after you instead. And your armor will adorn my tent as I make love to my lady that night. And maybe I will take your woman from you too, once she sees me in action on the field and thinks I may be even more exciting in the bed chamber!"

Odysseus smiled widely at her words.

"Talk all you want, Amazon," he said. "I am always ready to oblige you, though I won't make the first move. And you will find Achilles far more than ready, should your paths ever cross."

She glared at him, then wheeled her horse and rode away. Agamemnon and Odysseus broke into a hearty laughter, and left to seek out Achilles as the Amazons continued fighting in small clusters around the huge battlefield. Odysseus found Achilles sitting in front of his tent, working to sharpen the point of his great Pelion ash spear. Achilles lowered his spear point when he saw him coming. He always enjoyed time spent with the clever Odysseus.

"What brings you to the camp of the Myrmidons?" asked Achilles. "Didn't I hear battle cries earlier today? I thought you were in the field."

Odysseus pulled up a stool and sat next to Achilles. A servant hurried over and gave him a cup and filled it with watered wine, then filled the cup of Achilles again. The sun was hot, and they were both perspiring just by sitting.

"I bring you word of a challenge," said the Ithacan, leaning forward.

The smile faded from his face as Achilles nodded again, wanting to hear more.

"From a woman," he continued. "The queen of the Amazons."

Achilles frowned.

"I heard Amazons had arrived last night. Did she really ask for me to fight? Aren't there enough warlords out there? I am taking a break from the war as you know. Now that Patroclus has been avenged, my heart is not in the battle as much as it once was."

He leaned back, taking a sip of his wine, regarding Odysseus.

"I mentioned to her that you might not be all that interested in fighting a woman, but she didn't seem to care for that answer," Odysseus said. "She said she would challenge me if I didn't deliver the message...and take my woman from me."

Achilles leaned back and slapped his hand on his thigh, chuckling. Odysseus laughed, too.

"Of course, I haven't had a woman since I left Ithaca, and poor Penelope," added Odysseus.

That made Achilles laugh again. Odysseus was known as a family man who loved his wife and son. But he was also a lusty adventurer through and through and always kept an eye on the women who came into the camp. He would pick out ones that reminded him of Penelope, those with long black hair, a plump behind and a thick waist, and a pretty face.

"Tell her I am not interested in fighting women," said Achilles, dismissing it from his mind. They began talking about other matters, until Antilochus came striding up. He wore a pained expression as he pulled up another stool and sat down next to Odysseus. Achilles motioned for wine to be brought for him, as well.

"Achilles, you had best come out," said Antilochus. "Penthesileia, the queen of the Amazons, has killed ten warriors today. She is standing by the Scamander shouting your name, and calling you a coward. She is crazy, I believe. Too many years in the wilds, living like a man. She really thinks she can kill you, I believe."

"Perhaps she has a death wish," said Odysseus.

Achilles frowned. He didn't like how the situation was developing.

He had no interest at all in fighting a woman, no matter how skilled she was. But he did not care to be called a coward, either. He stood abruptly, walking toward his tent. He came back moments later with his helmet, but without his armor. He was stripped to the waist, wearing only a kilt and greaves.

"Let's go see this mad woman," he said. "Maybe I can talk some sense into her."

Penthesileia was sitting by the Scamander resting with her troops gathered around her when she saw the chariots coming her way. She squinted, then stood up. A slow smile ran over her lips when she heard the words of Alexandros. The prince had come to congratulate her for her victories, and he pointed at the chariots.

"It is Achilles!" he mumbled. "He is coming!"

She smiled widely, pulling her war helmet on. She strode forward as her warriors stood up behind her, watching the scene unfold.

Odysseus stopped his chariot, Achilles at his side. The slim Achaean forces on the field were gathering behind them. Achilles had not even bothered to call his Myrmidons into action. He stepped from the chariot and walked to the Scamander, staring across at Penthesileia.

"I am Achilles," he said forcefully. "I am told you wish to fight me."

"No, that is not true," she said boldly. "I wish to kill you! For the way you treated Hector in death."

Achilles felt his jaw tightening. He did not like her words, nor the way she scowled at him.

"I choose not to fight you," he said. "Go away." He turned and walked back toward the chariot, but her next words cut the air and made him halt in his tracks.

"Coward!" she screamed. "Let the world know that Achilles runs from Penthesileia, queen of the Amazons. That he dares not face her in combat to the death."

The hair stood up on the back of his neck and he felt the anger coming to him. He turned and faced her again.

"You are doubtless tired from a long day's battle," he said, his words hard. "I will come here tomorrow, at dawn. If you are here, I will kill you."

He turned and strode to the chariot, stepping up on it. She walked back to her troops, a cruel smile on her lips. She had achieved her aim. That night, she sat in her tent with her woman, stroking the young woman's hair and singing softly to her. When the song was over the woman cuddled up to her.

"Why do you insist on fighting the best of the Achaeans tomorrow?" asked the woman, much prettier and smaller than Penthesileia.

"What if... he kills you? What will happen to me?"

"Why, you will end up in the tent of some man," teased Penthesileia. "And then you will appreciate my skills all the more, sweet Narcissa."

Word of the challenge had spread though both camps and the Achaeans and Trojans poured out of their gates at dawn to witness the incredible fight that was brewing. Achilles rode next to Automedon, still not wearing his breastplate armor, an angry scowl on his face. Automedon knew not to speak to him, for Achilles was in no mood for talk. Behind then came the Myrmidons, silent as usual.

When he arrived at the Scamander, he saw that Penthesileia was there waiting for him, standing by her horse, a huge army of Amazons and Trojans behind her. Automedon stopped the chariot at the river's edge and Achilles shouted at her.

"So, you are determined to continue this mad scheme," he yelled. "Then, let us begin."

He nodded at Automedon. The horses splashed into the river and came out on the other side. She ran to her horse the moment she saw the chariot start across and both sides began shouting and streaming toward the river. In a matter of moments, it appeared that Ares, the god of war, had taken over once again. The armies flew at each other in a great clamor; the Achaeans, knowing now how skilled the Amazons were, fought with a renewed fury.

Achilles reached out from the chariot and killed a Trojan who was unlucky enough to be in his way. The chariot thundered toward Penthesileia, who charged toward it on her horse. She thew her spear and it flew over the head of Achilles. He cocked his arm to throw, but decided against it. She thundered past on her horse, surprised he had not cast at her. She wheeled the horse violently, trying to catch him unaware. But Odysseus had told him how skilled she was with the horse, and he remembered his days on Mount Pelion in games with the centaurs. Achilles knew exactly how to deal with skilled horses and their riders.

He was ready for Penthesileia. He leaped out of the chariot and stood facing her, both hands gripping his huge Pelion ash. She wanted to have her horse chasing after the chariot at full speed, but she could not turn him around quickly enough and get him moving at full speed in such a short distance. She realized that Achilles had outmaneuvered her by not allowing her horse the time it needed for a true charge.

"Curses on you!" she shouted, leaning down to try and strike him with her sword. He easily evaded her thrust and as the horse thundered past he raced after it, with greater speed than she had ever seen before. This time, she was just turning the horse around again as Achilles was upon her. With both hands, he rammed the Pelion ash spear upwards with all the power that was in his mighty arms. The spear drove deep into the side of the horse.

It screamed wildly, rearing high, its front hooves pawing the air as the shadow of death overtook it.

Penthesileia fell backwards off the horse, landing with a heavy crash on the ground, the wind knocked out of her. In what seemed like a distant world, she heard her horse crying out in terrible pain and she staggered to her feet, the helmet knocked from her head, laying twenty feet away. She still clutched her sword, somehow, and she lifted her free hand to wipe the dirt and grass from her mouth.

Before her eyes could adjust, she felt an incredible pain in her stomach. Her feet were jerked off the ground and she flew backwards, landing with a sickening sound in the dirt. Her sword went flying; her hands gripped the sword that was now sticking halfway into her abdomen. She stared up at Achilles standing over her, her eyes glazed. Her legs thrashed helplessly and she pulled at the sword to no avail, her hands thick with blood.

"Foolish woman!" croaked Achilles, gaping down at her.

Her Amazons halted fighting, shattered by what they saw. Several of them were struck down by Achaeans who did not care that they had ceased fighting, but other Achaeans pulled up in order to watch the incredible drama. Several of the Amazon leaders stumbled toward her, staring down at her. One knealt beside her, taking off her own helmet and cradling Penthesileia's head.

"Your wish has come true, finally," croaked the other Amazon. "You can now have your peace."

The Amazon holding her queen tightly looked up at Achilles.

"It took the best of the Achaeans to do it," she said, to both Achilles and Penthesileia. "Let your shade go now, down to the Elysian Fields, where the great warriors of the past will greet you as one of them."

Penthesileia tried to talk, but the words would not come. And then her body quivered violently and she was gone.

"What talk was that?" asked Achilles. "Why did she want to die?"

"Many years ago, she killed her sister, Hippolyta, in a hunting accident," said the Amazon, tears streaming down her face. "She has hated herself ever since. She has fought recklessly in war after war, always winning. When Priam sent word that Troy needed her help she was eager to come, being a distant relative to Priam and the royal family. She had heard of you and was anxious to test herself against you, knowing full well that this might be the result."

Achilles shook his head. He knelt down beside her and looked into her face. He pushed the long hair back from her face, then stood. The armies were all around, swords hanging in their hands, waiting for Achilles to tell them what to do next.

Thersites, an ugly man with a mean spirit, scrambled up to look at Penthesileia. He spit upon her and began jabbing at her with his spear. Achilles grabbed the spear and swung his fist to Thersites' jaw, knocking him to the ground unconscious.

"Get him out of here!" shouted Achilles to the Locrians of Little Ajax, whose tribe Thersites belonged to. They came and dragged him away. Then Achilles turned to the Amazons.

"Take your leader and honor her," he shouted. "And go home, back where you came from, unless you want to see the death of Troy. For I vow that Troy's end is near, and if you are here when we come again, you will all die."

He gave one last look at the slain queen of the Amazons and then he stormed back to his chariot.

"Go back to the camp," he said to Automedon. "Quickly, before I vomit and they all see me."

The Son of the Dawn

There were no more battles on the plain the following week. The Trojans were totally disheartened by what had happened to them, losing both Hector and Penthesileia in such a short span of time. The funeral was held hastily the next day, far from the city, in a small cove of tress. Then, most of the Amazons departed, leaving on the same trail they had come on just a few days earlier. However, a few decided to stay and fight and moved into the city.

In the third week, the Achaeans received news of another large troop coming to Troy and several of the warlords rode out to watch. The army was long and all of the warriors were ebony skinned. They wore animal skins over their entire body, with no visible armor, most of them carrying long bows. A spy told Agamemnon they were Ethiopians, and had come all the way from the land of the sunrise, where Helios stables his chariot each night. They were led by a huge, fierce warrior named Memnon, who was himself born of a goddess; he was known as the Son of the Dawn.

"He is as large as Ajax, maybe even bigger," said the spy. "Just to look at him causes most men to shrink away. The Trojans are exultant. They welcomed his troops into the city by throwing flowers at them and singing songs. Many a cup of wine is being drunk tonight in Troy, for they feel they have a champion that is the equal of Achilles."

Once again, Achilles had decided to take a respite from the fighting. He visited Polyxena on Mount Ida again for three days, the nights filled with intense lovemaking. He found it difficult to leave when the third morning came. She had told him that Troy was praying that Memnon would slay Achilles, and that such a defeat would cause the invaders to give up all hope and sail away.

"Achilles," she whispered, clinging to him. "I could not stand the thought of losing you. Please, fight no more."

He laughed lightly at her words, hugging her tight.

"So, you think I am growing old and can no longer defend myself," he said, smiling down at her.

"No, that is not true," she said. "It's just that you have fought so many battles in the ten years of the war. How many men have you killed and when will the gods finally turn away to help some other hero, instead of you?"

Her words had made him think on the journey back to the camp. As he passed Troy at night, he wondered if Memnon was indeed as big as Ajax. Arriving in the camp, he found the warlords meeting at the tent of Agamemnon. Automedon was waiting for him and told him that his presence was urgently requested the moment he came back.

He heard the raised voices and the shouting as he neared the tent. It was late and the tent needed many oil boats to provide enough light. The herald outside jumped to attention when he saw Achilles and raced in to announce him. The tent drew silent as Achilles walked in.

There were twenty warlords sitting or standing. All eyes turned on him as Agamemnon raised a cup to salute him.

"It is good of Lord Achilles to join us once again," said the high king. "Troy has a new hero, it seems. And," he paused, looking around the tent, and then slamming his fist hard onto the table, "not one of our champions dares to meet him in single combat! Not one, damn it to Hades!"

Achilles glanced around the tent. They were all there – Great Ajax, Diomedes, Little Ajax, Odysseus, Menelaus, Idomeneus and other warlords. He could not believe what he was hearing from Agamemnon.

"Is this Memnon so frightening that no one will face him?" asked Achilles, looking perplexed. "Can this be true?"

He looked around the tent again.

"Where is Nestor?" he asked. "Why is he not here?"

There was along silence before Agamemnon spoke up.

"Antilochus accepted Memnon's challenge today. It was like a man fighting a boy. Memnon killed him and took his body back to Troy. Nestor collapsed in anguish. After he was revived, Nestor went looking for you, to beg you to avenge Antilochus. Not finding you, he went mad with grief at losing his son. We all loved Antilochus. He was like Patroclus, dear to us all."

Achilles pulled his hair in sorrow then slammed his fists on the table. He lifted his face at last, looking around the table at each warlord, one by one, his eyes narrow and his gaze hard.

"Answer me….why did no one else accept his new challenge?" he growled.

No one responded, all sitting with eyes downcast. Then Ajax stood slowly. Achilles turned to face his cousin, aware that he suddenly looked very old and tired.

"It is true," Ajax said, his voice low. "As for me, I am battered, from too many battles. I have wounds that just won't heal." He held his right arm out, showing that it was bent at a strange angle. "My arm won't work right since I was hit with a large rock a month ago. I no longer have the strength I once had." He looked around at the other warlords, sinking back into his chair.

The others nodded grimly, rubbing their arms and thighs. Achilles turned to look at Diomedes, who had never shrunk from a fight at any time.

"He is simply too large and too powerful," said the leader of the Argives. "I saw him today in battle, Achilles. He is too big. And very skilled. I could not defeat him, and his challenge is that if he defeats our champion we must all sail away."

Odysseus spoke next.

"Achilles, we are unanimous in our viewpoint that only you can defeat this Memnon. And," he said, with a long pause, "it won't be easy. He too is the son of a goddess."

Achilles glanced around at them, one by one.

"Tell Nestor that tomorrow I will seek out Memnon and slay him, and avenge Antilochus," he said. He nodded at them and then left the tent. There was a long silence until they were sure he was out of hearing range, and then they began talking among themselves. Not all of them were sure that even the mighty Achilles, by far the best man they had ever seen, could stop Memnon.

He went first to see Nestor and offer his condolences. The old man was sitting in his chair deep in his tent, his hair disheveled and his features drawn. He looked far older than his sixty years. He seemed almost one hundred. He rose on shaky legs to grasp the forearms of Achilles, then fell back into his chair. Achilles sat across from him staring into his watery eyes.

"Antilochus is a fine warrior," began Nestor finally, still speaking of his son as if he were alive. "But he never had a chance against this monster. Memnon laughed at him as he struck him down, running his spear though his neck." He stopped, hands quivering. "I saw the fight; I had heard the war cry of Antilochus, then a large shout from our troops, then silence. I ran to where they were fighting."

He couldn't continue for some time; Achilles leaned back, biting his lower lip, trying to remain patient. Memnon had caused tremendous fear in the Achaeans in a very short amount of time, he realized.

Finally, Nestor looked straight at his visitor.

"You must avenge my son, Achilles!" Nestor pleaded, voice quivering. "He admired you like no other. He worshipped you, like the godson that you are."

He paused again, still staring at Achilles.

"But, be cautious, great Achilles. I have never seen a warrior like him, not since the days of Heracles. He is a mighty warrior with great skills."

Achilles nodded, standing tall, gazing down at Nestor.

"You have been like a father to me in the absence of Peleus," said Achilles, "and next to Patroclus, I liked Antilochus the best of all the Achaeans gathered here. I will avenge his death, Nestor."

Even Automedon was visibly nervous as he brought the chariot up. Achilles emerged from the tent in full armor, calling for the Myrmidons. They gathered around him and he ran his eyes over them, proud of all they had done in the ten years at Troy.

"I hear that Troy has a new hero!" he shouted. "I go to meet this Memnon, the son of the Dawn, and to slay him. I ask you to fight as you have never fought before, when you see Memnon go down. This defeat will dishearten Troy once and for all and then we will sack the city."

He paused before continuing.

"We came here ten long years ago to win glory and booty for Peleus and for Phthia," he said. "We have taken over twenty cities during that time, but not yet have we entered Troy through the Scaean Gates. Many of our comrades have died. We lost the best of us all when we lost Patroclus. It is time for us to end this war, to take Troy, to set sail for home!"

He raised his spear, shaking it, and the Myrmidons responded with a great roar. Over and over, the battle cry split the crisp morning air as they headed for the gate. They were met by warriors from all the other camps; every warlord had turned out his troops this day, in the expectation of seeing Achilles defeat the greatest champion Troy had yet known, a warrior who appeared to surpass even Hector.

The vast army poured out of the gates and the warlords were surprised to see the Trojans and all their allies already on their side of the Scamander. Achilles scanned the horizon, then spotted the chariot carrying Memnon. The black prince was taller than any warrior Achilles had ever seen, more than two heads taller than his chariot driver. He wore a black helmet with a high crest, also in black. As they neared one another, Achilles realized that Memnon was wearing animal skins, but he suspected there was bronze armor underneath the skins.

Suddenly, they were separated by a mass of soldiers surging in between them and Achilles was immersed in fighting. He swung his sword back and forth, cutting down Trojans right and left. Whenever a foe saw who he was facing, he tried to turn and flee but Achilles was too fast for him. He killed ten soldiers when at last Automedon pulled the chariot into a small clearing....and he was suddenly face to face with Memnon.

As the two warriors stared at one another, Achilles felt a hot tremor run down his back. Truly, this was a warrior who would severely test him. He had never seen such a huge man in his entire life. Memnon stepped down from his chariot and strode toward Achilles.

"Come down, little man, and let us see who the gods favor, and who is the best," said Memnon. But it was in a tongue that Achilles did not understand at all. He had never heard such language. He leaped from his chariot and raced toward the giant.

Neither carried a spear, both preferring to settle their destiny with swords. Automedon screamed the war cry and the Myrmidons all came running to watch. So did the black troops of Memnon and the Trojans. In a matter of moments, all fighting ceased across the plain as soldiers from both sides stood transfixed, awaiting the greatest single combat they would ever witness.

The charge by Achilles surprised the giant. In all his life, no one had ever attacked him. He grunted and swung his sword. It clanged against the shield of Achilles with such force that Achilles was knocked sideways, almost losing his footing. He had never been struck so hard and the hair stood up on the back of his neck, not from fear but from pure excitement. He loved the moment.

He responded with a tremendous blow of his own, causing Memnon to reel backwards, equally shocked by the force of the blow. They stared at one another in silence, both knowing this would be the greatest challenge either would ever know.

"Come, giant," grunted Achilles. "I have waited my entire life to find a foe like you. The bards will sing of this battle forever."

They charged into each other, Memnon towering over Achilles, slamming tremendous blows onto his shield. Achilles threw the shield up high, trusting it to hold back the blade hammering against it, and swung his sword at Memnon's middle. The giant was amazingly quick; he avoided the thrust easily and came at Achilles again.

The Myrmidons gasped as the giant drove Achilles back. They had never seen Achilles forced to take a backward step. Automedon grimaced, his throat thick. Even Odysseus leaned forward, his eyes narrowing. Had Achilles met his match at last, he wondered.

As Achilles absorbed the blows he felt the giant's strength waning. Then he responded. He charged into Memnon, ramming his shield up into the giant's head, knocking him back. It was a technique the giant had never seen. He growled and charged into Achilles. They locked bodies, straining, gasping, struggling to force the other backwards, each mindful that one slip could give the other the opening to end it.

Achilles fought for his breath, experiencing fatigue for the first time in years of battle. The giant was so huge that to move him took far more strength than Achilles could have realized. He felt his legs weaken….and a sense of dread crept into his heart. The giant forced him back with his shield, swinging his sword wildly. Over and over the blows came, in an unending stream. Automedon groaned, wondering how much more his master could take. He felt as though he might vomit and the Myrmidons began to chant, loudly.

Odysseus screamed at Achilles: "Remember Peleus! Achilles, think of Peleus!"

Achilles gasped heavily, his left arm weary from holding the shield so high for such long a time. His temples pounded from the exertion, both physically and emotionally. He found it extremely difficult to swallow.

And then his opening came. Bending low, he saw the giant's legs. He swung his sword as hard as could, in a horizontal arch. He felt the blade bite deep into the giant's calf muscle and heard him scream hideously. Memnon jerked wildly, howling, and tried to move away on one foot, to catch his breath. A huge gash in his leg was spitting blood. Achilles straightened up, his sword ready to strike again.

Memnon was hopping on one leg, tears streaming down his face from the pain. He tried to place the foot on the ground, but the pain was too much and he jerked it back up. As he did so, Achilles charged at him. Memnon groaned, jerking his shield up just as Achilles slammed into him with all his might. The giant flew backwards and sprawled in the dust, rolling wildly, then struggled desperately to stand back up. But Achilles was too quick for him. He lifted his sword and drove it forward in a blinding flash, the blade plowing deep into the giant's throat. Memnon's mouth flew open, trying to scream, but no sound came out. Slowly, he stood, the sword jutting out of his throat in front, Achilles still gripping it. Gritting his teeth, Achilles pushed it in until the blade broke out the back side of Memnon's neck. The giant jerked free, twisting, and staggered toward his men, his eyes wide with disbelief, hands clutching the sword blade. And then he tumbled headlong into the dirt.

An incredible roar went up from the Achaeans. No one had ever seen such a battle in all their days. Odysseus stared numbly at Achilles.

"Surely, you are a god!" he mumbled. "There has never been a warrior the likes of you, Peleusson. Never!"

Agamemnon gaped, unable to speak; Menelaus stood by his brother's side, gripping his arm tightly, gawking at the scene before him.

"Achilles has opened the door wide to victory!" shouted Menelaus when he was able to regain his composure. "We must take advantage of it. Zeus is with us!"

Agamemnon raised his spear and screamed out the Mycenaen war cry. The army leaped into the action, filled with inspiration by the greatness of Achilles. Staring down at the giant lying before him, Achilles turned him over and jerked his sword free. The Ethiopians weren't even determined to retrieve the body, they simply turned and ran toward the city as fast as they could. Seeing them, the Trojans broke and ran, as well.

Achilles ripped off Memnon's war helmet and threw it toward Automedon. He then tore into the animal skin covering the huge body and found the armor. He was going to strip it when the rage came over him. He stood, shaking with lust for battle, a feeling he had not known since he fought Hector. He threw back his head and screamed the war cry of the Myrmidons. Nothing could stop him now, he knew. Nothing, not even the gods of Olympus!

The Scaean Gates

The Trojan army was fleeing, once more panic stricken by the sight of Achilles and the Myrmidons racing amok across the plain. Their dreaded war cry filled the air, over and over, mixing in with the screams of injured horses and dying men. On the walls of the once proud city, Priam stood with Helen, watching in horror, unable to believe their eyes. Memnon had been their brightest hope, a hope that had been ruined once again by the might of Achilles. The moment they had feared for ten long years was upon them, and there was no turning back. No one could stand before Achilles and the Myrmidons. Priam sagged against a tower wall, his hand on his chest, unable to catch his breath. His heart was about to fall unto the ground, he felt as he clutched at his chest with feeble fingers.

"Open the gates," he mumbled. "All of Troy is lost! Nothing can stop the Deathdealer now."

Achilles was in a frenzy; instead of growing more weary, he seemed to grow stronger. It was as Chiron had said many years earlier on Mount Pelion, that Achilles possessed a stamina that he had never seen before in any other human, not even Heracles. And that quality served him magnificently on this day. He shouted to Automedon, issuing directions by pointing the Pelion ash spear. Warriors who saw him coming dropped their weapons and fled; his chariot sparkled with the brightness of the sun god. To the Trojans and their allies, it seemed as if Ares, the god of war, had taken human form and was running wild against them.

For what seemed like an eternity, Achilles rampaged. Alexandros was among the warriors who turned and fled, his legs pumping as hard as they could. He ran to the Scaean Gates, then turned breathless, gaping behind him, sweat mixing with dust to stream his features. His chest was heaving from the exertion, and he felt a sickness in his stomach that made him want to vomit. He pulled his blue-crested helmet off and leaned against the massive gates; he stuck his head behind one, and wretched hard, giving up what little food was still in his stomach. He wiped a hand across his face, then looked upward. He saw figures darting along the wall, he heard the wailing of women and the screaming of children.

"I am the cause of this horror," he told himself. "I have caused the death of thousands of brave men and of Hector, the bravest of them all." He pulled himself up straight and reached back into his quiver, pulling out an arrow. He reached for the pouch that he had stuffed inside the quiver earlier in the day, removing it gently. With shaking fingers, he untied the leather strings and opened the pouch, then peered in. The little pile was still there. He held the arrow's shaft and dipped the stony tip into the slime-like potion, wiggling it around, and then pulled the arrow out. He gaped at the sticky substance on the end of the tip.

"I must find the courage to send one poisoned arrow at him," he mumbled. "Somehow, I must find the courage...."

He staggered out from behind the gate, a mere shadow of the splendid figure that had sailed to Sparta ten years earlier to steal a woman's heart and give reason for a war that would change the life of thousands. He stumbled past the soldiers and chariots streaming around him, heading in the opposite direction, for safety behind the Scaean gates. He held the arrow in one hand, the bow in the other....a forlorn figure, lost in a world gone mad.

He stopped, shaking, and looked up.

"Apollo, if you ever cared for Troy and its citizens – if you ever cared for me and my father's house....please, help me send this arrow."

It was his victory at an archery contest in Troy many years earlier that had caused Alexandros to become known by his family and to be accepted as a member of the royal household. Those archery skills had saved him in battle on many occasions; now, he prayed that this same talent would perhaps rescue all of Troy from the fearsome force raging toward it right now.

He saw the chariot of Achilles off to the right and he gaped at the splendid figure with the gleaming armor. Automedon was bent over the railing, whipping the horses, Achilles at his side, shaking his terrible spear and shouting the Myrmidon war cry. But suddenly, the chariot stopped and Achilles leaped out. He had his back to Alexandros and was now a long stone's throw away. Achilles was facing a group of Myrmidons, issuing orders.

Alexandros could not believe his luck. Surely, Apollo had decided to intervene; how else could one account for Achilles stopping so close, with such disregard for his own safety? Achilles apparently gave no thought of attack for the entire Trojan army was in total flight. He had slain so many warriors that none were left before him.

Alexandros fit the arrow to the bowstring, trying to steady his nerves. He lifted the bow until he could see the great Achaean in full view, still in front of him, his armor and sword stained with Trojan blood. Alexandros fought to desperately steady his hand, took a deep breath, prayed to Apollo – and let the arrow fly.

Achilles was about to turn back to the chariot when he felt an incredible pain in his left foot. He twisted wildly, lifting his foot, and saw an arrow deeply imbedded in his heel. He bent over and gripped the shaft and tried to pull it out, but it would not come. He gritted his teeth, pulled again, and it slid out, covered with gore and blood. He cast it aside and stood tall, his headcrest shaking, his eyes gleaming from inside the war helmet. He took several steps, searching for the man who had sent the arrow. A burning sensation shot up his leg and he halted abruptly.

The sounds around him suddenly seemed far off, distant. There was a strange noise echoing in his ears. He dropped his sword, clasped his hands to his head, and groaned. The fatigue of the incredible fight with Memnon and many other battles throughout the day was racing through his body, he reasoned. But in a matter of moments he knew it was far more than mere fatigue that had such a grip on him.

Those near him stopped, stunned and staring. Trojans swallowed and backed up, while the Myrmidons closed about him.

"Achilles!" shouted Automedon running to his side. "What is wrong?"

"Poison," he muttered, glancing down at his foot, now throbbing with pain. "I have been shot with an arrow dipped in a deadly snake's poison. I can....feel it working in me....moving up my leg."

There was a deathly silence all around him as warriors moved slowly forward, anxious to comprehend what they were seeing. Was it truly possible that Achilles was injured? They shook their heads and began chanting the war cry, hoping somehow to scare off the demon that had infected their warlord. Achilles listened to them and grimaced weakly. He lifted his hands to his war helmet and pulled it off, his golden locks falling to his shoulders. Then, slowly, he knelt on one knee, staring at the ground as the Myrmidons surrounded him. Finally, he turned his gaze up to Automedon.

"I will never see grassy Phthia, or my father again," he said softly. "Here, the ground will hold me. Troy has become my homeland forever."

Automedon stared unbelieving as Achilles sagged to the ground. The poison was working feverishly, moving to his great heart. His face touched the earth and he lay silent....warriors gaping at him, numb with disbelief. They were seeing the death of a godson, and they could not fathom it.

The dust mingled with the blood to fill his mouth, and he lifted his head for the last time. Dimly, he saw a mighty figure striding toward him and he felt a strange calm deep inside. The giant comes and will protect my body, he thought. No Trojan will wear this armor as long as Ajax still breathes.

The poison had him in a death grip and he could no longer hold his head erect; his face sagged back into the dust. His mind was racing with visions of Chiron, Peleus, Thetis, Deidamia and Polyxena. He thought briefly of his son, Neoptolemus, and then he saw a vision of Patroclus walking towards him, a ghostly figure in the afterlife.

"Patroclus," he croaked, "I am coming...."

Somehow, he knew that great Zeus had not cheated him and that the glory was his for all time. And then the spirit of Achilles fled his body and the two armies fought for possession of his mortal remains.

The Fall of Troy

The funeral games of Achilles were the finest ever held. The Achaean warlords spared no expense and held nothing back in honoring the best warrior any of them had ever known, or would ever know. The games lasted for seventeen days and wonderful prizes were given to all who competed – horses and slave women going to the victors and lesser gifts to the others. Since wrestling was the favorite sport of Achilles, it was honored the highest, with boxing and mock combat close behind. Chariot racing, the discus throw and races were also contested.

The greatest prize was the armor of Achilles, rumored to have been fashioned by the blacksmith god and given to Peleus as a gift on his wedding day, so long ago. Since Ajax had carried the body of Achilles from the battle and Odysseus had covered him from behind, fighting off any Trojans audacious enough to try and stop Ajax, only those two were considered worthy to receive the armor. As a means of determining which warrior deserved the armor the most, Agamemnon asked ten Trojan captives who the city feared the most between Ajax and Odysseus.

The Trojans replied that every man dreaded the thought of meeting Ajax in single combat but said the entire city feared Odysseus for his cunning, and thus the Ithacan was given the armor. Ajax sulked off, bitterly stung by the decision. He drank in his tent for two entire days and then ran out at night with his sword, killing dozens of sheep held in a pen nearby, shouting the name of Odysseus. Many of the Achaeans watched the mad spectacle and when Ajax came to his senses and realized what he had done, he walked slowly back to his tent. His half brother Teucer found him the next morning, lying prone on his own sword, dead. Ajax had killed himself rather than live with the humiliation.

News of the death of Achilles had caused immense joy in Troy, but it was short-lived. In ten years, the city's denizens had seen the death of so many great heroes – from Hector to Memnon, and now the greatest warrior of all. None, it seemed, could escape the chains of their own mortality; if Achilles could die, the soldiers reasoned, then no one was safe for very long from the painful and sorrowful trip to Hades.

When Polyxena received word of his death she fell to the floor of her hut, trembling and gasping for breath. To think that Achilles was gone left her weak in body and soul. She made the trek down to Troy, then went to the camp of the invaders on the last day of the funeral games intending to throw herself onto the funeral pyre, but did not. Instead, she watched as the flickering flames consumed the body of Achilles and then returned to Troy, broken in spirit. She sought out her mother, Hecuba, and tried to explain her pain and confusion.

"Is it wrong to love Achilles when he had caused so much suffering to my family and to all of Troy?" she whispered, clinging to the queen. "I am so torn inside."

"War does this to all who fall into its grip," the aged queen told her. "Ares, the god of war, can be incredibly cruel. And yet he is the brother of Aphrodite, the goddess of love. I am told they often stroll hand in hand through the halls of Olympus. And they cast their spell over all mortals at one time or another.

"If you loved Achilles, do not feel shame or contrition. It was the work of Aphrodite. You were powerless against her spell."

The ashes and bones of Achilles were placed in a golden urn and buried next to the tomb of Patroclus. The Myrmidons marked the burial spot with a huge mound of hard-packed earth so that men for generations could pay their respects to the memory of Achilles as they sailed past windy Troy and up the Hellespont.

Agamemnon did not want to give Ajax a burial fit for a warrior who died in battle and planned to leave his body naked to be picked apart by scavengers. But Odysseus and Diomedes insisted that he be buried with all the dignity accorded to a mighty warrior.

"Ten years of valor and prowess on the battlefield outweigh one night of insanity," declared Diomedes in making the case, and all agreed. Ajax was not cremated but his body was laid to rest in a fresh mound just a short distance from where his mighty cousin was buried.

Within a matter of days, the Achaeans had lost their two greatest warriors. Odysseus saw the dark mood that was enveloping the army and acted quickly. He proposed two bold plans, the second even more audacious than the first. The first plan sent him to the island of Skyros, where he convinced Deidamia to allow the son of Achilles to come to Troy and take up where his father had left off. Odysseus believed that the appearance of the son of Achilles would breath new life into the Myrmidons and the entire army. Though just barely ten years of age, Neoptolemus was tall and handsome and already starting to show the muscular frame of his father. He was eager to join the expedition and came willingly.

Secondly, Odysseus devised the clever scheme that would end the conflict once and for all. He asked Agamemnon to have a massive wooden horse built and to position it before the gates of Troy. Hiding inside would be twenty warriors waiting for the pre-arranged signal to descend from the horse's belly and open the gates to the city. Meanwhile, the Achaeans would desert their camp, sailing away to the nearby island of Tenedos. There Agamemnon would look for the signal from the walls of Troy to bring the army back.

"Weary from the ten years of war, the Trojans will be desperate to believe we have given up and sailed for home," said Odysseus, eyes narrowing as he gripped his wine cup hard, watching Agamemnon. "They will bring the horse into the city and get drunk on wine and the barley drink. Then, in the middle of the night our warriors will slip out of the horse's belly and run to the gates, opening them for your warriors."

"What makes you so sure they will bring the horse inside the walls?" asked Agamemnon with skepticism. "That would be foolhardy."

"I have it all figured out," Odysseus said. "We will provide a story they will not be able to resist."

He paused to let his words sink in, then continued: "It will be the death of Troy; it will be like slaughtering sheep," he growled. After much discussion by many warlords, Agamemnon finally nodded his approval at the brash plan. And it was set.

Shortly before the horse was finished, the Trojans returned to the field of combat for a half-hearted attempt to rout the invaders. Teucer, the finest archer in the Achaean host, sought out Alexandros and challenged him to a battle to the death with bows. Alexandros had been frightened to leave Troy ever since shooting the arrow that had brought down Achilles and he was not anxious to accept. But his fellow soldiers accused him of cowardice and even Helen said she was ashamed of him for not accepting the challenge outright. Reluctantly, he donned his armor and took to the field to comfort Teucer.

The two expert archers faced each other at a short distance and each had several misses. But Teucer's fourth arrow wounded Alexandros in the thigh. He screamed out in pain and turned to flee, limping badly. The Achaeans laughed loudly and called him names, the Myrmidons shaking their spears at him and shouting curses. Both he and Teucer had dipped their arrows in the poison that had come from the snakes on Mount Ida, and Alexandros knew he was a dead man. He fell into the arms of a comrade and begged him to administer the ointment that he had brought with him from Mount Ida, the only cure for the snake venom. But the vial he kept the ointment in was empty…and Alexandros realized with a sudden terror that the gods had deserted him.

So the prince who had started the entire war ten years earlier by stealing the queen of Sparta died before the gates of Troy, in almost the same spot where Achilles had fallen. Few in Troy other than the king and queen who had sired him mourned his passing. Even Helen showed little emotion and shortly after was claimed as a wife by Deiphobus, one of Alexandros' many brothers.

The plan of the wooden horse worked to perfection, thanks to the actions of a man named Sinon. He was planted so that the Trojans would find him and he could plead the case of the horse as a fabulous tribute. Sinon told Priam and the Trojan leaders that the Achaeans had decided to give up the battle and sail for home. But they wanted to placate Athena with a tribute to her favorite animal, in the hope of securing a successful trip back to their homeland.

"The wooden horse was built large enough so that it would be difficult for you to bring it into the city," said Sinon to the throng of Trojans surrounding him on the plain, his voice quivering. In front of him sat the majestic horse, staring impassively at the walls of Troy.

"It has magical powers and will protect the city against any further wars if brought inside," he added. "The Achaeans want to honor Athena but do not want you to share in it."

Odysseus had instructed him carefully on what to say and how to act and Sinon was successful in his ruse. He even explained why the platform on which the horse sat had rollers under it, so that it could easily be pulled from the construction area to the front of the camp. Of course, the rollers would also make it easier for them to pull the horse into the city, but Sinon did not dare tell the Trojans that lest it all seem too contrived.

Odysseus, Diomedes, Neoptolemus and seventeen others hid in the dark belly of the horse, clutching their swords and spears as they listened to the debate below on what to do with the huge wooden object. One group was for burning the horse where it stood, while another group argued that it should be brought into the city. At one point, a spear was hurled up at the belly of the horse and the spear point broke through the wood near Neoptolemus. He showed no expression, merely glancing at Odysseus in the dark interior.

The hidden warriors sighed with relief when the decision was made to pull the horse into the city. They huddled together, sweat dripping from their faces as the hours ticked away, listening to straining and shouts beneath them as the huge horse was pulled into the city. After the horse was inside the walls, the city became wild with excitement. Everyone danced and feasted and drank deep into the night. Finally, the noise faded as the weary Trojans either passed out where they sat or trudged off to their homes.

After an hour of eerie silence in the streets, with Diana riding high, Odysseus gave the signal. Diomedes opened the trap door, peering down into the dark. Finally, he gave a nod and climbed down the rope ladder, followed by Odysseus, Neoptolemus and the others. They moved quickly to the Scaean Gates, killing several drunken Trojans who stumbled into their path. They opened the gates just slightly and one of the men slid outside. He lit a torch he had carried with him, swinging it back and forth. The signal was seen by a warrior standing on the tomb of Achilles, where it was relayed to another and yet another, all the way to Tenedos. Hours later, in the dark of early morning, the entire Achaean army was moving quickly toward the gates.

Troy was caught totally unaware. With most of the men lost in deep slumber after hours of drinking and celebrating, few of them had a chance to fight. Most were cut down in their beds or as they ran from their houses into the streets, stunned by the hideous screaming and war cries.

Releasing the frustration of ten long years of siege, the invaders were insatiable. Brutality ran amok from street to street and house to house. Priam was cut down in his palace, and Hecuba was dragged by her long, gray hair down the steps of the altar of Hera, where she had run for shelter. Helen's new husband, Deiphobus, was confronted by Menelaus in their bedchamber. Exhausted from the night's play, Deiphobus tried feebly to resist with just a short dagger in his hand and no armor. Menelaus sliced off his hand with a wild swing and as Deiphobus fell to the floor, begging for mercy, he was cut to pieces. Helen cowered in her bed watching, too numb to even cry out. Bloody Menelaus grabbed her by the wrist and pulled her wildly into the street, where he planned to kill her in front of his Spartans. But confronted with her unmatched beauty once again, Menelaus found his resolve fading and had her carried off to his tent.

Neoptolemus led the Myrmidons into Hector's chambers and found Andromache hiding there with her servants, clutching her young son, Astyanax, to her bosom. Upon discovering who she was, Neoptolemus claimed Andromache for his own and two Myrmidons carried her away as Astyanax was ripped from her grip and taken captive. The four-year-old son of Hector was flung from the highest wall, killed by warlords fearful that he would grow to manhood and some day seek revenge on the men who had sacked his city.

The slaughter continued all through the morning. Anything that could burn – the wooden huts with grass tops, the stables full of hay, many of the shops – was set on fire. The invaders ransacked the treasure vault of Priam and of several other warlords. Cartloads of it were brought to the tent of Agamemnon to be counted and divided up.

Agamemnon took many captives, including the princess Cassandra, who had once foretold Troy's doom because of Helen. Hundreds of Trojan women and children were split up among the many Achaean warlords. Agamemnon doled out the gold and the other spoils, such as armor, vessels, vases and fine horses, and within several days the army was ready to sail.

Once proud Troy was now a shambles, savaged and deserted. The smell of rotting flesh and burning wood hung heavy in the air for many days and a heavy cloud of smoke hovered over the city like a giant vulture. One by one, the ships of the invaders departed, until the harbor was alive with black hulls and brown sails. Nearly one thousand ships had come to Troy ten years earlier, and nearly that many were now sailing back to the mainland and to the island kingdoms which were part of the Achaean confederacy.

The Myrmidons were among the last to depart. They packed their tents and weapons and spoils of war slowly as they watched the ships moving out to sea. Automedon had assumed the leadership at the request of Achilles himself. Achilles had told all the war chieftans that if he was killed, then Patroclus was in charge. If they were both gone, the leadership would pass to Automedon, who had become his trusted driver and companion.

Automedon was busy with the ordeal of having the ships loaded for departure when he was approached by five Myrmidons and a young woman in a tattered gray tunic. Automedon was immediately struck by her beauty and wondered who she might be. The soldier leading the group explained that she was taken captive in Priam's palace and several warriors had fought for her, seduced by her beauty. When they found out who she was they knew they must turn her over to Automedon.

"She is…. Polyxena," said the first warrior.

Automedon felt a hot tremor run down his back. Achilles had confided in him of his great love for Polyxena and he in turn had instructed the Myrmidons prior to the final assault to look for her and treat her with great care. He was stunned to find her standing before him now. He took her hand and led her to a quiet place, where they found two chairs to sit upon.

"Tell me, have you been treated well?" asked Automedon nervously. "If any soldier or any Myrmidon has…."

"No," she said softly. "No one has violated me in any way. Once they discovered my name, they have treated me with great respect. Somehow, they must have known."

The two who had been so close to Achilles sat in awkward silence, sharing their love for him yet knowing they had nothing else in common. And then she made a request of him. It was a simple request, but one that took his breath away. They talked quietly for a long time, until at last he nodded solemnly at her.

"It will be as you ask," he said gently.

Upon the death of Achilles, Agamemnon had given Briseis back to the Myrmidons as a gesture of good will. On the day of departure she and Automedon walked together down the sandy beach, toward the tomb of Achilles. Neoptolemus marched next to Automedon. Behind them came the surviving Myrmidons, less than seventy of them now despite several reinforcements from Phthia through the years. And in their midst walked Polyxena, dressed in a white chiton.

They stopped at the mound that held the burial urn of Achilles, tears streaming down many of their faces. Automedon motioned to the warriors standing around Polyxena and they touched her arms, guiding her forward. Eyes wide and breathing heavily, she walked up to the tomb of Achilles, Automedon at her side.

"Great Achilles, you loved us in life and we loved you," Automedon said, voice choking with emotion. "But none did you love more than this woman from Mount Ida. After the death of Patroclus, you yourself told me of your love for her and of your trips to be with her, as a husband is with his wife. And she has told me of her great love for you and her desire to be with you in the Elysian Fields. Therefore, I send her to you now, great Achilles, to have as your bride forever."

Polyxena stood before him, small and helpless. He drew his dagger slowly, gasping for his breath. He gripped her right arm with his free hand and, grim faced, he slid the dagger into her breast, driving it deep. She shrieked and fell forward onto the mound, her white chiton now awash in blood.

"Your last wish – is my command," muttered Automedon to the dying princess of Troy.

Polyxena was wrapped in fine linens and buried next to Achilles' urn. At dawn the following day, the Myrmidon ships pulled away from the coast of Troy. Automedon stood at the back of his ship, staring out at the deserted plain where so many men had fought and died. His eyes wandered to the walls of the once proud city, now destroyed and deserted. His gaze shifted to where the Myrmidons had camped for ten long years and to the large mound earth tomb that held the ashes of Achilles, Patroclus and the body of Polyxena. And then he turned away, his throat tight and his eyes locked on the wine-dark sea before him.

The last of the heroes

The bard was excited to be finally meeting the most famous man in all of Hellas. As a young boy, he had heard the tales of Odysseus's grand adventures and they had stirred his imagination like no other stories ever had. Even the voyage of Jason was nothing compared to what Odysseus had gone through. Not only had the king of Ithaca fought at Troy for ten long years, but he had actually taken another ten years to reach his home, surviving peril after peril in breathtaking fashion.

And when he reached his palace at last, what transpired was even more incredible. His kingdom had been overrun by a band of ruffians who wanted to take everything he once owned, including his beautiful wife. Everyone had assumed that Odysseus was long dead and that Penelope was a widow. One hundred suitors had taken up living in the palace that once belonged to brave Odysseus and had ravaged his food supplies, humiliating his wife and young son with their barbarous actions.

The people of Ithaca knew that young Telemachus was not near the man his father was. "Oh, if only Odysseus would come back, the price these suitors would then pay," was what many an old man was saying, when gathering with friends at the taverns, or while relaxing on the little farms when the day's work was done.

But no one expected Odysseus to return, not after ten long years had passed since the fall of Troy. And then, one day an aged beggar showed up at the palace, asking for a handout. The suitors ridiculed him and tried to run him off, but Telemachus was hospitable to him. On the third day after his arrival, Penelope, under great duress, consented to marry the suitor who could string the huge bow of Odysseus and shoot an arrow through a row of axe handles.

None could string that bow; it not only took tremendous strength but skill as well. There was a trick to stringing the bow that only

Odysseus knew. When all the suitors had tried and failed, the old beggar had asked for chance. Everyone laughed and laughed; what a joke that was.

But the old beggar handled the bow with ease and slipped the string on like it was a play thing. Then he threw off his old clothes and stood tall and proud. Odysseus had come home at last. He leaped atop the huge banquet table and Telemachus, as prearranged, fed him the deadly arrows. One by one, Odysseus shot down the suitors, until none was left alive and the banquet hall was filled with crimson, everywhere.

Odysseus had a great reunion with his wife and son and the loyal servants and villagers. But shortly after, he had to leave for a period and travel to lofty Delphi to cleanse himself of the murders.

That had taken place thirty summers ago and now the young bard was trembling as he sat in the small waiting room, outside the throne room of Odysseus. He had requested an audience with the great hero of the Trojan War and it had been granted. He had traveled all the way from Athens and now, at last, he was going to meet the famous Odysseus.

The bard was shocked when Odysseus finally made his appearance. He was bent and hobbled and walked with a cane. He seemed much smaller than the bard had thought he would be and he wore a purple tunic that hung to his knees. He had long scraggly hair that was solid white, and a short, neatly trimmed beard that was just as white. At his side was his son Telemachus, now an aging man himself, and two young servants. The bard stood as the king entered the room and approached him.

"So, you are the young man who wants to meet old Odysseus," said the king. The young man bowed and stood straight. He saw the twinkle in the old man's eyes, and he suddenly felt very comfortable with him. The king reached out a foreman; as they gripped one another's arm the bard felt the sinewy muscles.

"I am Odysseus," said the king. "I welcome you to the palace of Laertes, and of Autolycus. Laertes was my father, and Autolycus was my grandfather. Together, the three of us, we have ruled here for nearly a hundred years." He paused, and glanced at his son. "And soon, my son Telemachus will become king. My days are now numbered and the number is small."

Telemachus protested, taking his father's arm.

"You have many years left, father," he said. The bard saw the deep respect that the son held for the father, as if he were looking at an Olympian immortal.

The bard was nervous but found his voice.

"I am Critus," he said softly. "I sing songs….mostly about the deeds of heroes. Great sir, I would like to know more about your deeds, and of the great Achaeans who fought at Troy. Sir, if you would allow me some time, I would be most grateful."

Odysseus regarded the young man for a while, saying nothing. Critus glanced nervously at Telemachus, then back at the old monarch. He was afraid that somehow he had offended the great king and would be asked to leave. But then Odysseus smiled.

"Very well, he said. "Today, we will talk about my voyage back from Troy. It took nearly ten years, you know."

For hours, Odysseus held the young bard captive with his marvelous tales of adventure. He told of the strangest sights a man had ever seen and of exotic lands and strange beasts. He talked of the one-eyed monster known as Cyclopes, and of the clashing rocks and the land of the lotus eaters. He leaned forward and spoke softly of beautiful women who could hypnotize a man and then seduce him, making him stay under their spell for years and years, and of many other things. And then he called a halt and they enjoyed a feast of roasted pig, thick slices of bread smothered in honey, boiled vegetables, and sweet watered wine.

After the long day of story telling and the feasting, Odysseus had to excuse himself in mid evening. He stood and walked slowly to where the young bard was sitting, still holding his drinking cup, and stared down at him.

"Tomorrow," said Odysseus, a very stern look on his face, "we will talk of Troy."

Critus watched the old man limp away, his head spinning with the prospect of their next discussion. It was Troy that he wanted to hear about the most.

The next day, Odysseus slept late and the bard could hardly contain himself. Odysseus kept him waiting until dusk. They finally met in the same room. Again, Telemachus was with his father.

"You are very fortunate that he is meeting with you to talk about Troy," said Telemachus in a hushed voice, while his father was paying tribute to the goddess Athena at the far end of the room. "It is not often he will discuss Troy. It makes him sad to think that all the heroes are now long gone and he alone is left to contemplate the greatest adventure ever undertaken by man."

When Odysseus returned, the bard saw that his eyes were wet. He sat on a large bench with a high back, covered with thick furs in front of Critus, who sat on a bench opposite his. The bard could hardly contain his excitement.

Odysseus stared at the young man before him.

"So, you want to know of the heroes, do you?" he said softly. "I will tell you about Agamemnon, Ajax, Diomedes and the others."

He took a deep breath and began:

"Agamemnon was the high king, but he was not a great man," he said. "Yes, he ruled over more men than any of the others, but he himself was ruled by greed. He always wanted more and more and more. It is a fault that traps many men and even I have been seduced by the god of greed. But Agamemnon was greedier than most. He sacrificed his own daughter, Iphigenia, so that he could get the blessing of the Olympian gods to sail to Troy. Ah, what a mistake that was. His queen never forgave him and when he returned to Mycenae expecting a conqueror's welcome, Clytaemnestra was waiting. She and her lover, Aegisthus, butchered Agamemnon in his own bathtub, cutting him to pieces. Oh, he died a horrible death.

"Great Ajax went mad one night, after I was awarded the sword and spear of Achilles at his funeral games. In order to decide who should have the great weapons, the warlords asked ten captives who the Trojans feared the most of all Achaeans, now that Achilles was no more. They replied that everyone feared to meet Ajax in single combat, but that the entire city feared my plotting more than they feared Ajax's sword. That made Ajax so furious that he lost his mind, slaughtering sheep and then falling on his own sword in his tent. That was a great loss to the Achaeans, so soon after the death of Achilles. We almost left Troy at that point. But then Athena visited me once more, and I came up with the idea of the wooden horse.

"Some say it was Palamedes who had the idea, but it was mine alone. I also devised the plot of leaving Sinon behind to tell the Trojans what the purpose of the giant wooden horse was. Sinon was a great actor; yes, he was indeed."

He paused to shake his head and sip a little wine.

"The Trojans – to think they actually brought that horse into the city. What a foolish act. They should have listened to Cassandra and the head priest, Laccoon, I think was his name. Sitting in the horse, we could hear them shouting that the horse was a trap and would cause the city's undoing. But no one could figure out how a wooden horse could be a danger. If only they had known the horse's belly was filled with the most courageous of the Achaeans.

"It took great courage, and discipline, to sit in that wooden trap and hear the debates on whether to take the horse into the city or burn it on the plain. Sinon did a great job of acting, telling them that the horse was a tribute to Athena and we had built it large enough that it could not be taken into Troy. Oh, that caused Priam and others to insist it be brought in, as a final insult to the vanquished invaders."

He paused again, sighing deeply.

"What a slaughter it was. The entire army was waiting outside the gates. They triumphed, but many had tough returns to contend with.

"Little Ajax was drowned at sea on the voyage from Troy, along with many of his Lycians. Diomedes sailed back to Argos and ruled there for many years, until he was killed in a chariot accident. He was a great warrior, one of the Achaeans I admired the most, both in battle and in counsel.

"Nestor returned home to Pylos as an old, old man. He never got over the death of his son, Antilochus, and simply faded away from mourning. A sad ending for a great king.

"Idomeneus returned to the great land of Crete and ruled happily for many years."

He paused, asking Telemachus for a little wine. Telemachus motioned to the servants at the far end of the room, and they came and filled all the cups.

"And what of Menelaus and Helen, the two for whom the war was supposedly fought?" Odysseus took several sips of his wine. "What a joke that is," he continued. "Helen was beautiful, I concede that, but was she worth an entire war? Of course not. The war was fought over passage and trade rights to the Black Sea and for possession of Priam's treasure. Not for any woman.

"But," he said with a wink, smiling at Critus, "you can say it was about Helen. That sounds much better, doesn't it? It makes us Achaeans sound far more noble.

"Well, Alexandros was killed by a poison arrow shortly before the city was sacked. Helen married one of his brothers, Deiphobus by name, and Menelaus cut him to pieces in his own bed chamber, right in front of Helen. Menelaus was going to kill her too, for her wicked ways, but she turned her charms on him and his resolve to punish her withered away. Helen and Menelaus returned home to Sparta and lived for many years together, raising their family. But they did not live happily, I am told. There was great animosity between them, as one might expect. And they died not long ago, spent and bitter."

He paused again before continuing.

"The Trojans drew a miserable lot. We sacked that city and just about everyone was put to the sword. There was much brutality; the Achaeans were frustrated after ten long years of trying to subdue those people. Oh, there was much brutality. We divided up the spoils – the treasure trove of Priam and of the lesser princes, and the women who were not killed."

He leaned back, and shook his head as if the memories were stirring great pain in him. Then he looked up.

"What more do you want to know?" he asked.

The bard took a deep breath and sighed. He leaned forward.

"Can you tell me about Achilles?" he asked. "Was he truly all they say he was? Was he the son of a goddess?"

Odysseus looked away for a long time, his eyes locked on a tapestry hanging on the far wall. It was of brilliant colors and showed warriors fighting before a walled city. He turned back to Critus, a new sparkle in his eyes.

"Achilles!" he said, letting the name roll off his tongue. "I saved him for last. I knew you would want to know about the best of the Achaeans.

"I discovered him, you know. He was at the court of Lycomedes, dressed as a maiden. His mother, she had drugged him and hypnotized him. She was a goddess, they say, and she knew the art of seduction like few others. My own eyes have seen women like her, some were witches, with incredible powers. But his mind was too strong to stay under the spell for long and just the sight of his great love, a warrior's weapon, brought him back to reality."

The old king paused again and placed his hand over his chest.

"Some times, I have great pains here, in my breast," he said to the young bard. "You know, I have seen eighty summers and I have outlived all the other heroes by many years. I have survived Achilles by over thirty years. That proves that being the greatest does not mean you will live the longest."

He paused again. Critus, waiting. He knew much more was coming, that he must be patient. Finally, the hero continued.

"I have never seen a man like Achilles," said Odysseus. "He was the best at everything he did. Everything. He was the swiftest, the strongest, and the most courageous. He was the best with the spear and with the sword. And he was such a wrestler that none of us would test him....not even me, although Great Ajax did once, before they sailed to Troy.

"Hector was a great fighter but he had no chance with Achilles. Nor did Memnon, who came all the way from the Land of the Dawn. He was a giant and a magnificent warrior and all of the Achaeans were afraid of Memnon. Even Great Ajax, weary from ten long years of war, did not want to meet the dark prince of Ethiopia. But Achilles...." He paused, shaking his head in awe, "Achilles cut him down like a man cuts down a tree in the forest.

"It was the greatest single combat these eyes have ever seen," said Odysseus, a far-away look in his dark eyes.

He sat silent for a long time, sagging against the back of the bench. The bard was afraid he had fallen asleep, or worse. But Telemachus simply smiled at Critus as if to say his father was resting.

Finally, Odysseus opened his eyes and leaned forward again.

"His mother was a goddess, of that there can be no doubt. She was even more beautiful than Helen, and walked as though her feet did not touch the ground. Oh, how she hated me. The day I took him from Skyros, she leveled a threat at me, saying the sea god would punish me." He paused, shaking his head. "I guess she was right after all. It did seem that Poseidon enjoyed tormenting me, keeping me from home and sailing his seas for ten long years. There were times when I imagined I could see Thetis laughing at me.

"His father, Peleus, was a magnificent man, a mighty warrior in his own right who became a good king. Achilles was taught by Chiron, the centaur, you know. Achilles grew up on Mount Pelion and learned things that no other mortal knew. He could play the lyre like a musician and he could heal wounds. Only Machon knew more healing than Achilles, and Machon was our best medicine man at Troy."

After another pause, the bard wanted to ask a question; Odysseus sensed that and nodded for him to speak.

"How did Achilles die?" Critus asked. "Who could kill such a man?"

"Only the gods could kill Achilles," said Odysseus. "No man could ever do that. Apollo had a hand in it, that much is certain. First, he provided Alexandros the thought and then the courage to do the deed, for Alexandros had neither the intelligence nor the fortitude to do this by himself. No, I saw Apollo's hands on this deed, through and through. He was the one who guided the arrow.

"That bastard who began the war concocted some sort of poison and dipped his arrows in it and shot an arrow. It almost missed, but struck Achilles in the foot, of all places. The poison was drawn from the most venomous of snakes; it killed him in a matter of minutes.

"I have heard the stories – that Achilles was invulnerable everywhere except the heel, that as a baby his mother dipped him in the River Styx to make him immortal and held him by the heel. That is the story men are telling, and that is well and good. Men need to explain how it is that one warrior can be so much greater than all others, and this story helps them to understand why Achilles was so wonderful.

"But the truth is this!" said Odysseus, pointing a crooked finger at the bard to make his point. "The gods loved Achilles and blessed him with a body and a mind that others could not approach. In that sense, he was like a god himself. Achilles was alone in the world, isolated by his greatness. He knew he was better than everyone else, and that difference made him alone.

"He could love, like all men; I think he loved Deidamia, to a point.

But I know he loved Briseis and Patroclus.... her as a wife and him as the brother he never had.

"But his true love was Polyxena."

There was a long silence, Critus trying to digest all that he had heard thus far while Odysseus collected his thoughts.

"What ever became of Briseis and Polyxena, of Deidamia and his son?" asked the bard. Odysseus sighed before answering.

"Achilles had a son by Deidamia; his name was Neoptolemus. He came to Troy from Skyros after the death of Achilles and he was a fine warrior, though not like his father; but then who was like Achilles? He was very, very young, as well. Just a boy. Neoptolemus was one of the twenty soldiers that hid in the Trojan horse with me. I picked him because he knew fear not at all and deserved to be there for all Achilles had done for us. He fought hard during the sack of the city. Neoptolemus sailed back to the mainland, but I do not know what became of him.

"Polyxena was captured in Priam's palace by the soldiers of Little Ajax, the Locrian, and handed over to the Myrmidons. They sacrificed her on the tomb of Achilles the day before they departed for home. I was there and she went willingly to her death, hoping to live with Achilles forever in the Elysian fields of heroes.

"Briseis was taken back to the Phthia by Automedon and she married him, I am told. They sought the blessing of Peleus, who gave it to them, knowing that Achilles cared for them both very much. They had many children; one of their sons was named Achilles.

"Peleus was told of the wonderful deeds of his son at Troy and died an old man, content in the knowledge that he had indeed sired a son who was greater than he himself was. A fine statue of Achilles was erected before Peleus died and sits in front of the palace. And Deidamia ruled as queen of Skyros for many years, never taking a new husband. They say she wept for Achilles until the end of her days."

"And what of Thetis?" asked the bard gently, spellbound by all he had heard.

"Who knows what happens to the gods and goddesses," said the old king. "Don't they live forever? I heard she was at Troy when Achilles sulked in his tent after the terrible argument with Agamemnon, but I never saw her there. So, who knows?"

Odysseus was weary and leaned back again, shutting his eyes. Critus leaned back, too, lost in all he had heard, his mind swimming with visions of the gallant men who fought and died at Troy. He would hardly have imagined that he would have heard such wonderful stories ever in his lifetime. He gazed in awe at the man sitting across from him, a man who had lived a life that no one else would ever match, he suspected. The men Odysseus had fought with and against, the incredible ten-year voyage back from Troy – a voyage full of monsters, strange lands and enchanting women. No, there was only one Odysseus, and only one life like his!

Finally, Odysseus rose slowly, as if his legs would give out from under him. The bard saw the tunic rise up for a moment, and gasped as his eyes beheld the famous scar left by a wild boar on the inside of his leg. It was a scar that was etched into his flesh nearly seventy years ago while Odysseus was still a young boy. It had been carved on his body before Troy had carved its memories on his mind and his psyche.

Odysseus walked to the wall and stood by a long spear that was hanging there, and a sword hanging in a sheath. He ran his fingers over them, staring at them for a long time.

"The ashes of Achilles were buried next to Patroclus, not far from the Myrmidon camp. Most of his great armor was buried with him," he said, his voice quivering. "Here, on my wall, are his Pelion ash spear and his bronze sword. They hang here as a reminder of the great adventure and of the greatest hero of all."

He turned to the bard and the flickering firelight from the center hearth danced on his features. He drew himself up, tall and proud. Critus gaped at him in awe; he seemed suddenly a figure from another life, from another world. He seemed more than just mere legend; he seemed like a god.

"Go, and tell your stories," said Odysseus. "Talk of the Achaeans, who were victorious. You can speak of the death of Troy and the tragedy of the Trojans. You can sing about the deeds of the heroes, on both sides, for there were many, that is certain. Hector and Aeneas and Sarpedon and Memnon....yes, the Trojans had many heroes, as well.

"But when you speak the name of Achilles, whisper it. Speak it in awe. He was the greatest man I ever knew, the greatest warrior who ever lived. His fame will endure for as long as men love great deeds and value courage."

He started to leave and then paused, facing the bard.

"There is something else about Achilles," he said, his brow wrinkling in thought. "He had a sense of direction that I have never seen in any other man. Like the rest of us, he came to Troy seeking riches and glory, but at the end they no longer mattered to him.

"I have given that considerable thought through the years," he said, shaking a crooked finger at the bard. "That....was what really made Achilles different from all the rest of us!"

And then Odysseus walked slowly out of the room. The bard never saw him again as he died shortly thereafter. But Critus began singing stories of Odysseus and of the great heroes who fought at Troy, so that their deeds would never be forgotten. He traveled the land of the Achaeans and other bards began to copy him, and sing the tales, as well. Critus sang of Troy on thousands of occasions and always he closed the same way.

"For who can match Achilles?" he asked, his voice wavering and tears welling in his eyes and in the eyes of his audience. "He who can must be more than hero, more than man."

Postscript

Achilles was immortalized in *The Iliad* of Homer. He is considered, along with Heracles, one of the two greatest heroes in all of Greek legend. His deeds at Troy were known and celebrated throughout the ancient world and he was worshipped for centuries as a cult figure of mythic proportions. Alexander the Great so idolized him that he could recite long passages from *The Iliad* by heart and insisted he was a direct descendent. Landing his vast army at the site of ancient Troy nearly eight hundred years after the Trojan War, it is said that Alexander ran naked around the tomb of Achilles.

In his magnificent book, *Homer and the Heroic Tradition*, Cedric D. Whitman brilliantly dissects the character of the Homeric hero and, specifically, Achilles: "The highest heroes are not men of delusion," writes Whitman. "They are men of clarity and purity, who will a good impossible in the world and eventually achieve it, through suffering, in their own spiritual terms." Such is the case with Achilles.

Most historians believe the Trojan War occurred around 1186 B.C. and was a trade war between the Trojan confederacy and the powerful mainland Greeks, called Achaeans at the time. The excavations of Frank Calvert and Heinrich Schliemann on the mound known as Hisarlik, at the mouth of the Hellespont, have shown there were at least eleven major cities known as Troy. Most likely, the one called Troy 7B was the city of Priam.

The location of the tomb of Achilles on the Troad was known for centuries and many great figures in history stopped to pay homage to his memory when they first arrived in Asia Minor. Today, no one knows where the tomb is. But the fame of Achilles is such that his name is known throughout much of the civilized world some three thousand years after his death.

About the Author

Mike Chapman first read Homer's *The Iliad* and a small book called *The Wrath of Achilles* as young boy in Waterloo, Iowa. He has studied the Trojan War era and the nature of Achilles off and on for nearly forty years. He retired from a long career as a newspaper writer and editor in 2002 and is now a freelance writer. His work has appeared in numerous national, regional and state publications. *Achilles: Son of Peleus, Scourge of Troy,* is his fifteenth book and his third historical novel. He lives on a small acreage near Kellogg, Iowa, with his wife, Beverly.